Genetic counselling

Genetic counselling should be viewed from many perspectives. To understand the ethical issues raised by genetic counselling, it is necessary for the practitioner, the detached observer and the student to be aware of these different perspectives. This book includes contributions from health professionals engaged in genetic counselling, and from observers and critics of genetic counselling with backgrounds in law, in philosophy, in biology, in the social sciences and in advocacy on behalf of those with mental handicap. This diversity among the contributors will enable health professionals to examine their activities with a fresh eye, and will help the observer-critic to understand the ethical problems that arise in genetic counselling practice rather than imaginary encounters. It is natural for health professionals to focus their concern on the immediate questions raised by individual clients, and for detached observers to consider the broader social implications of genetic counselling; this book will aid the process of mutual understanding.

The book consists of an introduction and eleven chapters. Five chapters have been written from the perspective of those engaged in genetic counselling or screening, and examine the ethical issues raised. Six chapters have been written from contrasting, critical perspectives.

This volume differs from other studies of ethical issues raised by genetics in that it focuses on genetic counselling and screening as such, rather than the new technologies applied to human reproduction. The breadth of the multidisciplinary perspective is also unusual, and will make the book of interest to health professionals, social scientists, philosophers of science and of ethics, lawyers and bioethicists.

Professional Ethics

General editors: Andrew Belsey and Ruth Chadwick
Centre for Applied Ethics, University of Wales College
of Cardiff

Professionalism is a subject of interest to academics, the general public and would-be professional groups. Traditional ideas of professions and professional conduct have been challenged by recent social, political and technological changes. One result has been the development for almost every profession of an ethical code of conduct which attempts to formalise its values and standards. These codes of conduct raise a number of questions about the status of a 'profession' and the consequent moral implications for behaviour.

This series, edited from the Centre for Applied Ethics in Cardiff, seeks to examine these questions both critically and constructively. Individual volumes will consider issues relevant to particular professions, including nursing, genetics counselling and law. Other volumes will address issues relevant to all professional groups such as the function and value of a code of ethics and the demands of confidentiality.

Also available in this series:

Ethical Issues in Journalism and the Media
Edited by Andrew Belsey and Ruth Chadwick

Ethical Issues in Nursing
Edited by Geoffrey Hunt

Ethical Issues in Social Work
Edited by Richard Hugman and David Smith

The Ground of Professional Ethics
Daryl Koehn

Genetic counselling

Practice and principles

Edited by Angus Clarke

London and New York

First published 1994
by Routledge
11 New Fetter Lane, London EC4P 4EE

Simultaneously published in the USA and Canada
by Routledge
29 West 35th Street, New York, NY 10001

Reprinted 1995

Typeset in Times by
Ponting–Green Publishing Services, Chesham, Bucks
Printed and bound in Great Britain by
T.J. Press Ltd, Padstow, Cornwall

Printed on acid-free paper

British Library Cataloguing in Publication Data
A catalogue record for this book is available from the
British Library.

Library of Congress Cataloguing in Publication Data
Genetic counselling: practice and principles/edited by
  Angus Clarke.
     p.   cm. – (Professional ethics)
  Includes bibliographical references and index.
  1. Genetic counseling–Moral and ethical aspects.
  I. Clarke, Angus.   II. Series.
  [DNLM: 1. Genetic counseling.   2. Genetic screening.
  3. Hereditary Diseases.   4. Abnormalities.
  5. Sociology, Medical.   6. Ethics, Medical.
  QZ 50 G3241 1994]
RB155.7.G463   1994
174'.2–dc20
DNLM/DLC

ISBN 0–415–08257–7 (hbk)
ISBN 0–415–08258–7 (pbk)

Contents

Notes on contributors

A. CAROLINE BERRY is a consultant geneticist at Guy's and St Thomas's Hospitals, London and is responsible for genetics services for the South East Thames Health Region. She is a member of the Church of England's Board for Social Responsibility and chairs the Medical Study Group of the Christian Medical Fellowship.

ANN WILLIAMS has been Clinical Nurse Specialist in the Institute of Medical Genetics, Cardiff, for the past five years, specializing in the field of inherited malignancy. She is presently studying for a Master's degree in Health Care Ethics. With a background in teaching she contributes to many educational programmes and conferences. HELEN HUGHES is a Consultant in Medical Genetics at the University Hospital of Wales, Cardiff. Her clinical interests are in the field of dysmorphology.

DAVID BALL, a research psychiatrist, worked with the Huntington's disease research group in Cardiff for two years counselling those seeking presymptomatic testing. He is currently a training fellow and honorary senior registrar, at the Institute of Psychiatry in London, funded by the Peacock foundation. AUDREY TYLER trained as a Medical Social Worker. She joined the Huntington's disease team at the Institute of Medical Genetics as a fieldworker in 1976, retiring from it in 1992. She has lectured and written extensively on psycho-social and ethical issues and is a member of the World Federation of Neurology's HD Predictive Testing Committee. PETER HARPER is Professor and Consultant in Medical Genetics at the University of Wales College of Medicine, Cardiff. He has worked particularly in the field of inherited neurological disorders, especially Huntington's disease and the muscular dystrophies, and is author of the book *Practical Genetic Counselling* (1991).

EVELYN PARSONS is currently responsible for the psychosocial evaluation of the all-Wales newborn screening programme for Duchenne muscular dystrophy and teaches sociology to nurses and midwives. Trained as a sociologist in the 1960s she has more recently developed a research interest in medical genetics, in particular, the concept of genetic risk and the implications of presymptomatic genetic testing. DON BRADLEY is Director of Newborn Screening for Wales though he trained originally in pharmacy and organic chemistry.

MARGARETHA WHITE-VAN MOURIK obtained nursing and midwifery qualifications in the Netherlands and then worked in various countries throughout Europe and the Middle East. For ten years she was the Scottish Coordinator of the Medical Research Council Vitamin Study on neural tube defects and consecutively studied the psychosocial aspects of a termination of pregnancy for fetal abnormality. She was a member of the working party on Biochemical Markers and Detection of Down's Syndrome for the Royal College of Obstetricians and Gynaecologists.

BENNO MÜLLER-HILL was born in Germany in 1933. He is a Professor at the Institute of Genetics in Cologne University. He is interested in gene regulation and protein-DNA recognition and has published a book on Human Genetics in Nazi Germany, *Murderous Science* (1988).

ABBY LIPPMAN, PhD, is a Professor in the Department of Epidemiology and Biostatistics and in the Centre for Human Genetics at McGill University, Montreal, Quebec. She is also chair of the Human Genetics Committee of the Council for Responsible Genetics (Cambridge, Mass.). Her research examines the applications of genetics from a feminist perspective, emphasizing the increasing geneticization of health and illness and the biopolitics of biomedicine.

LYDIA SINCLAIR is a solicitor in private practice, practising in the field of Learning Disability, Mental Health and Disability Law. She was formerly Legal Director for MENCAP (The Royal Society for Mentally Handicapped Children and Adults), and is a member of the Law Society Sub-Committee on Mental Health and Disability. She is also a member of the Mental Health Act Commission. MATTHEW GRIFFITHS is a specialist adviser to MENCAP. He has worked extensively on educational, human and civil rights and ethnical issues in the field of mental handicap for more than 20 years. He is currently involved in: 'Learning for Life' which will support all staff working with people with profound intellectual and multiple disabilities; 'Towards the Future', in collaboration with the East European Partnership and the government of Albania, to change practice in a range of institutions in Albania; and the national advisory group to implement the recommendations of the Mansell Report on services for people who have a mental handicap together with very difficult behaviour or a mental illness

JONATHAN MONTGOMERY is a Lecturer in Law at the University of Southampton. He is co-author of *Nursing and the Law* (Macmillan 1989), co-editor of the *Encyclopedia of Health Services and Medical Law* (Sweet & Maxwell 1991) and has written numerous articles on health care law. His textbook, *Health Care Law* is to be published by Oxford University Press in 1994. He is the chief law examiner for the Institute of Health Services Management, a member of the Ethics Advisory Committee of the British Paediatric Association, the Southampton and South West Hampshire Research Ethics Committee and the Wessex Regional Committee on Genetic and Antenatal Screening. He is also a non-executive director of the Southampton Community Health Services NHS Trust.

PAULA BODDINGTON studied philosophy at the University of Keele and at Corpus Christi College, Oxford. She lectured in philosophy at Bristol University before moving to the Australian National University where she currently teaches in the Faculties Philosophy Department. Her main field of teaching and research is in Applied Ethics.

MAUREEN RAMSAY is a Lecturer in Political Theory at Leeds University. Her research interests are in the application of normative theory to contemporary social and political issues. She is author of *Human Needs and the Market* (Avebury 1992).

General editors' foreword

Applied Ethics is now acknowledged as a field of study in its own right. Much of its recent development has resulted from rethinking traditional medical ethics in the light of new moral problems arising out of advances in medical science and technology. Applied philosophers, ethicists and lawyers have devoted considerable energy to exploring the dilemmas emerging from modern medical practice and its effects on the doctor–patient relationship.

But the point can be generalized. Even in health care, ethical dilemmas are not confined to medical practitioners but also arise in the practice of, for example, nursing. Beyond health care, other groups are beginning to think critically about the kind of service they offer and about the nature of the relationship between provider and recipient. In many areas of life social, political and technological changes have challenged traditional ideas of practice.

One visible sign of these developments has been the proliferation of codes of ethics, or of professional conduct. The drafting of such a code provides an opportunity for professionals to examine the nature and goals of their work, and offers information to others about what can be expected from them. If a code has a disciplinary function, it may even offer protection to members of the public.

But is the existence of such a code itself a criterion of a profession? What exactly is a profession? Can a group acquire professional status, and if so, how? Does the label 'professional' have implications, from a moral point of view, for acceptable behaviour, and if so, how far do they extend?

This series, edited from the Centre for Applied Ethics in Cardiff, seeks to examine these questions both critically and constructively. Individual volumes will address issues relevant to all professional groups, such as the nature of a profession, the function and value of codes of ethics, and the demands of confidentiality. Other volumes will examine issues relevant to particular professions, including those which have hitherto received little attention, such as journalism, law and genetic counselling.

Andrew Belsey
Ruth Chadwick

Acknowledgements

I would like to thank a number of people for their assistance throughout the gestation of this book: Ruth Chadwick, for inviting me to compile the volume; my family, for their forbearance over the past two years; the contributors, for their hard work and toleration of my editing; Jean Dunscombe, for her tireless efforts to impose a degree of organization upon myself as editor and the other contributors; Heather McCallum and Emma Cotter at Routledge for their processing of the volume through the various stages of publication; and, finally, Margaret Deith for her painstaking work in reading the manuscript, criticizing it so constructively, and providing such encouragement.

Introduction

WHAT IS GENETIC COUNSELLING?

Any answer to this question will inevitably reflect the perspective from which it is viewed: in my case, the perspective of a practising medical geneticist. Genetic counselling is what happens when an individual, a couple or a family asks questions of a health professional (the genetic counsellor) about a medical condition or disease that is, or may be, genetic in origin. The persons seeking information are usually known as 'clients'; the word 'patient' would suggest that they were suffering from a disease, which is very often not the case. The counsellor may well be medically qualified, but need not be. Certainly in the USA, many genetic counsellors are paramedical, having a distinct training and qualification. Whether the genetic counsellor is or is not medically qualified, however, the counsellor will be dependent upon a medical diagnosis or – if no firm diagnosis is available – upon a careful medical assessment of the affected individual in the family.

Clients may want information about a condition that has affected one or more relatives, and which may be said to 'run in the family'. Might they be affected by it? Or their children? What treatment is available? How may the condition show itself? In the event of a pregnancy, could testing for the condition be carried out, to see whether the child would be affected? What would be the chance of having an affected child?

In responding to these questions, information is provided that could help clients decide about plans for having children in the future, or about making other important decisions.

Another common question that arises when a couple attends a genetic counselling clinic concerns a child they already have, and who has a set of problems. Why is our child like this? Why does our child have these difficulties with his/her development? Or these behavioural problems? Or these physical health problems? Or this physical appearance?

In this situation, an explanation for what has happened is being sought. This may relieve the guilt felt by mothers who have blamed themselves for their child's problem because of something they did (or did not do) during the pregnancy. If a diagnosis can be established, this can be very helpful to the family, as well as to the health professionals; it allows some sort of guidance to be given about the likely future course of events (if the child has a progressive physical illness), and about possible future health problems that can usefully be anticipated. It allows the family to feel that they are not alone, and that other families have had similar experiences; it may allow them to contact other families whose children have been given the same diagnostic label, for mutual support. It may also allow accurate information to be provided about the chance of another child in the family being affected by the same condition.

Thus the core task of genetic counselling is to provide information about (possibly) genetic disorders to clients who seek this information. The clients may be looking back in time, seeking an explanation, or they may be looking forward in time, wanting to know about what might happen in the future. Therefore, the process of counselling must begin with *listening*, to find out from the clients what their questions are. If their questions relate to a specific disease, or to an individual in the family affected by a particular disorder, then it is important that the *diagnosis* of the affected individual is confirmed or clarified as far as possible. It may be necessary to search out information about the condition in question, if it is uncommon and the counsellor is unfamiliar with it; it may be necessary to undertake calculations to determine the risk of recurrence of a disorder from a knowledge of the family tree, if that is what the clients want to know. The information requested by the clients must then be *communicated* to them, in a form that is appropriate to their level of knowledge and understanding. It is obvious that the information given to a school biology teacher, who would already understand the biology but perhaps not the concepts of risk, would not be presented in the same way as to a bookmaker, who would understand risks but perhaps not the biology.

Once clients have been given the information they sought, that may be the end of the genetic counselling. However, if the clients are to make reproductive decisions on the basis of this information, they may find it helpful to talk through the implications of the information provided, and to discuss the various possible scenarios that could arise. This provision of support during the process of decision-making is also an aspect of genetic counselling, although it is approached very differently by different counsellors. The decisions may relate to planning a pregnancy, or having a prenatal diagnostic test or a termination of pregnancy. *Scenario-based decision counselling* entails suggesting that the client thinks through in anticipation their own likely emotional responses to the various possible options, and considers the likely responses of their partner, family, neighbours and others. Quite often, clients will anticipate a conflict between the decision they would like to make and the decision that their partner or others would like them to make; only they can make the final decision, but it can be helpful for them to anticipate any such potential conflict so that they make the decision that will leave them with least cause for regret over the coming months and years. Of course, many couples make decisions together, as couples; but it is always the woman who makes the final decision about a termination of pregnancy.

Individuals or couples making reproductive decisions in the face of a risk of genetic disease often experience their predicament as being a no-win situation; they can live with the sadness of childlessness; they can take a chance, and risk having a child (perhaps a second child) affected by a cruel disease, with the sorrow and suffering this may cause; or they can decide to subject a pregnancy to prenatal diagnosis, and perhaps to terminate the pregnancy if the test result is unfavourable. Opting for prenatal diagnosis can bring with it all the joy that comes with a reassuring result, or the anguish that comes from causing a miscarriage (if the testing of the pregnancy is followed by miscarriage), or the remorse that may come from terminating a wanted pregnancy (if the result shows that the child would be affected by the disorder in question). Discussing the various outcome scenarios for each possible course of action can help clients to weigh up their feelings and come to a decision.

The final component activity of genetic counselling to be listed here is to provide *ongoing support* to all families living with the decisions they have made, and to individuals affected by, or at risk of developing, genetic disease. Those at risk of developing an adult-onset disorder such as Huntington's disease may live most of their lives in the shadow of the illness; they may never actually develop the condition, but may have watched a parent and other relatives begin to show signs of the condition, then to become progressively more seriously affected and then to die from it, while they are wondering all the time whether their turn will come to be affected in the same way. Such individuals can benefit greatly from contact with specialists dealing with the disorder who take an interest in the whole family, not only those who are obviously affected at that moment.

Another way in which 'post-counselling' support may be provided is by practical involvement in the management and care of individuals with the disorders for which counselling is provided. This may take several forms:

1 regular management clinics for patients with specific conditions (clinical geneticists have differing backgrounds and experience, and are able to offer this type of support for patients with different types of disorder);
2 the long-term co-ordination of care for those who need regular surveillance for complications provided by a team of appropriate medical or surgical specialists (e.g. eye and heart specialists for those with Marfan syndrome; gastroenterologists for those at risk of developing tumours of the colon, as in familial adenomatous polyposis coli);
3 occasional clinic appointments offered for general review to ensure that problems are anticipated and identified early and that the family is given new information as it becomes available;
4 follow-up support in the family's home provided by specialist genetic co-workers or fieldworkers (in Britain, they often have experience in nursing and/or health-visiting). This may be particularly appropriate when a family has a need for emotional support but when the medical issues have been largely resolved; it may be necessary for this long-term support role to be transferred to members of the local primary health care team, because the specialist co-worker could otherwise be swamped by this aspect of her (or his) work. In many countries, this type of support service is simply not available. I would like to see such support accepted as an integral part of any genetic counselling or prenatal diagnosis programme, although the purchasers of health care (in the new British health system) may wish to purchase the 'prevention' without the 'support'.

What issues confront the genetic counsellor?

From what has been presented so far, the reader could be left thinking that the ethical issues involved in genetic counselling are indeed difficult, but that they have to be confronted by the clients and not by the professionals. While there is much truth in this, in that our clients certainly may be confronting difficult ethical issues which we do not have to face in our role as professionals, this approach is inadequate. As professionals working alongside families in difficult situations, we also encounter a set of ethical issues. The issues that we meet are not the same as those confronting our clients, but it is some of these issues – the issues that we genetic counsellors face as professionals – that this book hopes to address.

The ethical issues raised by genetic counselling can be considered as issues of practice, and as issues of principle and of social context.

ISSUES OF PRACTICE

Listening

This is generally regarded as a non-controversial activity, but it may be neglected none the less, and its importance cannot be overstated. It is essential for the genetic counsellor to discover what the clients want to find out before proceeding further; the agenda for a genetic counselling session is drawn up by the clients, not by the counsellor. In many centres, it is regarded as helpful for co-workers to visit clients before they attend clinic to gather background information about the clients' worries and questions, about the family structure, and about the condition that affects family members and that family's particular experiences of the condition. At this meeting, on the client's home ground, it is possible for the ethos of the genetic counselling service to be conveyed to the clients: 'We listen to your questions, and respond as best we can; you set the agenda.' Where home visits are not possible, telephone contact can be a very good second best.

Such pre-clinic discussions can help to allay the suspicions and fears of those who have been referred for genetic counselling without their knowledge. Some clinicians in other branches of medicine still expect genetic counsellors to give their patients instructions as to whether they should have children or be sterilized or undergo prenatal diagnosis and possibly have a termination of pregnancy (genetic counsellors do not do this); they may make inappropriate referrals of families who do not wish to be seen. A preliminary discussion on home ground is often also very useful in helping clients to formulate the questions they wish to discuss in the genetics clinic.

Establishing or confirming the diagnosis

This may also be thought of as non-controversial, but that would be a mistake. There may be no difficulty if the affected person is the client, or the client's child, and if the diagnosis is medically straightforward. But if the affected person is dead, the confirmation of diagnosis from records may be difficult; if the affected person is alive but no precise diagnosis has been reached, it may be because there is unavoidable diagnostic uncertainty; if the affected person does not want his/her medical records reviewed by geneticists on behalf of other family members, there may be a potential ethical problem of the control of access to medical records.

Finally, the family may not be ready to accept the diagnosis. They may not yet have come to terms with their child's developmental problems, and may not be ready to accept a diagnostic label that would indicate a very poor outlook for the future. There is then the difficulty of deciding whether one's primary duty is to the referring professional (who wants a diagnosis made, if possible), or to the immediate family (who want time to accept their child's set of abilities and problems), or to the extended family (if another branch of the family might want the diagnosis established because of implications for them), or to the child in question (whether the child is best served by being diagnosed and thereby categorized, or by remaining undiagnosed and therefore a unique individual).

Communication of information

Again, ethical problems abound beneath the calm and reassuring surface of everyday clinical genetics. For example, how do we communicate notions of risk to our clients? How do we distinguish between degrees of risk? Between low or 'acceptable' risks, and high or 'unacceptable' risks? Do we provide information about reproductive risk and prenatal diagnosis even when it has not been requested? If so, what implicit message does that convey to clients?

If an offer of prenatal diagnosis is declined by the client, what words do we use to describe this decision by our client? Has she (have they) 'chosen to proceed without prenatal diagnosis', or has she 'declined the offer', or has she 'refused it', or 'rejected it'? While these phrases convey much the same information about the client, they give very different pictures about the response of the counsellor to the client's decision.

Have we managed to communicate information about the availability of a prenatal test, without thereby implicitly recommending that the prenatal test should be accepted? The communication of information about such matters in a value-free manner may not be impossible, but is at least very difficult – and it certainly requires a conscious intention to avoid bias.

'Scenario-based decision counselling'

Many clients find decision-making after genetic counselling to be very difficult (Frets 1991), and some of the factors involved are not likely to be influenced by such counselling (Frets 1990). In this context, how many of the possible outcome scenarios for prenatal diagnosis will an individual client want to discuss? Does it not cause too much distress to the pregnant woman to bring up all the various possibilities?

On the other hand, is it not grossly paternalistic to decide on a couple's or a woman's behalf that they/she would not want to know about some of the possible outcomes of the decision that is about to be made? Why not find out what they/she would like to discuss?

Many professionals (I include myself) find it difficult to discuss all the possible outcome scenarios. There is the common presumption that genetic counselling is provided simply so as to make prenatal diagnosis available; it can be difficult and embarrassing to raise issues such as the remorse and depression that may follow a termination of pregnancy, or the possible conflicting views of different family members and the likely impact of these conflicts on personal relationships in the future. To raise these issues conveys implicitly to clients that the 'right' decision for some couples would be to have, or risk having, a child with a genetic disorder, rather than having prenatal diagnosis or a termination of pregnancy. This makes it clear that there are no rules set by the professionals, and effectively grants them permission to consider what they would like to do themselves. Not all clients want to make up their own minds in this way.

Unless we help our clients to discuss all options in advance of making firm decisions, we are not providing an authentic counselling service. And if we are merely regulating access to reproductive tests, without providing counselling and support, then how do we escape the accusation that (whatever we think or claim that we are doing) we are in fact acting to promote genetic testing and 'fetal quality control', rather than providing information and choice? Given the low priority that counselling skills are accorded in the training of medical geneticists, there may be good reason to hold these opinions.

To avoid discussion with clients about the difficult areas such as remorse, guilt and personal conflicts following either pregnancy termination or the birth of an affected child is effectively to decide what a client would like to discuss without asking her. Such decisions may be particularly unhelpful when the client belongs to a minority ethnic or religious group, and her likely views are decided without consultation, being determined largely by the stereotyped picture of the client's minority group that is held by the counsellor.

Ongoing support

Genetics departments cannot hope to provide the ongoing clinical management for everyone affected by genetic disease; it would simply be impossible. And why should clinical geneticists be involved in clinical management at all? Not all clinical geneticists would concur, but some feel that their involvement in clinical management encourages a useful degree of humility while simultaneously providing motivation for their research. This management role keeps us in contact with the practical problems of people with genetic diseases, and reminds us of the limitations of medicine in general and medical genetics in particular. To be involved in genetic diagnosis and counselling, in teaching and research, but not at all in the management of the practical difficulties of life for those with disabilities and genetic diseases, could slowly but progressively distort a professional's perspective on the very diseases with which he is engaged in the abstract.

ISSUES OF PRINCIPLE AND SOCIAL CONTEXT

Informed consent

There are two particular ways in which informed consent can cause difficulties in genetic counselling. First, there is the issue of complexity: the choices with which our clients may be confronted can be technically complex, but without adequate understanding the clients cannot give informed consent. We may try our best to explain the tests at an appropriate level of technical sophistication to suit the client, but do we succeed? Do clients understand the risk of error in the test result, or the risk of miscarriage caused by a prenatal diagnostic procedure? This becomes an ethical problem when we fail to explain the choices adequately to our clients; the involvement of specialist genetics fieldworkers to provide ongoing support to our clients can help to identify families who would like another chance to discuss points of continuing uncertainty.

The other context in which informed consent raises particular ethical questions concerns genetic screening programmes. In such programmes, it would require a vast input of resources for every client to have an hour-long one-to-one discussion about the proffered test with a qualified counsellor; in practice, many genetic screening programmes offer minimal information and cursory discussion. This is true of much antenatal clinic screening for Down syndrome (trisomy 21) and neural tube defects (spina bifida and anencephaly) and of 'routine' fetal ultrasonography; such tests will often be presented as 'routine' procedures, and detailed discussion of the testing may not be encouraged (Marteau *et al.* 1992a, 1993).

Population screening to identify carriers of autosomal recessive disorders such as haemoglobinopathies, cystic fibrosis and Tay-Sachs disease is another setting in which the validity of clients' informed consent may be problematic. In the past, some such programmes have generated enormous social problems – such as racial discrimination against black Americans found to carry sickle cell disease (Whitten 1973; Hampton *et al.* 1974), or have generated less visible but still substantial problems of stigmatization of thalassaemia carriers (Stamatoyannopoulos 1974). Furthermore, 10 per cent of carriers in one North American study of screening for haemoglobinopathies were unable to state that their health would not be affected (Loader *et al.* 1991). Screening for Tay-Sachs disease carriers has been shown to leave about one-fifth of carriers with long-term residual worries (Zeesman *et al.* 1984), and carriers are less optimistic than they were before being tested about their own future health (Marteau *et al.* 1992b).

Proposals to introduce widespread population screening for cystic fibrosis (CF), now that most carriers can be identified by molecular genetic methods, have so far not been adopted. The resource implications of screening whole (adult) populations in Europe or North America are enormous, and if adequate standards of pre-test and post-test counselling and informed consent were to be implemented, the costs would be prohibitive (Wilfond and Fost 1990); it should be remembered that approximately 1 in 25 individuals in Britain carries one faulty copy of the CF gene.

While provision for population screening may be costly, the costs of treatment for CF continue to rise as the expected lifespan of affected individuals increases, so the cost–benefit arguments in favour of population carrier screening will continue to be promoted with increasing vigour. The introduction of effective gene therapies for CF may add to the costs of caring for affected individuals, while diminishing the motivation for members of the public to accept carrier screening and prenatal testing. Screening programmes may then need to justify their existence by achieving high rates of uptake and significant shifts in reproductive patterning; to do this, they may need to adopt marketing strategies and promotional techniques to maximize their impact. What would informed consent mean in such a context?

Some advocates of CF carrier screening have devised cheap means of screening large numbers of pregnant women and their partners in the 'natural screening turnstile' of the antenatal clinic (Wald 1991). This is of particular concern because it is already known that many women find it difficult to decline (refuse) the offer of antenatal screening tests (Sjögren and Uddenberg 1988); perhaps every woman should attend an assertiveness training course before becoming pregnant. When carrier screening programmes are judged by the uptake rate achieved and by the money 'saved' by terminating pregnancies, rather than by the impact of screening on those offered the test, we will know that cost–benefit-based, 'public health genetics' (eugenics) has truly arrived.

Genetic testing in children

Where a child stands to gain as the result of genetic testing – where medical management can be modified appropriately – the ethical issues may be fairly straightforward, although informed parental consent should surely still be obtained even for newborn screening for treatable disorders (and properly informed parental consent is not usually obtained in this context) (Smith *et al.* 1990; Statham *et al.* 1993). However, where parents, doctors or social agencies (local authorities or adoption agencies) request predictive genetic testing for an adult-onset disorder or susceptibility, or carrier testing that will be of no relevance to the child until (s)he is of an age to make reproductive decisions, there is a potentially serious problem. Some adults prefer not to be tested for late-onset disorders or to determine their carrier status, and the child's future autonomy will be infringed by testing in childhood: it will have deprived the child of his/her future right not to undergo testing. It has been argued that the child's parents have the right to have such tests performed, because they are the guardians of the child's interests (Pelias 1991). This view would not generally be supported in Britain by the legal profession (see Chapter 9), particularly since the Children Act (1989) has established that parents have duties towards their children rather than rights over them; if the acquisition of information about a child's genetic status could prove damaging to the child's long-term interests, then parents and professionals would be obliged to refrain from carrying out such tests. Furthermore, the international medical community has declared its opposition to childhood testing for Huntington's disease (HD); a report from the World Federation of Neurology (1989) has advised strongly against testing children. The importance of this declaration has been emphasized by the requests for childhood testing received by HD test centres (Morris *et al.* 1988, 1989).

A consideration of predictive testing for HD is useful in any discussion of the genetic testing of children, because the issues are relatively clear. Many fewer at-risk adults have come forward for predictive testing for HD than had declared their intention to do so before the test was available (Tyler *et al.* 1992): when confronted with the reality of the test, many have preferred to live with uncertainty. Adverse reactions can occur in those given low-risk results as well as those given high-risk results (Huggins *et al.* 1992). Furthermore, even a 100 per cent accurate genetic test (such as has just become available for HD) would not prove that a child at risk of HD, and with possible symptoms of it, was actually suffering from the disease. The onset of HD in childhood is rare, and neurological symptoms in an at-risk child could have another explanation (Bloch and Hayden 1990). So predictive testing is chosen by a minority of at-risk adults, and even the potential medical diagnostic benefits of testing are few, because the diagnosis of symptomatic HD in childhood could not be confirmed by the genetic tests and might lead to the failure to diagnose a treatable condition.

In addition to the infringement of the child's future autonomy as an adult, there are other kinds of harm that could be inflicted on children as a result of genetic testing. The demonstration that their child is likely to develop a particular condition in adult life could influence parental expectations of the child's future health, abilities, reproductive plans and personal relationships; such altered expectations could distort the child's development as an individual, their educational and career achievements and their personal happiness, and could become self-fulfilling prophecies. Such problems could be generated by testing for susceptibility to multifactorial conditions (e.g. ischaemic heart disease) as well as testing for single-gene Mendelian diseases, with the added danger of family and professionals seeking to introduce preventive measures of uncertain safety and efficacy. Even the demonstration that the child is a healthy carrier of a recessive disorder such as CF could influence parental expectations of that child's reproductive future. Where there are several children in a family, and where they differ with respect to the genetic test in question, complex distortions of family relationships could arise. These issues have been raised elsewhere (Harper and Clarke 1990).

The control of personal genetic information

Information about a person's genetic make-up may be of interest not only to the individual but also to other members of their family, to their employer, their life-insurance company and possibly other agencies, including the state. When does this interest in a person's genetic constitution give the interested party a *right of access* to that information?

First, what it would mean for us to respect confidentiality? It would certainly entail making every effort to prevent the inadvertent breaching of confidences:

(i) obtaining consent before examining medical records, or genetic test results, on other family members;
(ii) obtaining consent before obtaining samples from, or carrying out genetic tests on, other family members.
(iii) taking care that confidential information about members of the extended family is not passed from one branch of the family to another. For example, when the family tree is drawn out, it may show the occurrence of pregnancy terminations, illegitimacy, adoptions etc. about which some members of the family may never have been informed. Care must be taken that such items of information are not revealed to those who did not already know

them (different versions of the pedigree may be needed for discussions with different branches of the family);
(iv) taking care not to reveal raw laboratory results to individuals in the family (which may include information about other family members), and only releasing the information that had been specifically requested;
(v) clearly distinguishing between samples taken for research purposes and those taken to provide information for the family; obtaining separate consent for these separate purposes.

These measures will help to prevent inadvertent breaches of confidentiality, but when might family members be thought to have a legitimate interest in the results of tests carried out on their relatives? They may be interested in such test results out of concern for their relative, or because the result may have implications for their own future health or the health of their children. If a person is found to carry a recessive gene defect (such as a mutant copy of the gene for cystic fibrosis – CF), relatives may be carriers too; they would be unaffected, but their children would have an increased chance of being affected if their partners also carried a mutant CF gene. Should a CF gene carrier be obliged to reveal this fact to his relatives? If Huntington's disease (HD) affects a man in the early stages of dementia (but with full insight) who does not want to give a blood sample for genetic testing – so that his children could be tested, if they so wished – should he be obliged to provide such a sample? Or should a sample be obtained from him by deception (the blood ostensibly being taken for some other purpose)? And if a profoundly handicapped child is found to have an unbalanced chromosomal rearrangement, and one parent carries the same rearrangement in balanced form, should that parent be obliged to reveal this to his/her family? Other family members may also carry the same chromosomal rearrangement, and be at considerable risk of having a similarly handicapped child.

Some commentators have been tempted to propose a legal framework of compulsion to deal with intra-family conflict over the right of access to such information. From the perspective of a clinical geneticist, however, I would regard such a development as being profoundly unhelpful. In practice, there are very few occasions where family members are not willing to share such information with their relatives; in fact, many families go to great lengths to trace relatives who live in different continents if there is any chance of its being relevant to them. Those who are at first unwilling to do so are often reacting with shock to a personal tragedy, and they do not usually refuse to discuss it with their families for very long.

In the very few circumstances where an individual has been reluctant to discuss the situation with his extended family, discussing the scenarios that could arise usually resolves the problem. The awareness that another branch of the family might experience the same sad problems as they have done, and would probably come to realize that they could have been warned in advance about the risks, almost always leads to a willingness to reassess the decision, and discuss the genetic issues with other family members after all. The introduction of legislation into this delicate area could cause great harm, leading individuals to fear disclosing a family history of genetic disease to any doctor. This could result in important clinical decisions being made without full information, as well as to ignorance of the risk of recurrence in the immediate or extended family. The chance of recurrence may be substantial, or may be mistakenly thought to be substantial when it is in fact minimal.

The introduction of compulsion into this area would also bring genetics into serious disrepute, adding weight to the historical perspective from which clinical genetics is viewed as a form of eugenic reproductive policing. Compulsion would contravene two of the central principles of medical ethics – confidentiality and autonomy – and its practical effects would be overwhelmingly harmful. While family members may have a legitimate interest in genetic test results on their relatives, these interests are not strong enough to justify their compulsory disclosure. The tested individual has a stronger claim to the information than other family members have. The parallels with the right to privacy for sexually transmitted diseases are helpful in considering these issues.

Individual autonomy in the area of reproductive decisions is not explicitly challenged even by those who challenge it with respect to the control of personal genetic information. However, the former sense of autonomy is implicitly under threat because the notion of harm being caused by the withholding of genetic information is intimately bound up with the notion of 'wrongful life', and this legal concept may come to be applied to children with genetic conditions or diseases whose parents decline prenatal testing. The sense of the word 'autonomy' is shifting from 'self-determination' to 'standing on your own two feet' or self-reliance (Chadwick 1993), so that individuals could be held financially accountable for their moral decisions. In such a climate, a decision made on moral grounds that resulted in the birth of a handicapped child could lead to the individual responsible for the decision (parent or other family member) being made financially responsible for the care of that child; society would not be willing to meet those costs.

What about the interests of third parties? Insurance companies may be fearful that someone found to be at high risk of a lethal disorder will take out health and life insurance without informing the insurance company, and the client's own doctor (likely to be submitting the medical report) may not be aware of the genetic situation. Should not the premium for someone at increased risk of ill health or death be raised? Otherwise, the company's other clients will be forced to pay higher premiums. Of course, the whole purpose of insurance is to spread the financial load of coping with such problems, when only a few individuals are likely to be affected; to alter premiums in this way could be held to run counter to this purpose. On the other hand, the prior knowledge of an increased risk may lead to the individual taking out more insurance than he otherwise would. A compromise has been suggested in which insurance companies would not seek the results of genetic tests unless a particularly large insurance policy was being arranged (Harper 1993).

Employers may wish to test their workforce to identify those at increased risk of occupational diseases. Such tests are not yet generally available, but could be considered to be potentially advantageous to the employer and the employee. However, the employee may not feel that (s)he has much to gain if a high-risk test result renders him/her unemployed. In addition, employers could screen the workforce for susceptibility to damage from pollutants as an alternative to reducing levels of environmental contamination; this might be disadvantageous to the workforce and to society as a whole.

More general concerns about the privacy of genetic information have been voiced in the USA, where health insurance is often arranged by employers. If employment prospects were to be harmed by genetic information being passed from insurance company to employer, then those with a family history of certain inherited diseases might be denied employment because they or their family were at increased risk of developing a costly disease. The employee might be at increased risk of developing dementia from HD; or his/her children might be at increased risk of developing a costly childhood disorder such as CF; in either case, the insurance company might face considerable expense. Such discrimination in the fields of employment and insurance against those who might come to be affected by disabling diseases has been recorded, despite the anti-discriminatory legislation contained in the Americans with Disabilities Act of 1990 (Holtzman and Rothstein 1992; Natowicz *et al.* 1992; Billings *et al.* 1992). Legislative efforts to regulate the control of genetic information are being pursued (McEwan and Reilly 1992), and in both Britain and America a legal framework is being constructed to control access to information held on genetic registers and databases (Harper 1992a; Reilly 1992). Until these protective measures are established and shown to be effective, there will be reason for concern about the potential misuse of genetic information held on individuals and families in ordinary medical records as well as in genetic registers. The compulsory disclosure of certain genetic diagnoses to state governments (eg chromosomal anomalies in California) would be a particular cause for concern when issues of privacy, stigmatization and inappropriate labelling are considered (Duster 1990).

The goals and evaluation of genetic counselling

One justification for genetic counselling services and genetic diagnostic laboratories is that they save money, that the termination of affected pregnancies results in fewer children with disorders that require expensive treatments (Chapple *et al.* 1987). Discussion of antenatal maternal serum screening for Down syndrome usually pay more attention to the potential cost savings of such schemes (Gill *et al.* 1987; Wald *et al.* 1992) than to their other effects (Blumberg *et al.* 1975; Donnai *et al.* 1981; Green 1990), particularly to the need for support after terminations of pregnancy carried out because of fetal abnormality (Lloyd and Laurence 1985; Elder and Laurence 1991; White-van Mourik *et al.* 1992). I have argued elsewhere that geneticists should divorce themselves from such simplistic notions of cost–benefit analysis, and should justify their diagnostic, medical management, counselling and support functions as much as their 'preventive' (reproductive options) activities (Clarke 1990). Client satisfaction with genetic counselling can be measured, although there is not much experience of doing this, and it seems to be influenced greatly by the information provided during counselling (Shiloh *et al.* 1990).

Cost–benefit analysis of medical genetic services can be presented in a more sophisticated form than the crude accounting used by those groups referred to above. Modell and Kuliev (1991) propose a model in which education of the population is a benefit and not a cost, and informed client choice is a benefit whatever the decision that is made. This certainly helps with the presentation of genetic screening as an enabling, informing activity that is not directing or coercing clients into making 'approved' decisions. However, it is not clear that the practice of such a screening programme is very different from that of a more directive programme that has been modified so as not to offend a sophisticated public. Furthermore, the adoption of autonomous decisions as the goal of genetic screening programmes is inadequate as the justification for the adoption by health service managers of any particular programme (why adopt one programme rather than another, when either results in clients making autonomous decisions?), and entails its own inconsistencies (Clarke 1991, 1993; Chadwick 1993).

The fact that a screening programme has been established suggests that 'society' and 'the medical profession' think it is A Good Thing, and that message may itself be experienced as directive (Clarke 1992, 1993). The promotion of national screening programmes for genetic disease could lead to the subordination of individuals' concerns and decisions to the broader, population-based goals (Harper 1992b), and that would bring such programmes uncomfortably close to the eugenic programmes of Nazi Germany and the compulsory sterilization programmes of the USA earlier this century. The promotion of population-based genetic programmes without adequate research into the social and ethical effects of such programmes is a particular cause for concern (Lippman 1991).

How can the quality and efficiency of genetic counselling services be measured while at the same time these traps are avoided? First, the core assessment can be the satisfaction of clients and of referring agencies, and peer review of practice can be used to determine that professional standards are maintained. However, much work will be needed to develop mechanisms of measuring client satisfaction that are reliable and that will be trusted by genetic counsellors as well as their employing institutions and the public.

History: eugenics

Doctors in the past have often given explicit instructions to patients to undergo a sterilization procedure, or to have a pregnancy terminated, because of a possible genetic disorder; these practices reflect attitudes that are no longer generally held by clinical geneticists (medical genetic counsellors), but they are still held by some other doctors, and they have influenced the public understanding of the medical approach to genetic issues. It is clear that many physicians who were involved in eugenics in Nazi Germany regarded themselves as worthy men engaged in thoroughly proper and responsible activities (Hanauske-Abel 1986; Müller-Hill 1988; Proctor 1988). It must not be forgotten that there were eugenicists in Britain too (Kevles 1985; Mazumdar 1992), and eugenic sterilization programmes operating actively in USA until at least the 1960s (Reilly 1977; Kevles 1985; Duster 1990).

It must be remembered, too, that the historical activities of eugenicists have contributed to the current climate of opinion and attitudes surrounding genetics. The expectation of many clients (and some medical colleagues) is that geneticists will give instructions about the 'patient's' future reproductive plans; they expect a medical geneticist or genetic counsellor to behave like any other health professional, and tell them what to do for the best.

Directiveness and social responsibility in reproduction

Even where the language of 'reproductive autonomy' and 'client choice' has entered the vocabulary of genetic screening programmes, clients may still be told what to do. In particular, clients may be subtly encouraged to take part in a programme (Marteau et al. 1992a, 1993). Taking part in a programme may be portrayed as the decision of the responsible citizen, or it may be presented as a matter of routine, with staff clearly expecting clients to participate. Such 'directive' practices reinforce the notion of 'social responsibility in reproduction'; failure to accept the test may be regarded by staff as a form of deviance. The decision as to whether or not to terminate a pregnancy affected by a sex chromosome anomaly (of minor importance in comparison to a diagnosis of Down syndrome) is influenced by the background of the person who gives the information: more terminations are performed if an obstetrician gives the information than if it is given by a genetic counsellor (Holmes-Siedle et al. 1987; Robinson et al. 1989). It is also clear that the framing of recurrence risk information in genetic counselling can influence clients' perceptions of the risk (Shiloh and Sagi 1989), so genetic counsellors may be influencing clients as much as antenatal clinic staff (who provide most pre-test information in connection with antenatal genetic screening programmes).

Is it in fact possible to be totally non-directive when counselling clients in genetic clinics? I have argued elsewhere that this is always difficult, and that it may be impossible in the context of genetic screening (Clarke 1991). Another view is that non-directiveness is unattainable, and that directiveness is acceptable as long as it is explicit; unacknowledged directiveness may be much more manipulative (Kessler 1992).

The notion of social responsibility in reproduction, coupled to the mistaken but increasingly popular belief that almost all genetic disorders and other causes of 'handicap' can be prevented by terminating affected pregnancies, is leading to the expectation that all babies will be biologically perfect. Where a baby is 'flawed', there must be someone to blame; if the medical profession has not been negligent, then it must be the parents' fault for not having had 'the tests', or for not having terminated the pregnancy. Such attitudes could have serious repercussions for the provision of care by society for those with congenital malformations and genetic diseases.

THIS VOLUME

In compiling this volume, I have been selfish; I have invited contributions from individuals whose views I have wanted to read. It is not possible in one volume to cover all the ethical topics raised by genetic counselling as a profession, and so I have been forced to browse among the possible topics and the possible contributors.

This introduction is intended to present to the reader the issues, as seen from the perspective of a clinical geneticist, and some of the literature concerning these issues. I have particularly aimed at including references to critical contributions to the discussions about genetic counselling. I have not attempted to cover the fields of the new reproductive technologies or gene therapy.

The first five contributed chapters have been written by individuals closely involved with the provision of clinical genetic services. The remaining six chapters are written from different perspectives. Despite the inevitable failure to cover every topic from every perspective, I hope that the contributions are of interest to those involved in genetic counselling and, more generally, in human genetics. I also hope that the book will interest students of philosophy and of the social sciences, as well as students of the health professions and concerned members of the general public. Finally, I hope that health service managers, civil servants and perhaps politicians may gain some insight into genetic counselling from this volume.

In Chapter 1 Caroline Berry has written an account of the issues faced every day by busy genetic counsellors, concentrating on truth-telling, abortion issues, confidentiality and autonomy.

Ann Williams follows this (Chapter 2) by considering the issues that confront a genetics co-worker (in Britain, usually a genetics nurse specialist). She is concerned to examine the relationships that are built by the genetics nurse with her medical colleagues and with her client families, and particularly to examine the boundaries of these relationships. How does the relationship with clients begin, and how does it come to an end? If the client needs to make a decision (perhaps about a pregnancy), how can the genetics nurse provide support during this process?

As an appendix to this chapter, I have included a document written to provide guidance to clinical research workers at the Institute of Medical Genetics in Cardiff. This was written by Ann Williams and Dr Helen Hughes, to help avoid the problems that may be generated by clinical research into genetic disease.

David Ball, Audrey Tyler and Peter Harper examine the issues raised by predictive genetic testing, concentrating upon the example of Huntington's disease (Chapter 3). They examine informed consent, childhood testing, and the need for confidentiality and autonomy in this difficult area. They consider how these issues will arise when testing is available for other, more frequent conditions, and when laboratory-based predictive testing is made available without coun-selling and support.

As an appendix to this chapter, I have included a discussion document written by Peter Harper about the boundary between research work and its diagnostic application in connection with DNA samples gathered from individuals in families with genetic diseases.

In Chapter 4 Evelyn Parsons and Don Bradley discuss informed consent for a screening programme (in which I am also closely involved) for newborns – screening for the (so far) untreatable disorder, Duchenne muscular dystrophy. They examine the re-negotiation of principles that has occurred in this programme as practical experience has accumulated – the programme's reflexivity.

Margaretha White-van Mourik examines the experiences of couples who decide to terminate a pregnancy on the grounds of foetal abnormality (Chapter 5). She reports that these couples are often given little of the support they need; she is able to recommend improvements in the way in which professionals deal with such families before the prenatal diagnosis is performed and following the termination of pregnancy.

Benno Müller-Hill, a biologist, has made a study of Nazi eugenics. He examines attitudes to 'racial mixing' in Nazi Germany, and the practice of sterilization for supposedly genetic defects of intellect or character or race in Germany and in Sweden (Chapter 6). He concludes that establishing counselling as non-directive, and declaring directive counselling to be unacceptable, is just the first of several necessary steps for the profession of genetic counselling, if it is to find its true function. 'Justice [is] lost where there is no help for the weak but when they are just left to be destroyed by the forces of the market.'

Abby Lippman's chapter is the one contribution that has been published before (Chapter 7). I am grateful to her and to the *American Journal of Law and Medicine* for permission to include the paper here. This contribution examines prenatal genetic screening from the perspective of a social scientist who is herself trying to examine such programmes as they are experienced by ordinary women. She critically examines the discourse of screening programmes, challenging their claims to provide 'reassurance' and 'choice'. She also examines the public health (cost) motivation for many such programmes, and their social consequences.

This critical approach is in the tradition of Farrant (1985), and of Rothman. The effect of prenatal screening on the relationship between a woman and her fetus has been examined by Rothman; even wanted pregnancies may be 'on approval' rather than being unconditionally welcomed. Rothman calls this phenomenon, *The Tentative Pregnancy* (Rothman 1986). Another way of providing reassurance that does not generate the same 'side-effects' (of anxiety, of miscarriages, of terminations of pregnancy) might be to provide a thorough scheme for the support of families with children who have physical or intellectual disabilities, including financial support, respite care and active community involvement.

Why, then, are genetic screening programmes proliferating, while the care for affected individuals is receiving less support and is even fragmenting? There may be a connection between these events and the phenomenon of 'geneticization', by which Lippman means the dominance of genetic modes of thought and genetic explanations for disability and handicap, as opposed to possible social and environmental explanations. Genetic contributions to handicap might be expected to be more difficult to remedy than social contributions, but this will be ignored where genetic modes of explanation are dominant.

It is tempting to link the growth of geneticization throughout the 1980s with wider political developments in Britain and the USA – the growth of individualism and the denial of the value of community. Thus, providing individual risk figures for Down syndrome in each pregnancy ensures that each woman/couple faces this in isolation. To ensure that families with an affected child are given the full support of their community is another possible way of reassuring pregnant women, but this could only happen in a society that valued the sense of community, and in which there was confidence that such values would persist.

The development of geneticization can be traced at least from Yoxen (1982), and is developed further by Baird (1990) and Lippman (1992). Müller-Hill's warning about 'the market' should prompt us to consider how to disengage the scientific component of geneticization from the accompanying political agenda of extreme individualism and the denial of community.

Lydia Sinclair and Matthew Griffiths both work for MENCAP, and their chapter examines mental handicap, and the needs of those affected by it (Chapter 8). How do decisions come to be made 'on behalf' of those with mental handicap? Their answer is that pragmatism dictates this, not ethical considerations. They assert that individuals with mental handicap can frequently contribute to decisions about their lives; they also argue that the promotion of prenatal screening and terminations of pregnancy so as to reduce the birth incidence of children with mental handicap results in discrimination against affected individuals and it adds to their exclusion from society. Families will 'choose' to terminate affected fetuses if they know that society's provision for such individuals is grossly inadequate.

Jonathan Montgomery is a Lecturer in Law at Southampton University. He has a strong interest in the law as it relates to children. In Chapter 9 he examines the rights of those with mental handicap and of children; he particularly sets out to distinguish the interests of children from those of other members of their family in relation to genetic testing. This chapter will be of interest to practising clinicians who are uncertain as to how the law in England and Wales (particularly the Children Act of 1989) relates to the debate about genetic testing in childhood. Where this is to the direct benefit of the child, there is no dispute, but clarification is needed where the test result concerns a late-onset disorder or the child's carrier status for a recessive disease or a balanced chromosomal rearrangement (topics that will not be relevant until the child makes reproductive plans as an adult).

Paula Boddington is a philosopher who discusses the issues raised by confidentiality in genetic counselling (Chapter 10). She considers the different spheres of confidentiality, and examines various challenges to the view that genetic information should be protected; in particular, she examines the concept of 'genetic harm'. She takes a critical view of a report on ethical issues in clinical genetics (Royal College of Physicians 1991).

Maureen Ramsay is another philosopher, interested in political theory, who examines geneticization and genetic reductionism in Chapter 11. She seeks to integrate biological and social explanations of genetic disease rather than according priority to either perspective. This allows the scientific findings of genetics to be acknowledged, while possible social and environmental remedies for health problems can be seriously considered.

A NOTE ON INHERITANCE

Genes are coded messages that instruct the growing body in how to develop and function. There are many thousands of different genes, which come in matching pairs; one of each pair of genes comes in the egg from the mother, and the other comes in the sperm from the father. When an adult produces an egg or a sperm, one member of each pair of genes is copied into the gamete (the egg or sperm).

Genes are too small to be visible even under the microscope. However, genes are organized into physical structures called chromosomes, which are visible under the microscope. Each chromosome can be thought of as a string of beads, with each bead representing a gene. There are twenty-three pairs of chromosomes in each cell in the body, with one of each pair being packaged into each egg or sperm.

Twenty-two of the chromosome pairs are the same in males and females; the other pair of chromosomes are the sex chromosomes, X and Y. A man has one X chromosome and one Y chromosome; a woman has two X chromosomes. The Y chromosome makes a man male, but does little else. Therefore if an X chromosome has a faulty gene on it, and if it is present in a male, that person is likely to show signs of the gene fault. Women who carry a faulty gene on one of their two X chromosomes are much less likely to be affected by it, because they have a second (spare) copy of the gene on the other X chromosome that will usually mask it. The X chromosome carries many genes that are quite unrelated to sex, so that the *sex-linked disorders* that are much more common in males than females include some types of muscular dystrophy (including the severe Duchenne type), haemophilia, colour-blindness and many more. Such disorders may arise as new mutations in a gene, or females in the family may be unaffected carriers. In that case, affected males will have carrier mothers, and the males will be linked in the family tree through healthy women.

Faulty copies of genes are common – everyone has at least one such gene fault (mutant gene). Most such gene faults cause no problem, because a single intact copy of most genes is enough to get by on without any difficulty. However, if a person inherits a faulty copy of the same gene from both parents, then that child will have no intact copy of the gene, and may have a genetic disease such as cystic fibrosis (CF) or a haemoglobin disorder such as sickle-cell anaemia or a thalassaemia. Because faulty copies of such genes do not usually manifest problems, these gene defects are termed *recessive*. Parents must be carriers of the faulty gene, and other relatives may be; brothers and sisters may be also affected, or other relatives if a carrier in the family has a partner who is also a carrier.

Some genes are sufficiently important that both copies must be intact for the person to avoid a genetic disease. Such gene faults give rise to *dominant* gene defects, which can be transmitted from one generation to the next (to 50 per cent of the children on average).

Chromosomes may also be involved in genetic disease. First, an egg or sperm may be produced that contains the wrong number of chromosomes. Many such conceptions miscarry early in pregnancy, but some survive to be born. Down syndrome occurs when a child inherits three copies of chromosome 21 instead of the normal two. Anomalies of the sex chromosome are common, and in liveborn infants they are not usually associated with major physical or developmental problems.

Another type of chromosomal problem arises when a rearrangement occurs – either with two small chromosomes joining together to form a single chromosome, or when two chromosomes exchange segments. Such rearrangements may cause no immediate problem, but if a person carrying such a rearranged set of chromosomes has a child, the child may be at some risk of a serious developmental disorder. The *balanced chromosomal rearrangement* may cause no difficulty because all the genes are present, just arranged differently. However, there may be a risk of such a person handing on to his or her children an *unbalanced complement* of chromosomes, that contains an incorrect set of genes. The rearrangement may also be handed on in the balanced form, so that several members of a family may carry such a rearrangement before it is recognized as the cause of physical or developmental problems in a child.

REFERENCES

Baird, P. A. (1990) 'Genetics and health care: a paradigm shift', *Perspectives in Biology and Medicine* 33: 203–13.

Billings, P. R., Kohn, M. A., de Cuevas, M. *et al.* (1992) 'Discrimination as a consequence of genetic testing', *American Journal of Human Genetics* 50: 476–82.

Bloch, M. and Hayden, M. R. (1990) 'Predictive testing for Huntington disease in childhood: challenges and implications', *American Journal of Human Genetics* 46: 1–4.

Blumberg, B. D., Golbus, M. S. and Hanson, K. H. (1975) 'The psychological sequelae of abortion performed for a genetic indication', *American Journal of Obstetrics and Gynecology* 122: 799–808.

Chadwick, R. (1993) 'What counts as success in genetic counselling?' *Journal of Medical Ethics* 19: 43–6.

Chapple, J. C., Dale, R. and Evans, B. G. (1987) 'The new genetics: will it pay its way?' *Lancet* i: 1189–92.

Clarke, A. (1990) 'Genetics, ethics and audit', *Lancet* 335: 1145–7.

—— (1991) 'Is non-directive genetic counselling possible?' *Lancet* 338: 998–1001.

—— (1993) Response to: 'What counts as success in genetic counselling?' *Journal of Medical Ethics* 19: 47–9.

Donnai, P., Charles, N. and Harris, R. (1981) 'Attitudes of patients after "genetic" termination of pregnancy', *British Medical Journal* 282: 621–2.

Duster, T. (1990) *Backdoor to Eugenics* New York and London: Routledge.

Elder, S. H. and Laurence, K. M. (1991) 'The impact of supportive intervention after second trimester termination of pregnancy for fetal abnormality' *Prenatal Diagnosis* 11: 47–54.

Farrant, W. 'Who's for amniocentesis? The politics of prenatal screening' in H. Homas (ed.) *The Sexual Politics of Reproduction*, Vermont: Gower.

Frets, P. G., Duivenvoorden, H. J., Verhage, F. *et al.* (1990) 'Factors influencing the reproductive decision after genetic counselling', *American Journal of Medical Genetics* 35: 496–502.

—— (1991) 'Analysis of problems in making the reproductive decision after genetic counselling', *Journal of Medical Genetics* 28: 194–200.

Gill, M., Murday, V. and Slack, J. (1987) 'An economic appraisal of screening for Down's syndrome in pregnancy using maternal age and serum alpha-fetoprotein concentration', *Social Science and Medicine* 24: 725–31.

Green, J. (1990) 'Calming or harming. A critical view of psychological effects of fetal diagnosis on pregnant women', Galton Institute Occasional Papers, 2nd series, no. 2.

Hampton, M. L., Anderson, J., Lavizzo, B.S. and Bergman, A. B. (1974) 'Sickle-cell "nondisease"', *American Journal of Diseases of Children* 128: 58–61.

Hanauske-Abel, H. M. (1986) 'From Nazi holocaust to nuclear holocaust: a lesson to learn', *Lancet* ii: 271–3.

Harper, P. S. (1992a) 'Huntington disease and the abuse of genetics', *American Journal of Human Genetics* 50: 460–4.

—— (1992b) 'Genetics and public health', *British Medical Journal* 304: 721.

—— (1993) 'Insurance and genetic testing', *Lancet* 341: 224–7.

Harper, P. S. and Clarke, A. (1990) 'Should we test children for "adult" genetic diseases?' *Lancet* 335: 1205–6.

Holmes-Siedle, M., Ryyanen, M. and Lindenbaum, R. H. (1987) 'Parental decisions regarding termination of pregnancy following prenatal detection of sex chromosome abnormality', *Prenatal Diagnosis* 7: 239–44.

Holtzman, N. A. and Rothstein, M. A. (1992) 'Eugenics and genetic discrimination', *American Journal of Human Genetics* 50: 457–9.

Huggins, M., Bloch, M., Wiggins, S. *et al.* (1992) 'Predictive testing for Huntington disease in Canada: adverse effects and unexpected results in those receiving a decreased risk', *American Journal of Medical Genetics* 42: 508–15.

Kessler, S. (1992) 'Psychological aspects of genetic counselling VII: Thoughts on directiveness', *Journal of Genetic Counselling* 1: 9–17.

Kevles, D. J. (1985) *In the Name of Eugenics: Genetics and the Uses of Human Heredity*, Harmondsworth: Penguin.

Lippman, A. (1991) 'Research studies in applied human genetics: a quantitative analysis and critical review of recent literature', *American Journal of Medical Genetics* 41: 105–11.

—— (1992) 'Mother matters: a fresh look at prenatal genetic testing', *Issues in Reproductive and Genetic Engineering* 5: 141–54.

Lloyd, J. and Laurence, K. M. (1985) 'Sequelae and support after termination of pregnancy for fetal malformation', *British Medical Journal* 290: 907–9.

Loader, S., Sutera, C. J., Segelman, S. G. *et al.* (1991) 'Prenatal hemoglobinopathy screening IV: Follow-up of women at risk for a child with a clinically significant hemoglobinopathy', *American Journal of Human Genetics* 49: 1292–9.

McEwan, J. E. and Reilly, P. R. (1992) 'State legislative efforts to regulate use and potential misuse of genetic information', *American Journal of Human Genetics* 51: 637–47.

Marteau, T. M., van Duijn, M. and Ellis, I. (1992b) 'Effects of genetic screening on perceptions of health: a pilot study', *Journal of Medical Genetics* 29: 24–6.

Marteau, T. M., Plenicar, M. and Kidd, J. (1993) 'Obstetricians presenting amniocentesis to pregnant women: practice observed', *Journal of Reproductive and Infant Psychology* 11: 3–10.

Marteau, T. M., Slack, J., Kidd, J. and Shaw, R. (1992a) 'Presenting a routine screening test in antenatal care: practice observed', *Public Health* 106: 131–41.

Mazumdar, P. M. H. (1992) *Eugenics, Human Genetics and Human Failings: The Eugenics Society, its Sources and its Critics in Britain* London: Routledge.

Modell, B. and Kuliev, A. M. (1991) 'Services for thalassaemia as a model for cost–benefit analysis of genetics services', *Journal of Inherited Metabolic Disease* 14: 640–51.

Morris, M., Tyler, A. and Harper, P. S. (1988) 'Adoption and genetic prediction for Huntington's disease', *Lancet* ii: 1069–70.

Morris, M., Tyler, A., Lazarous, L., Meredith, L. and Harper, P. S. (1989) 'Problems in genetic prediction for Huntington's disease', *Lancet* ii: 601–3.

Müller-Hill, B. (1988) *Murderous Science: Elimination by Scientific Selection of Jews, Gypsies and Other, Germany 1933–1945*, Oxford: Oxford University Press.

Natowicz, M. R., Alper, J. K. and Alper, J. S. (1992) 'Genetic discrimination and the law', *American Journal of Human Genetics* 50: 465–75.

Pelias, M. Z. (1991) 'Duty to disclose in medical genetics. A legal perspective', *American Journal of Medical Genetics* 39: 347–54.

Proctor, R. N. (1988) *Racial Hygiene: Medicine under the Nazis*, Cambridge, Mass.: Harvard University Press.

Reilly, P. (1977) *Genetics, Law and the Social Policy*, Cambridge, Mass.: Harvard University Press.

—— (1992) 'American Society of Human Genetics statement on genetics and privacy: testimony to United States Congress', *American Journal of Human Genetics* 50: 640–2.

Robinson, A., Bender, B. G. and Linden, M. G. (1989) 'Decisions following the intrauterine diagnosis of sex chromosome aneuploidy', *American Journal of Medical Genetics* 34: 552–4.

Rothman, B. K. (1986) *The Tentative Pregnancy: Prenatal Diagnosis and the Future of Motherhood*, London: Pandora (1988).

Royal College of Physicians of London (1991) *Ethical Issues in Clinical Genetics*. A report of a working group of the RCP committees on Ethical Issues in Medicine and Clinical Genetics. London: Royal College of Physicians.

Shiloh, S., Avdor, O. and Goodman, R. M. (1990) 'Satisfaction with genetic counselling: dimensions and measurement', *American Journal of Medical Genetics* 37: 522–9.

Shiloh, S. and Sagi, M. (1989) 'Effect of framing on the perception of genetic recurrence risks', *American Journal of Medical Genetics* 33: 130–5.

Sjögren, B. and Uddenberg, N. (1988) 'Decision making during the prenatal diagnostic procedure. A questionnaire and interview study of 211 women participating in prenatal diagnosis', *Prenatal Diagnosis* 8: 263–73.

Smith, R. A., Williams, D. K., Sibert, J. R. and Harper, P. S. (1990) 'Attitudes of mother to neonatal screening for Duchenne muscular dystrophy', *British Medical Journal* 300: 1112.

Stamatoyannopoulos, G. (1974) 'Problems of screening and counselling in the hemoglobinopathies', in A. G. Motulsky and F. L. B. Ebling (eds) *Birth Defects: Proceedings of the Fourth International Conference*, Amsterdam: Excerpta Medica.

Statham, H., Green, J. and Snowdon, C. (1993) 'Mothers' consent to screening newborn babies for disease', *British Medical Journal* 306: 858–9.

Tyler, A., Ball, D. and Craufurd, D. (1992) 'Presymptomatic testing for Huntington's disease in the United Kingdom', *British Medical Journal* 304: 1593–6.

Wald, N. J. (1991) 'Couple screening for cystic fibrosis', *Lancet* 338: 1318–19.

Wald, N. J., Kennard, A., Densem, J. W. *et al.* 'Antenatal maternal serum screening for Down's syndrome: results of a demonstration project', *British Medical Journal* 305: 391–4.

White-van Mourik, M. C. A., Connor, J. M. and Ferguson-Smith, M. A. (1992) 'The psychosocial sequelae of a second-trimester termination of pregnancy for fetal abnormality', *Prenatal Diagnosis* 12: 189–204.

Whitten, C. F. (1973) 'Sickle-cell programming – an imperiled promise', *New England Journal of Medicine* 288: 318–19.

Wilfond, B. S. and Fost, N. (1990) 'The cystic fibrosis gene: medical and social implications for heterozygote detection', *Journal of the American Medical Association* 263: 2777–83.

World Federation of Neurology (1989) 'Research Committee Research Group statement on Huntington's disease molecular genetics predictive test', *Journal of Neurological Science* 94: 327–32.

Yoxen, E. J. (1982) 'Constructing genetic diseases', chapter 7 in P. Wright and A. Treacher (eds) *The Problem of Medical Knowledge*, Edinburgh: Edinburgh University Press.

Zeesman, S., Clow, C. L., Cartier, L. and Scriver, C. R. (1984) 'A private view of heterozygosity: eight-year follow-up study on carriers of the Tay-Sachs gene detected by high school screening in Montreal', *American Journal of Medical Genetics* 18: 769–78.

Chapter 1

Genetic counselling

A medical perspective

A. Caroline Berry

INTRODUCTION

Clinical genetics is an unusual branch of medicine as it draws on the
resources of high technology (gene sequencing and manipulation)
and attempts to apply these to the problems of those who, through
life's random chance, are at risk of genetic disease in either themselves or their offspring.

The geneticist acts as interface between the two, first explaining
the technical aspects to the people concerned and then endeavouring
to work out with them what actions they wish to take. Where an
individual is at risk of developing malignant disease and early
diagnostic procedures are available then the way forward is relatively straightforward but where the decisions are concerned with
reproduction there may well be a number of options available. The
geneticist's role is to work through these with the potential parents
and try to sort out with them the best way forward.

For the geneticist to fulfil this role satisfactorily, first and most
obviously there is a need for an accurate diagnosis, accurate test
results and accurate interpretation of these findings. As genetic
diseases are often rare, there may be a need for detailed library
searches and access to appropriate computerized databases. This is
particularly important in view of the very rapid progress being made
in the field of gene mapping and identification. A disease for which
no molecular test was available last year may well be established as
readily detectable this year.

For the geneticist there is another very important aspect that will
need to be explored and that is the nature and needs of the person or
couple requesting the information. In order to make the detail of the

high technology tests available to those who usually have little technical knowledge it is important to communicate in a way that is appropriate so that the people concerned feel neither patronized by being talked down to nor overwhelmed by technical jargon. Preliminary discussion will usually provide some clues to the most suitable approach. Decisions about reproduction are not made solely on the basis of logical, scientific factors (Frets and Niermeijer 1990) so it is important to discover what aspects are paramount for the couple concerned: have they already decided that whatever the risk they are going to start another pregnancy (or have already done so) as the only way they can see of restoring self-esteem? Or is their confidence so devastated by a recent tragedy that they feel unable ever again to face the uncertainties of another pregnancy? What are their views on abortion? Who is the decision-maker and how do the couple relate to one another? An understanding of recessive inheritance may lead to the spontaneous comment: 'If I had married anyone other than you this would never have happened.' Where studies involving the wider family are likely to be necessary these relationships need to be explored too. Some families are close and supportive but in others there are long-term estrangements and dark secrets where there must be serious concerns about the effects of invasion of privacy and rekindling old 'forgotten' memories.

These ramifications of clinical genetics can inevitably give rise to ethical dilemmas and most geneticists will, if they analyse their daily routine, find numerous examples regularly arising. Most departments and individuals develop semi-standard ways of handling these and only call for debate as some new situation arises. However, it is important to review beliefs and practice regularly as there is no place for complacency. There is constant change not only in the technical aspects but also in the attitudes and expectations of those requesting advice or information.

Despite the uniqueness of clinical genetics, with its emphasis on personal choice and its involvement with families rather than individuals, the ethical problems that arise can be considered under the classic medico-ethical headings of:

Truth-telling
Abortion issues
Confidentiality
Autonomy

TRUTH-TELLING

Clinical geneticists *par excellence* are a group of doctors who believe they should give truthful answers to those who question them. If a couple want to know their risk of having a disabled child, the geneticist will give them as accurate information as possible irrespective of whether this is good news or bad. The consultands can only make informed decisions if they have been fully informed. This sounds self-evident and is usually straight-forward but there are a number of occasions when tensions arise because of conflicting interests.

The geneticist's personal concern

There are numerous occasions where the geneticist is unable to give a couple an accurate recurrence risk. If they have a child, or have lost a fetus, with certain abnormalities, a recessive syndrome may be the cause (with a 1 in 4 risk of recurrence). On the other hand the features may be atypical or may be so non-specific that their combination may well be a chance event. The geneticist must endeavour to give the couple as accurate an outlook as possible, remembering that it is as serious an error to give a couple an incorrectly high recurrence risk which may deter them from further pregnancies as to give them too low a risk, resulting in their having a further affected child. It is the latter event which is likely to damage the geneticist's reputation so the geneticist has to guard against giving elevated recurrence risks for self-protection. Fortunately, as prenatal diagnosis becomes more widely applicable such negative undercurrents have diminishing importance.

The impact on the affected individual

This is particularly acute with dominant conditions for which prenatal diagnosis is available. An individual who is only mildly affected with, for example, neurofibromatosis needs to know the full range of the gene's potential manifestations so that he or she can decide whether or not to take the 50 per cent risk of transmitting the gene to a child, or whether to request prenatal diagnosis if it is available. The fact that this is even suggested can be an affront to the self-esteem of the person affected, while the list of complications, if they are being heard for the first time, can give rise to considerable anxiety about personal health. This is further discussed below under 'Necessary versus unnecessary truth'.

The impact on parents of an affected child

If prenatal diagnosis is available for a condition such as cystic fibrosis which can be very variable in its severity or in the case of a very rare disease of which parents can have had no experience, there can be tension between the attitudes of paediatrician and geneticist. For the paediatric management of the child it may well be correct to adopt a positive attitude and to focus on the treatable aspects of the disease, perhaps avoiding mention of some of the untreatable complications that may arise. The geneticist, discussing the 1 in 4 recurrence risk and the availability of prenatal diagnosis, will need to give full details about the possible burden of the disorder and its complications. This can be particularly difficult when parents are still coming to terms with the diagnosis of their affected child and may have had no experience of the progressive nature of some diseases. The geneticist needs to keep fully informed about the effectiveness of new treatments and yet to remain realistic where these are still potential rather than recognized and evaluated procedures.

Sometimes family support groups, with their opportunity for meeting with other parents and learning from their experiences, may provide a better way of becoming acquainted with the truth than medical discussion.

With rare disorders even this may be difficult to arrange and it is also important to be aware of the impact on parents of seeing children well advanced in the course of the disease affecting their child. Parents visiting a school for the physically disabled may for the first time realize the full implications of the diagnosis of their son's Duchenne muscular dystrophy.

The dawning of such understanding cannot be forced and there may be times when the geneticist has to accept that parents may be unable, even at the subconscious level, to understand the full truth of what they are being told.

Necessary versus unnecessary truth

The geneticist must be careful to see the information from the client's viewpoint and be as sure as possible that what is being said is not only true but also useful and necessary. It is necessary for a person with Von Hippel Lindau disease to know that they are at risk of developing renal carcinomas and retinal lesions which, if untreated, can lead to visual impairment. The person concerned should be encouraged to attend regularly for the appropriate screening tests but these necessary words of explanation and instruction, if absorbed, remove the client from the world he or she normally inhabits and into a different, hospital- and medically-orientated world. Thus the genetic diagnosis brings a lifelong shadow of ill-health and high risks of having an affected child, with consequent heart-searching prior to starting a family, or guilt if children are already born. On top of this is the impact on the spouse, or, if there is no partner, loss of self-esteem and desirability as a potential partner. Chapter 3 is devoted to the problems associated with Huntington's chorea but other disorders can have as serious an impact. In fact, with a more variable condition such as neurofibromatosis the geneticist's difficulty can be more acute since he/she knows that only a proportion, perhaps 20 per cent of those affected, will develop serious problems; many are consequently made anxious unnecessarily. As our knowledge of the human genome increases, however, our predictions should become more accurate. On the other hand, with the increasing importance of cancer genetics and interest in other forms of screening for pre-symptomatic disease predisposition, the number of individuals whose lives will be affected is likely to increase rapidly. In each case the importance and usefulness of the genetic information to be imparted must be balanced against the potential harm it will cause by engendering stress and anxiety.

Genetic information may blight not only the lives of the young: it may also have a major impact on older people, and this needs to be considered carefully before blood samples are collected from grandparents and other relatives in any family study. There may be times when samples can be taken on the understanding that no results will be given. Often this is not practicable because if, for example, one grandparent is found to be a chromosome translocation carrier, then it is that side of the family that should be investigated further. Individuals usually request test results and if these are available it is unreasonable to withhold them. However, their impact must not be underestimated. For example, the grandfather of five young grandsons recently diagnosed as having Duchenne muscular dystrophy heard that he was a germinal mosaic who had transmitted the mutation to all the boys. There may be times when imparting such a truth can be avoided but whatever occurs it is essential that those involved are aware of the impact their words may have.

Suppression of the truth

On other occasions it may be the family who want to suppress the truth. Sometimes, as discussed above, this may be involuntary and part of the denial process, but on other occasions it may be quite deliberate. Parents may claim to be unaware of the need to inform their children of genetic risks or may deliberately suppress the facts. This can cause particular difficulty for those who practise arranged marriages. If a girl is shown, for example, to be a carrier for Duchenne muscular dystrophy, she may become a liability to her father by being potentially unmarriageable. The family may refuse testing until after marriage. One father, whose teenage daughter was tested and found to be a carrier, responded to this unwelcome news, 'We must keep this a secret mustn't we?' It was only possible for him even to discuss this further with a geneticist of his own ethnic background, and such a person is not always available.

Great sensitivity is needed when culture and tradition give women a low status. For a woman to find that she is a 'gene carrier' of any sort may result in loss of husband, security and status. This can even occur with heterozygosity for a recessive disorder (Naveed *et al.* 1992).

Thus, though telling the truth is fundamental to communication in clinical genetics, the geneticist needs to tread carefully and think ahead lest the truth does more harm than the genetic disorder might.

ABORTION ISSUES

Although in the future clinical genetics is likely to involve treatment of genetic disease and prevention of disease in those at risk, at present prevention is very dependent on prenatal diagnosis and selective abortion of affected fetuses. Couples at high risk of having seriously handicapped offspring may decide to have no children but this is quite unusual and where a prenatal diagnostic test is available the majority of couples make use of it. This, perhaps surprisingly, often includes couples who, until faced with the problem, would have considered themselves opposed to abortion.

The abortion issue is an emotive one but is very much part of the clinical geneticist's daily round.

Discussion prior to pregnancy

Appropriate requests

When parents are seen for counselling following the birth of a child with malformations or handicap, the majority ask whether a prenatal test would be available in a future pregnancy. If such a test is available, the couple need to be asked whether they have thought through the implications and how they would respond to an abnormal result. To many the answer is self-evident: they would request termination of pregnancy and when the condition is seriously handicapping no further ethical discussion is necessary. Some couples do not find the answer easy or obvious. Even though the condition is well established as warranting termination, a couple with, for example, a child with Down syndrome may feel disloyal to their living child if they request abortion next time. It is important to talk the matter through, though a decision will need to be left until a later date, particularly if the child concerned is still young and the parents are still coming to terms with the diagnosis.

Inappropriate requests

On other occasions parents may request prenatal diagnosis for what seems, to the geneticist, to be an insufficiently serious condition, such as, for example, cleft lip and palate. Ultrasound can be used to identify clefting in the second-trimester fetus but most parents, when they think about it, decide that they would continue the pregnancy even if the abnormality were found again, particularly if their affected child has had a good repair. Some will still prefer to have the investigation done so that they will be forewarned of the baby's appearance if it has reoccurred. The first sight of a newborn with severe cleft lip can be a very shocking and unforgettable experience for a parent.

Men with haemophilia sometimes request prenatal sexing and termination of female fetuses so that they can avoid having carrier daughters. However, careful discussion of the implications of being a carrier usually results in the couple viewing daughters more positively. This is a situation where choice of sex at conception might be a real advance and it is likely that this will be available for the daughters of men living today.

Prenatal diagnosis and termination of female fetuses is a further vexed issue. There is little demand by European parents but the problem is a real one for Asian and other couples. In the UK the terms of the abortion law are such that the abortion would have to be performed for social rather than genetic indications. A fetus of the 'wrong' sex is probably as much a social disruption as a fetus conceived at the wrong time but this leads to a discussion of abortion for social rather than genetic reasons and will not be taken further here. Most genetic centres avoid the issue as their resources are earmarked for medical problems. A few women are known to have a normal female fetus aborted after an amniocentesis done on grounds of advanced maternal age. The only such patient I have had contact with returned for a further amniocentesis in her next pregnancy unaware that the outcome of the previous pregnancy was known. When asked what she would do should another chromosomally normal female be found she was adamant that she would continue this time. The fetus was male so her resolve remained untested!

Low risk but anxious mother

Another very different difficult situation may arise: girls who have grown up in families with several boys affected with, for example, Duchenne muscular dystrophy may have been taught by their mothers that they may well be carriers and therefore should have the appropriate tests during pregnancy and avoid having sons. Recent developments have made it possible for some of these girls to be reassured that they are very unlikely to be carriers and they are therefore advised that no testing is necessary during future pregnancies. Despite this, a small proportion of such young women adamantly request prenatal testing and may even request termination of pregnancy if the fetus is male and has inherited the higher risk grandmaternal X chromosome.

Although the matter can usually be resolved to everyone's satisfaction by further discussion, this is not always the case. The geneticist may see the woman's behaviour as unreasonable but it must be remembered that it is very hard to reject long-held beliefs and that, although laboratory test results can be very impressive to geneticists, they have only an intellectual impact on a woman whose memories of affected males may be very powerful. The matter may be further confused by the 'survivor guilt' which is being shown to be an important factor in families receiving good genetic news (Hayden 1991).

Available but not necessary

Although the geneticist regularly meets parents requesting prenatal tests that seem inappropriate, the opposite situation may also arise: the geneticist is aware that prenatal diagnosis is available but is hesitant about raising the matter lest it cause offence to the client. This is particularly likely with autosomal dominant disorders. The fact that a test is possible does not mean that it is either necessary or appropriate and it is entirely possible for this to be made clear as the topic is introduced. Most couples are quite able to make their views known provided they are given an opportunity to do so.

Discussions during pregnancy

There are a number of occasions when fetal abnormality is detected unexpectedly during pregnancy. As ultrasound becomes more widely used and its definition improves, a large number of structural defects may be detected. Usually these will be discussed with the parents by the obstetrician who is likely also to involve the appropriate paediatrician. It is when an amniocentesis shows an unexpected chromosome abnormality that the geneticist is most likely to be involved. Most amniocenteses are done to test for Down syndrome, and when either a sex chromosome aneuploidy or some unidentified marker chromosome is discovered, the parents are faced with an exceedingly difficult decision, the pregnancy usually being well into the second trimester.

The role of the geneticist is to explain as far as possible the likely implications of the finding. Truthfulness is of paramount importance but inevitably the counsellor's personal views may have some influence on how the information comes across. Two reports (Holmes-Siedle *et al.* 1987; Robinson *et al.* 1989) show that the pregnancy is more likely to continue if the finding is discussed with a geneticist than when information is provided by an obstetrician only. The chief difficulty is the wide variation known to occur with the sex chromosome aneuploidies, so that predictions for any individual fetus cannot be accurate. 'Marker' chromosomes may be difficult to characterize and this makes it again almost impossible to give parents exact predictions. It is important at the outset to establish the couple's views on termination of pregnancy. Those who would only want it if the fetus were definitely expected to have mental handicap would most likely continue the pregnancy, while a couple faced with an unintended pregnancy after completing their family would be more likely to opt for termination. Often, however, the answer is not straightforward and it is a matter of trying to work out the right course of action for a particular couple.

While some couples will decide to continue a pregnancy because the condition found is not drastically severe, it is worth bearing in mind that there may be couples for whom continuation is a better option than termination when a fetus is shown to have a lethal condition, such as anencephaly or Edward syndrome (Trisomy 18). The majority will opt for termination in these circumstances but some will prefer to 'let nature take its course' and there is some evidence that those who do this have less guilt and distress than those choosing termination. The finding may, however, be explained by self-selection bias. In this delicate area it is important to give the individual couple as accurate a picture as possible of the likely prognosis and to work out with them whether termination or continuation of the pregnancy is the right way forward for them.

Risks of consumerism

A continual concern must be how and where the line is drawn between abnormalities that warrant termination of pregnancy and those that do not. Clarke (1990) has argued vehemently that society should not be allowed to drift but that thought and discussion must be focused on deciding for which conditions termination of pregnancy is permissible. At present the law states that abortion is legal if there is 'substantial risk' of 'serious handicap' in the fetus and this provides a reasonable guideline. Yet what is 'serious handicap'? With a condition such as Klinefelter's syndrome severe learning difficulties may occur but usually do not. Is a 1 in 20 risk of Duchenne muscular dystrophy a 'substantial' risk, bearing in mind the devastating nature of the disease? We need to keep the balance, remembering that it is the client not the geneticist who has to live long term with her decision, guilt at an unnecessary abortion or a lifetime with a handicapped child. On the other hand, we must beware of the consumerist attitudes that often characterize present-day society. It is entirely right and natural for parents to desire a healthy child and strive for that, but pregnancy remains full of uncertainties. The child who arrives is not an item of merchandise but a person to be cherished.

CONFIDENTIALITY

Confidentiality has been one of the essentials of the doctor–patient relationship ever since the time of Hippocrates. Clinical geneticists see their responsibility to the family as a whole, and so difficulty with regard to confidentiality at the individual level may arise.

Access to medical records

At the most mundane level is the matter of hospital records and the need to obtain information on an affected person so that the correct diagnosis is known.

For a relative to be given accurate information, it is essential to know whether the affected person suffered from Huntington's chorea or Alzheimer's disease, from dystrophia myotonica or one of the other muscular dystrophies. Ideally, the affected individual should give informed consent before the relative's geneticist is given access to medical information. In practice this can be difficult. The affected person may have died or be incapable of giving consent. The person requesting counselling may not wish other family members to know that (s)he is making the enquiry. At present there is a degree of acceptance that medical information can be passed in confidence from one medical practitioner to another, but this may change as medical paternalism diminishes. If so, the task of the geneticist would be made considerably more difficult, since access to medical records for confirmation of diagnosis is a prerequisite for accurate genetic counselling of other family members.

Withholding consent

In some families confidential information may be deliberately withheld from those to whom it is highly relevant. A young woman was found to carry a translocation which put her at 10 per cent risk of having a child with Down syndrome in any pregnancy. She had a large number of brothers and sisters but her mother forbade her to give their names and addresses to the genetic centre, or to allow her to inform them of their need for testing. The geneticists were thus powerless, though very uneasy with the knowledge that individuals were remaining ignorant of their risk of having a handicapped child. Is this a sufficiently serious public health hazard to warrant the more coercive measures that are permitted in relation to infectious disease?

Paternity findings

Paternity discoveries provide a further area where confidentiality can be difficult, since respecting one family member's confidentiality can have unfortunate implications for other family members. This is particularly important now that linkage analysis is regularly used for carrier detection and prenatal diagnosis. The apparent failure to identify a gene marker transmitted by the father can indicate either non-paternity or the mislabelling of samples. The entire family may need to provide new samples unless non-paternity can be satis-factorily proved by the use of 'finger-printing' techniques. Even this raises a difficult but very real ethical issue. If the family members concerned donated their blood samples in order that another family member's carrier state could be ascertained, is it right that a quite different type of test (paternity testing) is undertaken on that sample? Admittedly, the object of the exercise is still to ascertain carrier risks but the information obtained could well have much wider implications.

If the testing is done and non-paternity is found, there is then the problem of what information to give to the various family members. Sometimes useful results can be given independent of paternity so that that aspect does not have to be mentioned, whereas on other occasions the family have to be informed that it is impossible to give them any useful information without divulging the reason for it. Occasionally a private discussion with an appropriate family member can unravel the tangle.

The father's responsibility for a pregnancy

What rights has a woman to information about risks that her child or fetus may have inherited from its father? Usually parents start a pregnancy knowing, for example, that there is a 50 per cent risk of the fetus inheriting neurofibromatosis from its father. Unfortunately, with more casual liaisons, the knowledge of such risks is not always available; the following case report illustrates the problems that can arise. A young woman had become pregnant during a casual affair with a man she barely knew and with whom she no longer had contact. She asked for advice because she was aware that his marriage had resulted in children with cystic fibrosis. She also mentioned that he himself had some sort of tumour affecting his hearing. By showing that the woman did not carry any of the common cystic fibrosis mutations, the geneticist easily disposed of the original query. The second aspect caused the geneticist much more concern. The man was already known by a genetics centre research worker to have been recently diagnosed as having neurofibromatosis Type II (NFII). The information had been received as part of a research questionnaire and no details were given as to what the man himself understood of the diagnosis and its genetic implications. As the young woman was carrying his child, who now had a 50 per cent risk of developing NFII and would need screening from an early age for cataracts and acoustic neuroma, the geneticist felt a responsibility that she should be informed of the risk. On the other hand, there was also a responsibility to protect the confidentiality of the man concerned. Did he forfeit this by being responsible for the pregnancy? There was also concern that if the woman were informed she might know more about his condition than did the affected man.

The matter was fortunately resolved by his helpful and responsible general practitioner, who undertook to discuss the diagnosis and its genetic implications with him and to gain his permission for the woman to be informed.

Such conflicts of interest arise not infrequently and may not always be satisfactorily resolved. They raise the matter of an individual's right to withhold co-operation and this raises the questions associated with autonomy.

AUTONOMY

Patient autonomy and the importance of the patient's being involved in decisions about their own management is increasingly becoming recognized as an important development in modern medicine. Geneticists have in fact lived with such patient–doctor interaction ever since genetic counselling clinics first began soon after the Second World War. The geneticist has seen his or her role as a provider of information rather than a dispenser of definitive advice. In the UK geneticists have adopted non-directive techniques, encouraging clients to make their own decisions as to whether or not to have children. In Europe a more direct approach is often adopted but the evidence is that the final outcome is similar whether directive or non-directive techniques are used (*Lancet* 1982). Reproduction is an emotive area and parents' decision-making is not necessarily governed by rational adherence to well-meaning advice (Sorenson *et al.* 1987).

Who decides?

It could be argued that it is irresponsible of a geneticist to allow a woman to continue a pregnancy knowing there is a high risk of the fetus having a severe disorder such as muscular dystrophy. Should any pressure be exerted on such a woman to have the necessary prenatal test to obtain a definite diagnosis when she makes it clear that she wants no such test for fear of losing a precious pregnancy?

Here surely the parents' wishes must be paramount. The medical adviser may feel that the loss of the pregnancy is less of a disaster than having an affected child but it is the parents themselves who have to live for the rest of their lives with the result of their decision. Those suffering from autosomal dominant conditions may well feel less concerned than their medical advisers about the implications of having a child with the same handicap that they themselves live with (Phillips *et al.* 1982) and in many respects they are better informed than their doctors. Others, however, feel it would be irresponsible to bring an affected child into the world.

Family involvement

Accepting such autonomy for an individual patient is one thing, but where one person's autonomous decision can have major implications for other family members it is another matter. We have already discussed the problems when confidential information is withheld. Other tensions arise when important biological samples are withheld. It can be exceedingly important for members of the extended family for the exact mutation present in the affected family to be identified. This can only be done if a blood (or other tissue) sample is available from the affected family member. In most families relationships are good and the necessary samples can readily be collected. Where, however, there is family ill-feeling, key family members can, by refusing to provide a sample, block the possibility of relatives learning their own carrier state or being able to have a reliable prenatal test. Reasons for such refusal to co-operate vary. One family disapproved of prenatal diagnosis in principle; in another, one branch of the family had a grievance against the rest of the family. In yet another family where a marriage had split up, the father of a boy with muscular dystrophy refused consent for the boy to provide a sample as he had no wish to help his former wife to have a happy outcome to a pregnancy by a new partner.

In all these understandable domestic scenarios the geneticist feels helpless in the face of autonomous decisions by competent individuals. Should there be any form of compulsion to force people to assist those they have no wish to help, but to whom, it could be argued, they have important obligations?

This difficult matter of the conflicting rights of individuals to have access to genetic information is a new issue in medical ethics and one that needs further discussion by geneticists, ethicists and lawyers, as suggested by the recent report from the Royal College of Physicians (1991). Meanwhile, clinical geneticists will aim to remain sensitive to the interests of those who consult them and their relatives.

REFERENCES

Clarke, A. (1990) 'Genetics, ethics and audit', *Lancet* 335: 1145–7.

Frets, P. G. and Niermeijer, M. F. (1990) 'Reproductive planning after genetic counselling: a perspective from the last decade', *Clinical Genetics* 38: 295–306.

Hayden, M. R. (1991) 'Genetic testing and screening', Proceedings of the 8th International Congress of Human Genetics, *American Journal of Human Genetics* 49, Supplement 4.50.

Holmes-Siedle, M., Ryynanen, M. and Lindenbaum, R. H. (1987) 'Parental decisions regarding termination of pregnancy following prenatal detection of sex chromosome abnormality', *Prenatal Diagnosis* 7: 239–44.

Lancet (editorial) (1982) 'Directive counselling', *Lancet* (ii): 368–9.

Naveed, M., Phadke, S. R., Sharma, A. and Agarwal, S. S. (1992) 'Sociocultural problems in genetic counselling', letter to the Editor, *Journal of Medical Genetics* 29: 140–4.

Phillips, C. I., Newton, M. S. and Gosden, C. M. (1982) 'Procreative instinct as a contributory factor to prevalence of hereditary blindness', *Lancet* (i): 1169–71.

Robinson, A., Bender, B. G. and Linden, M. G. (1989) 'Decisions following the intrauterine diagnosis of sex chromosome aneuploidy', *American Journal of Medical Genetics* 34: 552–4.

Royal College of Physicians (1991) 'Ethical issues in clinical genetics', Report of a joint working party of the college committee on ethical issues in medicine and the college committee on clinical genetics, *Journal of the Royal College of Physicians of London* 25: 285–8.

Sorenson, J. R., Scotch, N. A., Swazey, J. P., Wertz, D. C. and Heeren, T. C. (1987) 'Reproductive plans of genetic counselling clients not eligible for prenatal diagnosis', *American Journal of Medical Genetics* 28: 345–52.

Chapter 2

Genetic counselling

A nurse's perspective

Ann Williams

THE ROLE OF THE GENETICS NURSE/CO-WORKER IN GENETIC COUNSELLING

It comes as a surprise to many people to learn that nurses are employed in such an unexpected area of health care as genetics, which is seen as a medical and scientific discipline where the skills of the nurse would be unlikely to find a place. In fact, all the Regional Genetic Services in the United Kingdom have, as part of their genetic counselling teams, co-workers who come predominantly from the nursing profession. Most of us seek to emphasize rather than repudiate our nursing backgrounds, and we locate our practice within the scope of the advanced practitioner requirements outlined by the Royal College of Nurses (1988).

A review of the membership of our professional body, the Genetic Nurses and Social Workers Association (GNSWA) for 1990/1 showed that 76 of the 80 members were registered nurses. This chapter is therefore written with a strong emphasis on the role of the nurse as co-worker in the genetic counselling services.

There is no formalized preparation for practice in genetic nursing and entrants to the speciality may come from a variety of nursing disciplines. The same survey of the GNSWA membership showed only four members without additional professional qualifications. Nurses working in genetics have a responsibility, as specialist practitioners, to identify their own educational needs and to recognize the need for continuing supervision and support. This is necessary for them to deal with the psychological burdens of their work. Individual practitioners are able to negotiate their nursing role within the requirements of local needs and policies, and taking into account their own interests, experience and skill.

This gives genetic nursing staff considerable autonomy in their day-to-day activities.

With professional autonomy comes personal responsibility. Nurses entering genetics find not only that they are expected to work towards defining their role, but come face to face with the need to identify and think out the ethical basis of their practice, perhaps for the first time. The most urgent of these tasks is to define the practical and ethical boundaries of their relationships with the families they care for.

In practice some of the role-related boundaries are defined by the situation of the specific client group with which they are in contact. Nurses in genetics may work with families seeking to understand the birth of a handicapped child or undergoing prenatal diagnosis and considering the possibility of terminating the pregnancy. They may be working predominantly with families suffering from one specific condition such as Huntington's disease, or a group of conditions such as the muscular dystrophies or the familial cancers. They may have a generic role in caring for families with a variety of conditions which may or may not have a genetic origin. Some genetics nurse/co-workers are assigned a specialized role, or may develop expertise in a particular area; for such individuals, the working out of role boundaries will be shaped by that pattern of work.

Whether they are working in a specialized or a broad generic setting, there are many issues that nurses in genetics have in common, and which they share with the medical staff. Contrary to popular belief both inside and outside the medical and nursing professions, not all these issues involve decision-making nor are they necessarily related to reproductive choice.

Some of these shared issues include: How far should one go in seeking and gathering family information? When and (equally importantly) how should other family members be approached when they may have relevant information but not be aware of their own at-risk status? How should the role of the professional be defined in all the various possible contexts, such as when the family members are to be approached for their own potential benefit, or for the potential benefit of other family members, or for the benefit or interest of the contacting clinician?

Nurses also share with the doctors concern about the provision of a caring environment for the giving of bad news or the discussion of painful or distressing subjects, and have a responsibility to offer care and support whilst recognizing that the families and their individual members have their own mechanisms of adaptation to their newly discovered situations and that they may seek help and support from professionals other than genetic staff or indeed from within their own family and social relationships.

Special attention also needs to be paid to avoiding misuse of relationships with families, leading to the disruption of family structures and interactions. This applies particularly to the process of ending a supportive relationship without giving a sense of abandonment, and leaving scope for a resumption of contact as family circumstances change. All in all, this is a tall order to deliver in practice. This issue is the central ethical problem for genetic nurses – how to manage a relationship with a family which takes account of these areas of concern while the nurse herself may have competing claims for her ethical awareness and thoughts.

These concerns fall in with many of the traditional values in nursing which are grouped together under the heading of 'caring'. They focus on doing one's best for one's patient, and within health care ethics they might be discussed in terms of the ethical principles which direct professionals towards promoting benefits and minimizing harms.

A further set of ethical considerations attracts the attention of the genetic nurse from the perspective of counselling. This, in its guise as support for families and family members, forms an important part of the day-to-day work in genetic counselling. These are the ethical values and directives encompassed by the principle of respect for autonomy. Indeed the concept of unconditional worth that underlies the counselling process resonates strongly with the ideas of the philosopher Immanuel Kant, who proposed that individuals should be regarded as 'ends in themselves' and not be used as means to other ends.

GENETIC COUNSELLING, INFORMATION AND AUTONOMY

The principle of respect for autonomy has come to play an increasingly important part in professional–client interactions in all spheres of health care. It is interesting and probably inevitable that the increasing awareness of individual patient autonomy and the development of the role of supportive counselling have proceeded hand in hand. The two are interwined and mutually dependent. For individual patients (or families) to exercise autonomy, they need sufficient information to enable them to understand and evaluate the options facing them.

The most significant expression of respect for autonomy is the issue of informed consent, and the importance that has come to be attached to it. For patient (or client) consent to be truly 'informed', what obligations are imposed on the professional? The discussion of these obligations has focused very much on the information given, how it is presented, how understandable it is, and how accessible it is to those who are having to make the decision, i.e. to give the 'consent'. The presentation of the information is obviously very important but is only a part of the process by means of which patients and families assimilate and assess the information they are given. As well as the intellectual activity of active comprehension there is also an emotional dimension to understanding. Families have to go beyond comprehension; they have to believe the information that they have been given and relate it to themselves in a meaningful way. This confrontation with the emotional consequences of assimilating the information may require that individuals face and address some of their deepest fears and anxieties. Clients may grieve their loss of normality, or of their image of themselves as normal, and set out on a painful path of adjustment to a new understanding of themselves and their place and role within their own social context.

In the definition of genetic counselling as a speciality, great emphasis has always been placed on the role of the practitioner in sharing information with the patient/client. Emery (1984) defines genetic counselling as the communication to those seeking it of 'information about the nature of the disorder, its severity and prognosis and whether or not there is effective therapy, what the genetic mechanism is that caused the disease and what are the risks of it occurring in relatives'. He further identifies the role of the counsellor as discussing the options available to reduce the risk of passing the condition on to future generations but does not include the discussion of courses of action which might be available to both affected and at-risk individuals for safeguarding their own health. This forms an important part of genetic care often overlooked in attempts to understand the process and aims of genetic counselling. The dangers inherent in viewing the process exclusively from the view of 'prevention' of handicap have been well aired by Clarke (1990).

The term 'counselling' as applied to a genetic consultation identifies the commitment of genetics services to a non-directive and non-judgemental approach in conveying information to families about genetic status and genetic risk. Unfortunately, the term has other connotations in general and professional use which might give expectations of what is being offered on the part of client or referring professional which are at odds with the service we hope to deliver. On the one hand, counselling is a term used to describe almost any activity involving discussion or information-sharing between client and professional inside health care and in other non-health care settings. On the other hand, counselling as psychotherapy is recognized within psychiatric practice as a problem-solving activity. It delves deep into the components of an individual personality and as such is a frightening prospect for many people who regard themselves as 'normal'. Through conversations with other genetic nurses I have confirmed my feeling that patients sometimes reject genetic *counselling* on the grounds that they are not mentally ill nor do they have family problems of the kind they expect to be amenable to such a process. It should be clearly understood that genetic counselling does not routinely entail therapeutic counselling of this sort, although the offer of such therapy may be appropriate for some genetic counselling clients in great distress.

MANAGING THE RELATIONSHIP WITH THE CLIENT

It can be seen that the phrase 'genetic counselling' brings with it a possibly implicit, unacknowledged set of beliefs, attitudes and values. Confronting the ethical questions arising out of genetic counselling will inevitably deal with these issues as much as with the consequences and outcomes of clinical practice. Providing a way of defining the boundaries of the relationship between professional and family is therefore the key to ensuring that this relationship is ethical and therapeutic. By therapeutic I mean not only a relationship which is helpful to the family in practical ways, but one which is conducted from its inception through its progress to its ending in such a way that it does not damage the dynamics of that family, or undermine its adaptive mechanisms.

The first contact between the referred family and the genetics service may be a visit to the family home by a genetics nurse/co-worker, and it is on that occasion that the relationship between them is negotiated, often against a background of stress and anxiety. For the family, home visiting has positive elements in the extent to which they may be able to maintain an element of control over the proceedings and to set the agenda, but home visiting has its own formality and structure. It is in no way an informal or merely social occasion. Social skills, whilst contributing to the successful conduct of a home visit, are not enough to carry through what is essentially a professional activity. The genetics nurse/co-worker is responsible for initiating the visit and will have certain tasks to complete during it. She therefore has to manage its progress, and much of the control of the relationship as it develops remains in her hands. However, the family permits the encounter to develop and shapes it by making clear the nature of their concerns.

Yoxen (1986) suggests that the exercise of autonomy by patients rests on their confidence in their own understanding and judgement. One constraint on this confidence is imposed by the institutional and hierarchical nature of hospitals and the rituals employed in such health care institutions to exert control over patients' behaviour. In taking the early contact between the patient and the service out of a hospital setting clinicians are attempting to 'empower' clients to handle the genetic consultation effectively. In doing so, however, we cross boundaries that have been long established. Far from empowering patients, relieving their anxieties or transferring control of their 'genetic career' to them, we may well be taking away signs and markers that patients recognize and use to guide them in their contact with the service. This could itself generate anxiety because of the loss of traditional roles and behaviour cues. It is not at all normal practice for a nurse to visit at home prior to an out-patient appointment. From the outset, therefore, we are in fact setting a new agenda for the delivery of care and we have an obligation to define clearly what is on offer and how it can be provided. For the genetics nurse/co-worker there is a clear duty to define the scope of her practice not only in practical terms, but to have identified and considered the conflicting ethical demands of such an approach to nursing care.

An effective way of approaching this task is to consider the limits of genetic nursing practice rather than its components.

MANAGING THE RELATIONSHIP WITH DOCTORS

The first set of boundaries to be negotiated are those between nursing and medical staff, and where the professional skills of nursing fit into the service as a whole. Donahue (1978) identified and discussed the role of the nurse as patient advocate, suggesting that the ethical duty of the nurse is to ensure that the patient obtains from health care those things to which he has a right and that she further has an obligation to protect him 'from every erosion of human dignity and value'. There are many instances in genetic nursing practice (and all other spheres of health care) when it is appropriate for the nurse to challenge and question the beliefs and decisions about certain patients made by medical staff. To hold a different point of view from the medical staff in areas where one is competent to do so, or to relay a patient's wishes to the same medical staff at the family's request, is not to act as patient advocate. Abrams (1978), in discussion of Donahue's earlier paper, identifies several possible models for the responsibilities and functions of the patient advocate. To take on an adversarial role on the patient's behalf is not only wearing for the nurse but, from the patient's point of view, may be counterproductive if the role of advocate leads the nurse to come between the patient and clinician and thereby to inhibit the development of the relationship between them. This will only add confusion to an already worrying and distressing situation. Furthermore, as Abrams points out, the possibility for conflict exists between the advocate's role in presenting the patient's wishes and the nursing obligation to act in a patient's best interests.

Another possibility is that nurses might be seen as the 'kindly face' of genetics, making up for insensitive or inept behaviour on the part of clinicians inside or outside the genetics service. Further, nurses in clinical genetics might be seen as trading on the goodwill patients feel towards nurses, encouraging them to accept clinic consultations or interventions which conflict with the individuals' own values, beliefs or wishes.

Opposing roles often emerge when the demands of care for the family conflict with the research imperative in medicine. Advances in the care of families with genetic disorders are made as clinicians gather information on the natural history and the clinical manifestations or presentations of disease processes, and when they identify families suitable for further study that may provide information on the genetic mechanisms operating to produce a defined set of symptoms. Medical staff rightly make a clear distinction between the two groups in their dealings with patients. Should nurses do the same, when the care needs of both groups are very similar? If research is aimed at discovering an appropriate intervention for family members, it might be the case that the supportive care offered by the nurse is actually more valued in families where few medical interventions are as yet available. For further discussion of the possibilities in the relationship between researcher and client, see the appendix to this chapter (pp. 56–62).

Defining an ethically acceptable role within the triad of doctor, patient and nurse, whilst avoiding extreme positions – neither patient's advocate nor doctor's aide – establishes the genetic nurse's position within the health care speciality.

This leads to the second area in which one must establish boundaries; the counselling context in which genetics nurses/co-workers operate, and the provision of supportive care for families. Unlike many other spheres of nursing practice, the relationship between nurse and patients or family is not incidental to the successful completion of the nursing task. The effectiveness of supportive counselling requires the establishment of an appropriate and defined relationship. There are no displacement activities in which to engage – the relationship is the care.

Socialization into the professional values concerned with caring and their associated goal of making the patient feel better may be perceived as being in potential conflict with a professional role which uses counselling skills to create a dynamic relationship between patient and client. The activity of counselling does not in itself make things better in the short term – it does not give the kind of instant symptom relief and comfort that nurses are expected to provide. Indeed, if these traditional nursing values were translated into a counselling context, it could lead to a highly paternalistic (or maternalistic) relationship in which patients' ability to experience the reality of their situation is compromised or even taken away from them.

While supportive counselling does not take the pain away or make the load any less heavy to bear, patients and family members can be helped to explore ways of bearing the pain, and genetic nurses can from time to time share the load with them without attempting or purporting to take it away. At the end of the relationship with the family, whenever that comes, it is the clients who will still have to face their worries and problems and incorporate them into their daily lives.

Once again the practical and ethical dimensions of practice go hand in hand. The nurse must define the space within which it is safe for patients to acknowledge and resolve their feelings of grief, anger, hurt and despair. To take away from patients the right to these negative feelings is not only psychologically inadvisable but, within the context of respect for their autonomy, it is also ethically unsound.

GENETIC NURSES AND FAMILY SUPPORT

The third area in which the limits of nursing practice require clarification relates to those situations in which decisions are being made. As I have already indicated, genetic counselling does not always compel the making of a decision, and when it does, it may relate to decisions about monitoring one's own future health, or establishing one's risk status through DNA testing for specific inherited conditions. Decisions about whether to conceive or continue with a pregnancy are not the only kinds of choices to be considered in the light of genetic disease.

The desire to respect autonomy and to support patient choice has led to considerable concern within medical genetics regarding the use of non-directive counselling approaches, the avoidance of professional bias and the possibility of transmission to family members of information loaded with the values of society, the profession or the professional. Clarke (1991) has explored this issue, and has questioned whether non-directive counselling is possible given the conflict in the delivery of genetic care between patient choice on the one hand, and the public health role of genetics in preventing handicapping conditions on the other.

In practice, in many areas of professional care, including genetics, clinicians have sought to distance themselves from a patient's decision-making process. Brody (1985) first suggested that this view of the doctor's responsibilities developed as a result of the rejection of the paternalistic ethos that had previously dominated medical practice. Nurses, equally fearful of compromising a patient's autonomy, have frequently taken the same route. If, however, one is working as a nurse with a specific remit to offer supportive care to patients, and if one recognizes that the time at which clients need most support is the time at which they are making these hard choices, then one has to look carefully for a way to fulfil both requirements – supporting the family while respecting their autonomy.

From the family's point of view, this worry for doctors and nurses can be profoundly unhelpful. People consult doctors and nurses because they want help, and they expect expert practitioners to provide it. In some families, individuals who are already attempting to cope with a difficult and distressing situation are further traumatized and confused by the behaviour of doctors and nurses who are afraid to get beside the patient in their distress for fear of compromising their own ethical values. Yoxen (1986) states that 'You do not always free someone by not getting involved in their decisions.' It is in no way respectful of patients and families to leave them floundering in a sea of worry and guilt as they attempt to grapple alone with decisions which they never expected to be called on to make.

The crux of the problem here of course is not that respect for autonomy and doing one's best to demonstrate it is wrong, but that the way in which autonomy is respected may be. It is the role of the nurse in supportive counselling to recognize the distinction between the decision being made (which must be the family's) and the process of deciding. Reviewing the options available, clarifying a patient's own values and beliefs, and considering the responses of other family members, neighbours and friends are all part of the process of deciding. Decisions are made in the turmoil of the emotions as well as in the calm and ordered rationality of the intellect. Autonomous decisions are not divorced from the rest of the patient's life, and do not depend solely on the information the genetic counsellor has provided. One further point to be made here is that families should at least be aware that they may subsequently be confronted with difficult decisions as a result of actions that they are considering at the present. Thus, the possibility of making decisions about the continuation of a pregnancy might be a later outcome of a decision to take part in an antenatal screening programme or to accept prenatal diagnosis. It would be dishonest on the part of the professional to enrol a patient in such a programme without making them at least intellectually aware of the possible agenda which may result.

CONCLUDING THE RELATIONSHIP WITH A FAMILY

There comes a time in the nurse's involvement with a family when it becomes clear that the need for supportive care is at an end. This should occur when they have arrived at what is, for them, an acceptable balance between the constraints imposed by their genetic condition and the particular social circumstances in which they live. For some families, acceptance comes quickly and the balance is easily achieved. The nurse's involvement will be brief. Indeed, in some circumstances, the helping relationship is rejected or deemed inappropriate by the family, who have personal resources or other sources of help and support to assist them in dealing with their particular worries and fears. Just as the genetics service recognizes that patients should be empowered to make their own decisions once they have accepted counselling, it is equally important to acknowledge they are also free to decline all or any part of the service that is on offer.

Even at the point of initial contact with a family, there is already latent within the relationship a recognition that it will come to an end. This ending must be planned so that both family and practitioner are left feeling that there are no unresolved issues, no emotional 'loose ends'. Occasions do arise, unfortunately, where the counselling skills of the genetics nurse/co-worker are insufficient to help the family and they need to be referred for more specialized help. It is important to bear in mind that genetic fieldworkers are nurses using, and trained in the use of, counselling skills but that they are not psychotherapists. Nurses are using their skills to help the family to an acceptance of their actual situation, however unacceptable this may initially appear to the family; this will entail supporting them through the emotional changes that may accompany this process. They do not have a responsibility beyond this in counselling patients with regard to the wider issues that may pertain in their lives. This is no denigration of the skills of the nurse specialists; just as patients will have physical difficulties unrelated to their genetic condition but still requiring treatment, so they may well have emotional and social problems requiring specialist help.

CONCLUSION

Not all familes come to accept and adjust to genetic problems in the way that professionals would regard as right or healthy. In seeking to help families accept their genetic situation and make positive adjustments, we may be promoting a view of the problem or a value-laden perspective on living that is inimical to the family's view of itself. Genetic disease can be functional not only for affected individuals but also for the family as a whole. It becomes integral to personalities, and provides the cement which holds the family together as a functioning unit. If the aim of supportive counselling is to enable families to incorporate genetic information into the pattern of their lives and their plans for the future, then, in families such as this, the task is already done, and in ways which suit the family, not the professionals. Having based the service on concerns about patient choice and respect for autonomy, can we thus logically impose a view of an appropriate response to genetic information which overrides the family's own pattern of acceptance? Veatch (1989) suggests that paternalism may be strong or weak and in its strong form it 'overrides an autonomous person's wishes'. To attempt to replace a family's coping strategy might well be paternalism in its strong form. Further, and rather more practically, it would be wrong to challenge or try to overturn patterns of living with genetic risk, even at the family's request, if one did not have the means required to replace those patterns with something preferable; and which of us can claim that with any certainty? This brings us again to defining the limits and boundaries of nursing practice.

Throughout this chapter I have attempted to look at the ethical dimensions of the relationship between the genetics nurse/co-worker and the family, and in doing so I have made the assumption that this is self-evidently important without taking any specific steps to justify this.

Suffice it for me to say that genetics is a speciality of medicine where awareness and consideration of the family is vital. Workers in genetics need to be aware that they are entering a family which has its own structure, and which may be very different from their own experience of families, and this should be respected. Families have a history and a future, not only in relation to the disease course, but also in relation to past and future contacts and relationships with health professionals. As such, the attitudes towards and expectations they have of staff may differ from that experienced in other clinical settings. Furthermore, the fact that professional relationships may exist with a number of different family members adds particular complications. Each of these family members may be a client by virtue of their family relationships. They are not just interested parties looking on, as in the rest of medicine, but may be intimately touched by decisions made by other family members. The flow of information between professionals and each family member must be carefully considered if the flow of information between family members is not to generate misunderstanding.

Families also, of course, have a history and a future totally unconnected with their disease or medical career. If great care is not taken in examining the psychological and practical issues in the care of families, and the ethical basis on which these considerations are founded, there is enormous potential for breaching the oldest directive of all in health care ethics: 'Above all, do no harm.'

ACKNOWLEDGEMENTS

I would like to thank my psychology colleague Joe Soldan for helpful discussions.

REFERENCES

Abrams, N. (1978) 'A contrary view of the nurse as patient's advocate', *Nursing Forum* 17 (3): 259–67.
Beauchamp, T. and Childress, J. (1983) *Principles of Biomedical Ethics*, New York: Oxford University Press.
Brody, H. (1985) 'Autonomy revisited: progress in medical ethics' (discussion paper), *Journal of the Royal Society of Medicine* 78: 380–7.
Clarke, A. (1990) 'Genetics, ethics and audit', *Lancet* 335: 1145–7.
—— (1991) 'Is non-directive genetic counselling possible?' *Lancet* 338: 998–1001.
Donahue, P. (1978) 'The nurse, a patient's advocate', *Nursing Forum* 17 (2): 143–51.
Emery, A. (1984) 'The principles of genetic counselling', in A. Emery and I. Pullen (eds), *Psychological Aspects of Genetic Counselling*, London: Academic Press.
Royal College of Nursing (1988) *Specialists in Nursing*, London: RCN.
Veatch, R. (1989) *Medical Ethics*, Boston, Mass.: Jones & Bartlett.
Yoxen, E. (1986) *Unnatural Selection?* London: William Heinemann Ltd.

APPENDIX TO CHAPTER 2: GUIDELINES FOR CLINICAL RESEARCH WORKERS, WALES REGIONAL GENETICS SERVICE

Welcome to the Institute of Medical Genetics, University Hospital of Wales. We hope that you enjoy your time with us and that your study goes well. These guidelines are intended to help you identify possible areas of difficulty to enable you to address these issues **BEFORE** embarking on your clinical activities. In this way we hope to ensure that your work proceeds smoothly and that departmental policies (which may differ in some respects from practices you have been used to elsewhere) are adhered to and understood.

The first section of these guidelines is intended to help you clarify your role with the families you will be seeing. Clinical staff will continue to have a responsibility for the care of patients and families whilst you are here and after you have left and it is essential that relationships between them and their patients are not damaged as a result of your activities.

Research or Service

It can be quite difficult to tease apart the overlapping requirements of research duties and clinical responsibility to patients. Families often find it difficult to differentiate between clinical care and research. This may be particularly true for patients and families who have an uncommon condition and who are able to get very little in the way of information through usual medical channels. A doctor (or nurse) with a lot of information who comes from a department with which they have already had clinical contact, and who has time to discuss things with them, is likely to be perceived as a clinical carer. The onus is therefore on the researchers to explain very clearly why they are in contact and what they can (and cannot) offer. The time-limited nature of your involvement should be explained at the outset.

Care must be taken not to give the impression that, as a provider service within the NHS structure, the Institute is 'touting for business'.

How Will You Ascertain [Identify] the Families?

1 *Through the Institute's own records.* It is likely that we already know of a number of families who could help your study. Initial contact with these families should be made through the responsible Consultant who will discuss with them their willingness to be part of any research project.

2 *Families in Wales who are Newly Identifed and Contacted by You as a Result of Your Study.* Special attention needs to be paid to defining your role with the family. Every area in Wales has a Consultant responsible for families in that area and discussion with him/her before contacting the family is advised.

3 *Families from outside Wales.* There may be less scope for confusion about your role with these families, who should have no expectation of a service from Cardiff. This cannot be guaranteed and you should discuss with your supervisor appropriate contact with their own Regional Service.

As a general point letters to families should state unequivocally your role as a researcher, the purpose of the study and a clear indication that there is unlikely to be any personal benefit from taking part.

What Will You Offer?

Families vary greatly in their response to genetic conditions. Indeed, individuals within families show great variation in their acceptance of and willingness to discuss their situation or problem. In recruiting families into your study and maintaining your relationship with them you need to be extremely careful not to offer or imply benefits that you cannot possibly hope to provide, or induce them to enter your study with unrealistic offers of help, support or improved outcomes, either during the study or upon its completion.

Although you will have defined the aim of your study in terms of benefits for affected families the only outcome that can be realistically predicted is additional qualifications/experience/ publications for yourself. In the short term you are unlikely to 'cure' the disease, make an enormous impact on the management of the condition in any individual family or develop helpful tests with early clinical usefulness. By the process of aggregation of information you are likely to make a contribution to all these areas. These distinctions must be conveyed to prospective research subjects, as must the distinction between the generation of DNA data and DNA testing, which yields results.

It has always been the policy of this department that blood samples taken purely for research purposes are kept and used separately from samples taken for service use or DNA banking. Particular care needs to be taken not to imply that those participants in the research will somehow have 'jumped the queue' when a test becomes available. **THE RESEARCH STUDY IS MORE IMPORTANT TO THE RESEARCHER THAN IT IS TO THE FAMILY!!**

How Much of a Service Commitment Do You Want to Take on?

Some of your contacts with families are bound to have a service component. You will be discussing with family members things *as they are now*. You may identify other people in the family who are 'at risk' or diagnose a hitherto unrecognized affected individual. This creates a need for information, counselling and support and possibly referral to clinicians outside the genetic service. You should clarify for yourself and negotiate with clinical genetic staff, both medical and nursing, how much of this service work you want or feel competent to take on.

Can You Counsel?

Most genetic appointments last about an hour. When did you last spend that length of time in conversation with a patient? Before contacting families you must spend time in clinic with experienced clinicians. You may have other experience or training which is pertinent, or we can help you with information about further learning and experience both within the Institute and/or at other centres.

The possession of a MB, a BN or RGN (medical or nursing qualification) **DOES NOT CONSTITUTE ADEQUATE TRAINING**.

Home Visiting

Most researchers find it necessary to visit families at home from time to time. Fortunately, the Regional Service is well supplied with Genetic Nurses/Fieldworkers who are experts on the organization and conduct of home visits. They can be found in Cardiff or at other genetic centres in Wales. You must spend time on home visits with them before arranging your own. Home visiting is not a social occasion although good social skills are required to carry it out effectively. It has its own structure and formality. Researchers from other countries (including England!) should take the opportunity to observe and discuss different behaviour patterns and cultural norms. The golden rule is: Never refuse a cup of tea. If no tea has been offered by the end of the visit, you should review its conduct critically, preferably with the aid of a fieldworker!

How Will You Handle a Refusal?

Although patients have every right not to co-operate in research, you may find a refusal difficult to accept, given its importance to you. It is essential that patients who decline to participate are left feeling that their relationship with the Department has not been damaged. If patients know how to make contact with you they may be in touch again at a later date.

Record-Keeping

It may become apparent in the course of the project that an initial research contact with a family has generated a service requirement.

At this point you should discuss with the relevant Consultant the opening of a service record to ensure not only that appropriate care is offered to the family but also that the work done can be accounted for in the audit and appropriate decisions can be made with regard to payment for tests and consultations.

Plans must also be made with regard to storage and use of data when the study is complete. The Institute has considerable expertise in the organization and management of computerized databases and registers and discussion with appropriate staff is advisable.

Confidentiality

Apart from the usual considerations, you should be aware that you may come to know more about the health, etc., of the family as a whole than do the individual members; maintaining 'internal confidentiality' is therefore particularly important as the work progresses.

For reasons of confidentiality you may decide to identify your blood samples with numbers rather than names. Where your study is collaborative, you should devise clear guidelines on the disclosure of information to other researchers, and similarly, when contacting Porton Down to establish cell lines.

Passing on New Information

If your study will generate results, you should plan in advance with colleagues and families how these will be given, by whom, and what support will be available afterwards. Results that you might consider 'good' might have profound effects on family dynamics and results both positive and negative should be handled with the same caution and consideration. You may consider it appropriate to share any new information about the condition with the families who have helped you, towards the end of the study.

Offering Local Back-Up

Whilst many people with genetic problems welcome any interest in their situation, the contact you make may provoke further questions, anxieties or worries, which you may feel unable to address or which might more appropriately be handled by existing teams at a service level. Giving all Welsh families the contact number of the local nurse/fieldworker and details of how to obtain a referral to a Consultant will ease this situation. If patient records are held outside Cardiff some record of your contact would be helpful, as would contacting the nurse/fieldworker to let her know that you are operating in her area. She might also be able to arrange a helpful introduction to a family or give useful insights into family dynamics.

Ending a Relationship with a Family

Planning the extent and scope of your involvement with every family also involves a consideration of how you will end your contact with them. Some families will only be seen by you on one occasion, perhaps in a clinic or at home so that you can verify clinical details or take blood samples.

Some families, however, might enter into a much closer relationship with you, either because of the nature of your research or because something in the family structure provides you with more data for your work than is gained from other families. Sometimes these deeper relationships develop spontaneously so that the line between professional contact and friendship becomes blurred in the minds of one or both parties. This is a particular danger if thought has not been given to the end of the relationship from the outset. As a result families, who already have chronic problems to cope with, are given an additional load of distress and resentment. You therefore have a responsibility to explain that you will not be able to provide ongoing support over an extended period, negotiate with the family a plan for ending the relationship and avoid saying unexpectedly at the end of a visit 'This is the last time we will meet', and establish or re-establish contact with service provision if this is appropriate.

There are three administrative matters that also need considering before you embark on your study.

Meeting People

The onus is very much on you to introduce yourself to clinical consultants, nurse manager and nursing staff and generally to familiarize yourself with personnel and ways of working.

You must also arrange a meeting with the Audit Officer to ensure that your work is 'accounted for' within the audit system.

How Much Will It Cost?

There are many hidden costs in research that the inexperienced researcher might not consider, including secretarial help and laboratory services. Additional tests arranged in Departments other than Genetics will also need to be paid for. Where laboratory tests are carried out within the Institute you should negotiate costs with the director of the laboratory concerned.

Medical/Legal Cover

You must ensure that you are appropriately covered to carry out research on patients. This may require Honorary clinical appointments and those registered outside the United Kingdom should take special care to ensure that these requirements are met. Again the onus is on you to demonstrate that you have made appropriate arrangements.

MRS ANN WILLIAMS AND DR HELEN HUGHES – NOVEMBER 1992

Chapter 3

Predictive testing of adults and children

Lessons from Huntington's disease

David Ball, Audrey Tyler and Peter Harper

Presymptomatic testing is not a new concept, but its scope has recently been extended by advances in genetic techniques which permit testing for an increasing number of genetic disorders, often without knowledge of the causal biochemical lesion. This development has raised multiple ethical issues, some of which have already been encountered in the field of medicine and others which are new. At present difficult ethical decisions are often made, sometimes by default, by those leading the field, whose perception and insight may be distorted by their individual background or research approach. The implications for the individual and the community may not be fully comprehended, for example in the introduction of genetic screening programmes. It has even been suggested that geneticists have 'added more confusion than clarity to ethical analysis in this area' (Benson 1992). Such issues should be debated by all sections of society and backed by legislation in order to protect the individual, society and genetic research.

Neonatal screening for such disorders as phenylketonuria (PKU) and congenital hypothyroidism is a form of presymptomatic testing that is now routine in most developed countries; if an abnormality is detected, treatment can be initiated. However, the rapid molecular advances that comprise the 'New Genetics' (Weatherall 1991) have resulted in techniques that permit presymptomatic diagnosis before any rational approach to treatment has been developed, for example presymptomatic testing for Huntington's disease. As the Human Genome Project fulfils its aim of identifying all human genes, the capacity for such testing will increase dramatically. Testing is already feasible for most single-gene disorders and in addition may become possible for many polygenic disorders such as coronary heart disease, depression and schizophrenia. It may then be feasible to predict future personal events by consulting a geneticist, rather than a fortune-teller, for an interpretation of a 'genetic lifeline'. Whilst of necessity the full awareness of ethical and legal issues lags behind these rapid scientific advances, it is essential that difficulties are anticipated and guidelines established, as has occurred for Huntington's disease following collaboration between the lay and professional bodies (World Federation of Neurology 1989 and 1990). Regulation is needed to ensure that misuse does not occur, and genetics thereby become discredited, as has happened in the past: for example, under the Third Reich it has been estimated that 3,000–3,500 compulsory sterilizations were undertaken for Huntington's disease (see figure 3.1); this disorder was specifically included in the list of conditions for which killing

Gesetz zur Verhütung erbkranken Nachwuchses
Vom 14. Juli 1933

(Reichsgesetzblatt I S. 529)

Die Reichsregierung hat das folgende Gesetz beschlossen, das hiermit verkündet wird:

§ 1

(1) Wer erbkrank ist, kann durch chirurgischen Eingriff unfruchtbar gemacht (sterilisiert) werden, wenn nach den Erfahrungen der ärztlichen Wissenschaft mit großer Wahrscheinlichkeit zu erwarten ist, daß seine Nachkommen an schweren körperlichen oder geistigen Erbschäden leiden werden.

(2) Erbkrank im Sinne dieses Gesetzes ist, wer an einer der folgenden Krankheiten leidet:

1. angeborenem Schwachsinn,
2. Schizophrenie,
3. zirkulärem (manisch-depressivem) Irresein,
4. erblicher Fallsucht,
5. erblichem Veitstanz (Huntingtonsche Chorea),
6. erblicher Blindheit,
7. erblicher Taubheit,
8. schwerer erblicher körperlicher Mißbildung.

(3) Ferner kann unfruchtbar gemacht werden, wer an schwerem Alkoholismus leidet.

Figure 3.1 Nazi Germany: compulsory sterilization law (1933). Huntington's disease was a specific indication for compulsory sterilization in Nazi Germany.

was indicated in the 'T4' extermination policy, although no data exist on the number of individuals killed (Harper 1992). Let us hope that the expensive lessons of history will be heeded, that these abominations will not be repeated, and that appropriate legislation will follow informed debate.

This chapter examines the ethical issues raised by genetic pre-symptomatic testing, using Huntington's disease as an example (Craufurd and Harris 1986). This disorder is a particularly salutary model for the following reasons: first, it is a serious and eventually fatal illness, usually of adult onset; second, there is currently no treatment that can prevent the inexorable progression of the de-generative process. The gene and mutation responsible for Hunting-ton's disease have recently been identified (Huntington's Disease Collaborative Research Group 1993), but all data on presymptomatic testing so far rely on linked marker studies within individual families. The late onset of Huntington's disease means that it is possible to make a genetic prediction of the disease in healthy individuals, as much as thirty years or more before they will develop symptoms (see Harper 1991a). Not surprisingly, such testing is fraught with multiple ethical problems (Berg and Fletcher 1986; Huggins et al. 1990; Morris et al. 1989). These issues are applicable to many other disorders, particularly those of adult onset (McGuffin and Sergeant 1989; Ball and Harper 1992).

HUNTINGTON'S DISEASE

Huntington's disease is named after George Huntington, who gave the first complete description of this condition in 1872 (Huntington 1872). It is an inherited (autosomal dominant), neurodegenerative disorder, usually of adult onset, and it demonstrates complete, but age-dependent, gene penetrance (i.e. all individuals who possess the gene will eventually develop Huntington's disease if they live long enough). Neurological symptoms include involuntary movements (chorea) and disturbance of voluntary movement (e.g. unsteady gait, motor impersistence and difficulty in swallowing) (see table 3.1). Psychiatric symptoms are common and include depression, irrita-bility and psychosis, whilst cognitive impairment frequently pro-gresses to severe dementia. Thus there is a slow, progressive physical and mental decline over many years and death, often due to chest complications, occurs on average some fifteen to twenty years after onset (see Harper 1991a).

Table 3.1 Clinical features of Huntington's disease

Inheritance
Autosomal dominant with age-dependent penetrance (100%)

Symptoms
1 Neurological:
   Involuntary movements (chorea)
   Impairment of voluntary movements
2 Vulnerability to psychiatric disorder
3 Dementia

Onset
Usually middle years of life (mode 40–45 years)

Duration
Average duration (mode 15–20 years)

GENETIC PRESYMPTOMATIC TESTING

In 1983 the gene which causes Huntington's disease was linked to a genetic marker on the short arm of chromosome 4 (Gusella *et al.* 1983); this marker and others found subsequently have permitted presymptomatic testing to be performed for individuals at risk (figure 3.2). The test uses a technique that attempts to identify a marker that is co-inherited with the disease gene and is informative regarding the transmission of the disorder in a particular family (Hayden *et al.* 1988). DNA samples from close family members are required, particularly those who are affected, as well as from the person requesting testing. Occasionally the linked marker and the disease gene will dissociate due to a recombination event between them during meiosis, thereby introducing uncertainty and the possibility of error (Shaw and Youngman 1991). Thus tests that use linked markers can only modify the estimated risk of carrying the disease gene up or down, rather than identifying its presence or absence absolutely; their accuracy depends on the distance on the chromosome between the marker and the disease gene. The capacity to modify risk estimates is dependent on the amount of genetic variation (polymorphism) in the marker used and on the available pedigree structure (Lazarou *et al.* 1993). Exclusion testing in pregnancy is a special approach that permits an at-risk parent to have children at low risk of carrying the Huntington's disease gene (figure 3.3). This

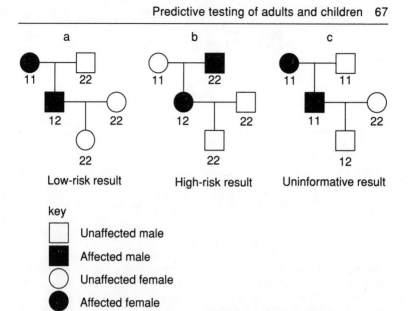

Figure 3.2 Presymptomatic testing using linked markers
Pedigree a   In pedigree a the affected man has inherited allele 1 and the Huntington's gene from his affected mother and therefore the disease gene is being co-inherited with this allele. His daughter requesting presymptomatic testing has inherited allele 2 from her father and is therefore at low risk of carrying the Huntington's disease gene.
Pedigree b   In pedigree b the affected mother of the individual requesting presymptomatic testing has inherited allele 2 and the Huntington's disease gene from her affected father. The man requesting testing has inherited allele 2 from his affected mother and is therefore at high risk of carrying the Huntington's disease gene.
Pedigree c   In pedigree c it is not clear which allele 1 is co-inherited with the Huntington's disease gene and therefore the result cannot be interpreted and an alternative marker must be employed.

test is of particular use for subjects who do not want their individual risk altered or for whom presymptomatic testing is not possible, usually due to pedigree limitations (Tyler *et al.* 1990). In essence this technique detects whether or not the at-risk subject has passed to the fetus the relevant part of chromosome 4 (i.e. the area close to the gene that causes Huntington's disease) that they themselves have inherited from their affected parent. Thus if they have passed on the chromosome region inherited from the affected parent the risk to the fetus would be the same as that of the at-risk subject (i.e. usually 50

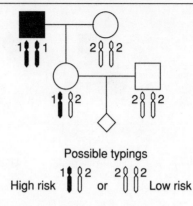

Possible typings

High risk   1 2   or   2 2   Low risk

Figure 3.3 Exclusion testing in pregnancy
The couple requesting exclusion testing in pregnancy in this example consists of an at-risk female (unfilled circle) and an unaffected male partner (unfilled square). Her parents are an affected male (filled square) and an unaffected female (unfilled circle). Using markers linked to Huntington's disease it is possible to detect whether the at-risk subject has passed to the fetus (diamond) the region containing the gene responsible for Huntington's disease from her affected or unaffected parent. In this situation the affected parent types 11 for the marker, whilst the unaffected parent types 22. The at-risk subject types 12 and her unaffected partner 22. If the fetus (diamond) types 12 then the estimated risk of carrying the Huntington's disease gene will be raised as it will have inherited that part of chromosome 4 which carries the gene responsible for Huntington's disease from the affected parent. However, if it types 22 then it will have inherited this region from the unaffected parent and will be at low risk.

per cent); however, if the fetus has inherited the gene from the unaffected grandparent, then the risk would be that attributable to the possibility of recombination between the marker used and the Huntington's disease gene (often less than 2 per cent). Thus the fetal risk is usually raised from 25 per cent to 50 per cent (that of the parent) or lowered to less than 2 per cent, whilst the parent's risk remains unaltered (Quarrell *et al.* 1987).

Linked marker studies are normally the only means of genetic prediction for a disorder until the causative gene is identified and specific mutation(s) isolated, whereupon direct mutational analysis becomes possible, allowing prediction to be made using a single sample from an applicant. In the case of Huntington's disease such mutation testing is now feasible, since a specific mutation has been identified in the form of an unstable trinucleotide sequence within a gene (IT 15) that codes for a protein with as yet unknown characteristics (Huntington's Disease Collaborative Research Group 1993). While this mutation is variable in extent within a single family, the same mutation appears to be responsible for virtually all cases of Huntington's disease (MacMillan *et al.* 1993; Snell *et al.* 1993). Further information on this recent development can be found in the special issue on Huntington's disease of the *Journal of Medical Genetics* 1993.

THE DEMAND FOR PRESYMPTOMATIC TESTING IN HUNTINGTON'S DISEASE

Presymptomatic testing in Huntington's disease has been available since 1987 in the United Kingdom and 248 tests had been performed up to the end of 1990 (Tyler, Ball and Craufurd 1992). Worldwide, over 1,400 tests have been performed in 19 countries (Harper 1991b; World Federation of Neurology 1993). In the United Kingdom a consortium of testing centres has been established to agree a common service protocol, set standards of good practice, collect data and provide a forum for debate (Craufurd and Tyler 1992). Criteria for entry into the testing programme include a confirmed family history of Huntington's disease, having an affected parent or grandparent, a potentially informative family structure, being at least 18 years of age and able to give freely informed consent (see table 3.2).

Table 3.2 Inclusion and exclusion criteria for presymptomatic testing in Huntington's disease using linked markers

Inclusion criteria
Confirmed family history
25–50% risk
Potentially informative family structure
18 years of age or more
Freely given informed consent
Exclusion criteria
Clinically affected
Current mental illness or drug misuse
Recent significant mental illness or drug misuse
Risk of suicide

Exclusion criteria include being clinically affected with Huntington's disease, suffering with current or recent significant mental illness or drug misuse, or being at risk of suicide (Tyler, Ball and Craufurd 1992). Those applicants presenting for testing who demonstrate symptoms and signs of the illness, of which they are unaware, present a very difficult counselling problem (Tyler, Morris *et al.* 1992).

The predicted risk of carrying the Huntington's disease gene has been raised in approximately one-third of subjects tested and lowered in two-thirds. Using data from the United Kingdom, the most common elevated and lowered risks were between 95 and 100 per cent (range 70–98 per cent) and 1 and 5 per cent (range 1–25 per cent) (Tyler, Ball and Craufurd 1992). The experience that has been gained in Huntington's disease is applicable to many other testing situations and is not limited solely to disorders of late onset.

SHOULD TESTING BE CONSIDERED IN THE ABSENCE OF AN EFFECTIVE TREATMENT?

When the value of testing is considered, it is important to examine the purpose, disadvantages and benefits. Whilst the last may be obvious if preventive treatment is available, the advantages may be less clear if such testing does not have therapeutic implications and only provides information. Before testing was offered for Huntington's disease, the lay organizations and samples of people at high risk were surveyed to discover whether such testing would be utilized in the absence of an effective treatment, and it was consistently endorsed (Tyler and Harper 1983; Mastromauro *et al.* 1987; Meissen and Berchek 1988).

The main reasons cited by applicants for requesting testing include making childbearing decisions, informing existing children and relief of uncertainty (Tyler, Morris *et al.* 1992). However, risk alteration may disturb relationships; for example, family dynamics may be altered by loss or gain of the 'sick role', and marital break-up has been reported, even when risk has been reduced (Tyler, personal observation).

A low-risk result provides relief from anxiety, often for an entire family, an opportunity to bear children with a minimal probability of their being affected and an increase in self-confidence and esteem. Thus most persons receiving a decreased risk have felt relieved and report an improvement in the quality of life, with fewer symptoms of depression. However, survivor guilt is not uncommon and between 10 and 50 per cent experience difficulties in adjusting to their new low-risk status (Tibben *et al.* 1992; Huggins *et al.* 1992).

A high-risk result indicates that a currently healthy individual is very likely to develop a lethal disorder, but provides no information about the age of onset, thereby altering the primary source of uncertainty. Such a prospect may have a deleterious effect on self-image and lifestyle and also places a great burden on partner and children. Symptoms of depression and anxiety are common and some experience a prolonged period of significant distress; however, most individuals given a high-risk result adjust to their new status within a year. They live with a heightened perception of the present but have increased difficulty in planning for the future (Bloch *et al.* 1992). Bloch *et al.* also highlight the risk of premature diagnosis in such individuals, which could have damaging effects. In addition, a high-risk status may preclude the use of denial as a defence mechanism when the first symptoms of Huntington's disease develop, which may result in increased distress and risk of suicide. Other possible disadvantages include stigmatization in the areas of employment, insurance and social relationships (Berg and Fletcher 1986). Possible benefits of a high-risk result include the ability to make better informed decisions, including marriage and childbearing plans, not only for the person tested but for their partner and children. Also the time prior to the onset of the disorder may be used for preparation, both practical and emotional, for future infirmity and hardship.

Ongoing support and counselling for all who have undergone risk alteration are crucial to the success of a predictive test programme, and medium and long-term effects of testing should continue to be monitored. Current experience indicates that presymptomatic testing in Huntington's disease is safe and acceptable, given adherence to a strict protocol, and very few attempts at self-harm have been reported as a result (Lam *et al.* 1988; Brandt *et al.* 1989). It appears to improve the quality of life for the majority of applicants and presumably their families, at least in the short term. In summary, there is no evidence to suggest that testing should be restricted and some to suggest significant benefits (Hayden 1991).

A more cogent argument concerns the use made of limited health resources. Presymptomatic testing is currently supported by counselling and requires significant laboratory work-up, both of which are extensive and expensive; however, the ultimate outcome for the individual remains unaltered. How can one measure the cost effectiveness of such a technique, and can it be justified given other competing claims on resources? This cost–benefit dilemma is not new, and wide-ranging consultation is needed to establish the emotional and financial criteria by which society will prioritize and fund such procedures (Klein 1992).

THE 'MYTH' OF INFORMED CONSENT

Fully informed consent implies the appropriate provision and comprehension of information, followed by a willingness to participate. For many treatments in medicine the issue of how much information should be provided has been difficult to resolve and has become the subject of litigation by aggrieved patients. Consent must be based upon a knowledge of the nature, consequences and alternatives associated with the proposed procedure. The first question to be addressed is the content of the information provided. An individual should not be exposed to a risk of harm unless they have agreed to that risk, and that choice cannot be made without sufficient information (Mason and McCall Smith 1991). Guidelines have been established by both the World Federation of Neurology in conjunction with the International Huntington's Association and the United Kingdom Huntington's Disease Prediction Consortium, which outline specific areas to be covered in detail (World Federation of Neurology 1989 and 1990; Tyler *et al.* 1990). However, the complex nature of the testing procedure may hinder comprehension, and consideration should be given to how best to communicate such complicated information to an individual with little or no understanding of science, let alone genetics. Certainly, knowledge of the precise scientific techniques employed is not essential to understand the implications and limitations of the testing procedure. Explanations should be targeted at the applicant's intellectual and emotional level, which can be inferred by background information and the subject–counsellor interaction. Verbal information should be reinforced by written and other material and questions encouraged. In addition, it is of vital importance to confirm comprehension by asking the individual to indicate that they have understood the information presented by gentle prompting and questions.

Unless information is complete and is presented impartially, the subject could be at risk of manipulation, either deliberately or subconsciously, by the counsellor. Is it possible for information to be presented in a way that is uninfluenced by personal background, experience, values, beliefs and personality? Some suggest that non-directive genetic counselling is impossible, given the need to supply information, and consider the term 'non-directive' inappropriate, proposing that it be limited to Carl Rogers's original psychological technique (Rogers 1942; Clarke 1991).

Perhaps the term 'consent' is also an inappropriate word when considering presymptomatic testing as it suggests a passive agreement to undergo a procedure rather than an active seeking. The aim of counselling should be to enable an individual actively to request or decline testing. Consent should be freely given but because others are often involved in the decision process, particularly close family members, it may be difficult to detect and prevent third-party pressure and imposition. In certain circumstances this may be obvious, for example when testing is requested directly by an insurance company or a lawyer, but it may be more difficult to identify subtle manipulation, in a suggestible individual, particularly by a family member. Testing should be postponed if there is any suspicion that an individual is not wholeheartedly in favour of being tested but is being subjected to a degree of coercion. Subjects may also seek testing during a crisis, such as a recent discovery that they are at risk, only to change their minds when they have adjusted to the situation. A careful exploration of motivating factors and reasons for seeking testing at this time is essential in all cases, and is of particular value if other issues are influencing the applicant, such as an impending court case.

Two groups that require special consideration include the psychiatrically ill and the cognitively impaired. In these circumstances individuals may be unable to comprehend fully or to assimilate information, and testing may be postponed, if the disorder is acute, or considered inappropriate if it is chronic.

TESTING OF CHILDREN

Understanding, essential to informed consent, has important implications also for minors. Testing of minors for Huntington's disease has been sought by parents, often to relieve their own anxieties. Two cases have been reported in which mothers have requested a test for their infant, as they felt that bonding could only occur with a child at low risk. In one of these cases the child, if found to be at high risk, would have been given up for adoption (Bloch and Hayden 1990; Tyler et al. 1990). In the event, neither of the children was tested. Testing has also been sought by adoption agencies as a perceived duty to provide information for potential parents (Morris et al. 1988; Tyler 1988).

If and when an effective treatment becomes available, it may be important to seek testing as early as possible in order to initiate preventive measures. However, we are not in that enviable situation and a test result does not have implications for treatment. Thus testing a child carries no medical advantage but puts the child at risk of harm, as a high-risk result may prejudice upbringing by either natural or adoptive parents, and may even result in stigmatization. It also removes the child's future autonomy regarding the decision to be tested (Craufurd *et al*. 1990; Harper and Clarke 1990). In addition, particular problems could arise should two or more sibs be tested and receive different results.

There is consequently a consensus that children should not be tested and that the decision whether or not to seek testing should be deferred until an individual is of sufficient intellectual and emotional maturity; this is currently deemed to be at 18 years of age in the United Kingdom (Craufurd and Tyler 1992).

THE LIMITATIONS OF PRESYMPTOMATIC TESTING USING LINKED MARKERS

Protein abnormalities and direct mutational analysis can be used to test for the presence or absence of a disease gene once this has been isolated and characterized. However, linked markers can only be used to raise or lower the estimated risk of carrying a gene and as such there is some residual uncertainty because of the possibility of recombination between the marker and the disease gene (see p. 66). There has been at least one report of a subject at risk for Huntington's disease being given a high-risk result, only to have it changed to a low-risk result on further DNA analysis, following the identification of new markers closer to the Huntington's disease gene and the availability of DNA samples from other relatives (Craufurd, personal communication). There has also been a report of a low-risk result being reversed to high risk, which caused considerable distress (Turner and Willoughby 1990). The possibility of recombination must also mean that a small number of individuals given a low-risk result will subsequently develop the disorder. Three such cases have already been reported in the USA and UK, and the emotional trauma caused to both subject and professional was intense (personal communications, anonymous). How subjects perceive such high- and low-risk results, and what they mean to them, needs further study. For example, the margin of uncertainty implied in a high-risk result, however small, is often an exaggerated source of consolation, whilst the uncertainty of a low-risk result is often ignored (Wexler 1992). There has also been a report of an individual who, following risk alteration from 50 per cent to 11 per cent, perceived herself to be at a higher risk than formerly (Huggins *et al.* 1992). Many who have received a high-risk result have indicated that they would not seek further risk refinement when the causative gene has been cloned and accurate mutational analysis is feasible, preferring to maintain the small degree of uncertainty and therefore hope. Those who have received a low-risk result are similarly reluctant to jeopardize this status by further risk refinement.

Linked marker studies require DNA from other family members and this relies on availability and co-operation, accurate diagnosis of those affected and diligent sample collection. Clinical diagnoses within the family must be conscientiously confirmed and preferably verified at post-mortem in at least one affected family member. Approaching relatives or medical practitioners involved with their care raises issues of confidentiality and privacy. For example, the genetic centre may have information concerning family members, particularly those affected with Huntington's disease, but whose condition is not known to the applicant, and a breach of confidentiality could occur if this information were revealed. Sometimes an informative result can only be obtained using the DNA of a key relative who may be demonstrating early signs of the disorder, but who is unaware of, or unwilling to consider, the probable diagnosis and to undergo confirmatory investigations. To press this person to seek medical advice could be considered an invasion of privacy. Occasionally there is a history of bitter family disputes which may be rekindled, for example, if an estranged spouse is approached for a blood sample. Also elderly unaffected subjects, required as escapees (i.e. who have reached an age at which they are virtually certain not to carry the HD gene), can become very anxious when asked to supply a blood sample for analysis. Clearly a 'cold' approach is not appropriate and counselling must be provided for all these persons, which entails a considerable demand on resources. That the need to respect privacy of other family members takes precedence over the desire of the person to be tested was stated in a UK national symposium on predictive testing for Huntington's disease (Tyler and Morris 1990).

The late onset of Huntington's disease often meant that, when an individual requested testing, the grandparents had died and samples were not available. Furthermore in any linkage study, family members from whom samples are essential may be unwilling to provide them, thereby rendering the testing procedure uninformative. What responsibility do these individuals have towards those requesting testing? Should society insist that they provide a blood sample? An example that is sometimes encountered is the parent who is not at risk refusing to provide a DNA sample, possibly because they disapprove of prediction, believing it to be harmful to their children. It has been argued that persons sharing a common genetic endowment have a duty to share the available knowledge with others who are also implicated (Royal College of Physicians Committees on Ethical Issues in Medicine and Clinical Genetics 1991). This argument has not yet been tested in court and it is not known whether it would command public support; it is likely that the moral duty of these individuals to provide this information would be upheld, unless there are compelling reasons to the contrary, but it is unlikely that society would ever sanction the use of force.

These issues again emphasize the need for expert counselling to ensure that applicants understand the implications and limitations of the testing procedure and stress the need for public discussion.

CONFIDENTIALITY, OBLIGATIONS AND RESPONSIBILITIES

A high-risk test result may lead to stigmatization, and questions of access to such information are therefore of great importance. To whom do the results belong and to whom should or can they be released? This will be of particular importance when genes which predispose to common disorders and attributes such as heart disease, cancer or intelligence are identified. Current practice assigns ownership to the tested individuals themselves (World Federation of Neurology 1989 and 1990). Results are only communicated to family doctors with the consent of the subject and all records are securely stored in separate notes.

How should the medical profession respond if, for example, insurance companies or the courts request access to such information? How should society react to the future prospect of a genetic profile being a prerequisite for personal insurance or employment, altering insurance premiums and job prospects? Such information is already being sought and requests for testing have been received from those at risk of Huntington's disease who wish to obtain a mortgage or employment in the armed services. It has been suggested that discrimination based on the outcome of genetic testing should be outlawed (Anonymous 1991) but could an individual use a low-risk result to their advantage?

Although the need for medical confidentiality is stressed by all professional bodies, it is subject to qualification in the United Kingdom, and the General Medical Council (GMC) lists possible exceptions (Mason and McCall Smith 1991). Those carrying the HIV virus who do not disclose it to their partners or significant others have highlighted the issue of whose rights are paramount. The GMC has stated that information can be passed on to a sexual partner in the absence of consent provided every effort has been made to persuade the affected individual to pass it on without success. This principle has been applied to genetics, where diagnosis in the patient has important implications for a partner or children. In the United States of America the President's Comission for the study of ethical problems in medicine (1983), when considering screening and counselling for genetic disorders, has also stated that confidentiality can be overridden under specific conditions, mostly relating to the avoidance of serious harm. Should this principle also be applied to the results of genetic tests? That an individual should be obliged to disclose a test result to offspring seems ethically unexceptional since this information materially affects their risk status and as such could be said to 'belong' to them. A Royal College of Physicians report suggests that as long as individuals have the right to decide for themselves whether to bear children it could be argued that such individuals should have access to the fullest possible information, including genetic, pertinent to that decision and therefore this should not be withheld. A case has been reported of a general practitioner informing a pregnant woman, without the permission of her husband, that he was at 50 per cent risk of developing Huntington's disease (Tyler *et al.* 1990). Following testing, could a general practitioner in similar circumstances believe that there was a duty to reveal the result? It has been argued that doctors can still preserve confidentiality by only informing children of their change in risk and not mentioning that of the parent; however, in Huntington's disease this distinction would be difficult to maintain since the implications are obvious (Glantz 1982).

Insurance companies and employers could be supposed to have a particular interest in the results of genetic tests. In the future direct questions regarding participation in molecular genetic testing could feature on insurance application forms, as has occurred for tests of HIV status. Currently problems arise when insurance companies seek a medical report and are informed of a previously undisclosed family history of Huntington's disease. Following predictive testing, should an individual and their general practitioner be obliged to indicate that testing has occurred and disclose the result in a medical report? This would appear to be the current legal situation in the United Kingdom. One problem could be that individuals receiving a low risk may wish to inform such bodies, and requests to write letters of support have been received by testing centres (Quarrell *et al.* 1989), but presumably those given a high-risk result would not wish to publicize it. In Minnesota test candidates are reportedly paying for testing directly, rather than through their insurance companies, to protect themselves from possible pressure to reveal a test result (Nance *et al.* 1991). Furthermore, this could have implications for the doctor–individual relationship as applicants may seek to prevent test information reaching their medical notes by not involving their general practitioner. At present genetic tests are not generally being used for insurance purposes and therefore a 'window of opportunity' exists to debate and resolve issues of whether and how they should be used before widespread application ensues. It has also been argued that there should be a moratorium on the use of genetic testing until guidelines have been issued, possibly within a legislative framework (Harper 1993a).

Given the extensive and expensive training for some occupations, it is very likely that employers will seek as much medical information as is available, including a genetic 'curriculum vitae' or profile. A survey in the United States of America has indicated that by the year 2,000 some employers are likely to use genetic tests to exclude workers from occupational hazards and screen job applicants (Wertz and Fletcher 1989). Can genetic testing be justified by the 'desire to protect' employees, the public and employers, particularly in adult disorders like Huntington's disease, where such tests give no indication of age of onset or likely severity? Published guidelines suggest that genetic screening should only be used where there is significant and serious risk of harm to affected workers and co-workers, and that the danger should be actual and not hypothetical (Murray 1983).

Much has been said on the importance of confidentiality and protection of individual rights. It has been suggested that parents may have a 'fiduciary' duty to descendants both born and unborn to seek testing (Lamport 1987). However, this is a difficult doctrine to promulgate, since it does not consider the possible harm done to an unwilling parent, which may be greater than that done to the children left in a position of uncertainty. Whilst there is a positive obligation to do no harm, there is no similar obligation to do good, although it can be argued that good and harm are merely positions on the same spectrum and that by not doing good, one is in fact doing harm. Should the individual tested always inform a potential partner or spouse of the risk alteration, as this will have important implications, particularly for childbearing decisions? What obligation should a subject have to inform an employer, especially if the occupation is potentially hazardous to self or others, and/or involves expensive training? What rights, if any, should society have over those of the individual? Where should the line be drawn between confidentiality and obligation, individual autonomy and duty? Detailed regulation and guidelines demand the careful study of relevant cases and many opinions should be sought.

ISOLATION OF THE HUNTINGTON'S DISEASE GENE: IMPLICATIONS OF DIRECT MUTATIONAL ANALYSIS FOR LATE-ONSET DISORDERS

Now that the gene responsible for Huntington's disease has been identified, direct mutational analysis is possible. This will simplify and accelerate the laboratory testing procedures, and collection of samples from other family members will be largely unnecessary. Counselling will then become the rate-limiting, and most expensive, aspect of the testing procedure (Harper 1993b; Simpson and Harding 1993). Such counselling is the essential foundation on which the applicant bases the decision to proceed with testing, gives fully informed consent and prepares for risk alteration. Crucial elements in this decision-making process include the exploration of the emotional impact of being at risk, the history of the disease in the family, and the applicant's exposure and reaction. As a result perceptions of themselves in relation to their at-risk status may change and unnecessary anxiety and myths may be dispelled. Even if testing is not pursued, subjects report that they have benefited from this in-depth discussion. For all these reasons it must be preserved to protect the applicant. This will be of particular importance when the test becomes available in commercial laboratories, where financial criteria may be paramount. There are already anecdotal reports from the United States which suggest that counselling protocols are not being observed (Chapman 1992).

Huntington's disease, as has already been noted, is a disease of late onset and families are often complete before the symptoms become manifest in a parent. Testing the adult children of an asymptomatic gene carrier by linkage analysis is very difficult without the co-operation of that parent, but direct testing is now feasible following the identification of a causal mutation. In this situation testing the child would of necessity alter the risk of the apparently normal intervening parent. Thus a negative risk result would reduce the estimated risk of the parent, whilst a positive result would imply that the at-risk parent was an obligate carrier of the gene. 'Testing through' an at-risk parent would therefore result in an unsolicited risk alteration. Whose rights should then prevail, those of the parent or those of the child? This dilemma has been the subject of much continuing and unresolved debate, which again raises the question 'To whom would the greater harm be done?'

Other problems of testing without knowledge or consent could arise. Testing of a DNA sample obtained surreptitiously, for example using a blood sample obtained for another reason, would be possible without the knowledge and consent of the individual concerned. Such a scenario could be envisaged if the partner of an at-risk individual, reluctant to undergo testing, was particularly anxious to know that person's risk because of existing children or childbearing decisions. Whilst one hopes that this situation would be identified by a conscientious laboratory, and the request rejected, this must remain a possibility.

EXCLUSION TESTING IN PREGNANCY

Exclusion testing in pregnancy is currently offered only to those parents who, after counselling, intend terminating a high-risk fetus, because otherwise the fetus would be subjected to risks associated with the sampling procedure for no alteration in management; these include an increased risk of miscarriage and fetal abnormalities (Firth *et al.* 1991). Termination of these, often desperately wanted, high-risk pregnancies, results in the loss of a fetus not carrying the Huntington's disease gene in approximately 50 per cent of cases, whereas those fetuses which carry the Huntington's disease gene could be expected to have forty years of potentially useful life. In addition, such therapeutic abortions are associated with psychological sequelae (Zolese and Blacker 1992).

These reservations should be balanced against the opportunity of raising an unaffected family, avoiding feelings of guilt associated with the transmission of the gene, and prevention of an economically and emotionally devastating disorder. However, some of these low-risk children will grow up in a family that is distorted by the presence of a parent affected with, or absent due to, Huntington's disease, with all the psychological and social sequelae. This reservation would also apply to prenatal testing when the parent has received a high-risk result.

Should the parents alter their mind and decide to continue with a high-risk pregnancy, as has occasionally happened (Brock *et al.* 1989; Bloch and Hayden 1990), then the fetal risk will be linked to that of the parent by the possession of the same short arm of chromosome 4, inherited from the affected grandparent. Thus, should the parent develop symptoms of Huntington's disease, the resulting child would be an obligate gene carrier, barring a recombination event.

For some the emotional cost of this technique for obtaining a 'normal family' is too great. However, there is general agreement that counselling prior to embarking on this procedure should be as extensive as that for presymptomatic testing and that this should be provided by those responsible for the specialized counselling for Huntington's disease, rather than being devolved to general prenatal testing services (Tyler *et al.* 1990; Wexler 1992).

To what extent exclusion testing will continue to be requested or offered, now that mutation testing is feasible, remains to be seen. It is likely that some individuals will ask for such testing to avoid altering their own risk. Others may seek a test for themselves and only embark on fetal testing should this prove positive. However, the psychological consequences of a double loss, that is, their future health and the termination of a pregnancy, if both tests prove positive should be carefully considered, preferably before conception.

Combining *in vitro* fertilization, embryo sampling and polymerase chain reaction techniques may in future allow the identification and implantation of a low-risk embryo, as is currently available for parents at risk of having a child with cystic fibrosis. This would have several advantages, including the knowledge that the fetus is at low risk from the outset, avoiding the risks and trauma of fetal sampling, and circumventing the need for termination of a high-risk fetus, but this approach will introduce additional ethical issues associated with such techniques.

PRESYMPTOMATIC TESTING IN OTHER GENETIC DISORDERS OF LATE ONSET

Presymptomatic testing is becoming available for other late-onset neurological disorders, including inherited prion diseases, Kennedy's disease and familial Alzheimer's disease. In these disorders direct mutational analysis allows presymptomatic testing in many families. However, uncertainty may still be introduced, for example because of incomplete penetrance, as in inherited prion disease (Collinge *et al.* 1991). Thus the same principles of counselling, formulated in the context of Huntington's disease, should be followed before and after testing. There are also relevant lessons for presymptomatic testing in late-onset disorders affecting other systems, such as polycystic kidney disease, myotonic dystrophy and familial cancers.

CONCLUSIONS

Presymptomatic testing in Huntington's disease provides a model for genetic testing in other disorders, particularly those of late onset. Ethical issues that have been encountered and examined during the first five years of testing provide a general framework by which other testing programmes can be examined and established. Important guidelines can be drawn from the Huntington's disease experience in areas which include informed consent, prenatal testing, testing of children, confidentiality and obligations. One consistent and essential factor is the need for expert counselling; this need will increase as more genes are mapped and must be considered when the future allocation of resources and training is being planned. Decisions involving resource allocation, priorities, ethics and future research should be made by a wide section of society following full and informed debate.

ACKNOWLEDGEMENTS

Thanks are due to the Huntington's disease families who have taught us so much, our colleagues in Cardiff, and those who have supported our research financially, including the Mental Health Foundation, Medical Research Council and the Huntington's Disease Association. We are very grateful to Kathleen Gillespie, Gary Houlihan and Angus Clarke for helpful comments.

REFERENCES

Anonymous (1991) 'Proposed ban on genetic testing in Denmark', *Lancet* 337: 1340.

Ball, D. M. and Harper, P. S. (1992) 'Presymptomatic testing for late-onset genetic disorders: lessons from Huntington's disease', *FASEB Journal* 6: 2818–19.

Benson, R. (1992) 'Why geneticists shouldn't do ethics', *European Society of Human Genetics* 46 (Abstract).

Berg, K. and Fletcher, J. (1986) 'Ethical and legal aspects of predictive testing' (letter), *Lancet* ii: 1043.

Bloch, M., Adam, S., Wiggins, S. *et al.* (1992) 'Predictive testing for Huntington's disease in Canada: the experience of those receiving an increased risk', *American Journal of Human Genetics* 42: 499–507.

Bloch, M. and Hayden, M. R. (1990) 'Predictive testing for Huntington's disease in childhood: challenges and implications', *American Journal of Medical Genetics* 46: 1–4.

Brandt, J., Quaid, K. A., Folstein, S. *et al.* (1989) 'Presymptomatic diagnosis of delayed-onset disease with linked DNA markers: the experience in Huntington's disease', *Journal of the American Medical Association* 261: 3108–14.

Brock, D. H., Mennie, M., Curtis, A. *et al.* (1989) 'Predictive testing for Huntington's disease with linked DNA markers', *Lancet* ii: 463–6.

Chapman, M. A. (1992) 'Canadian experience with predictive testing for Huntington's disease: lessons for genetic testing centers and policy makers', *American Journal of Medical Genetics* 42: 491–8.

Clarke, A. (1991) 'Is non-directive genetic counselling possible?' *Lancet* 338: 998–1001.

Collinge, J., Poulter, M., Davis, M. B. *et al.* (1991) 'Presymptomatic detection or exclusion of prion protein gene defects in families with inherited prion diseases', *American Journal of Human Genetics* 49: 1351–4.

Craufurd, D., Dodge, A., Kerzin-Storrar, L. *et al.* (1990) 'Testing of children for "adult" genetic diseases' (letter), *Lancet* i: 1406.

Craufurd, D. I. O. and Harris, R. (1986) 'Ethics of predictive testing for Huntington's chorea. The need for more information', *British Medical Journal* 293: 249–51.

Craufurd, D. and Tyler, A. (1992) 'Predictive testing for Huntington's disease. Protocol of the UK Huntington's Prediction Consortium', *Journal of Medical Genetics* 29: 915–17.

Firth, H. V., Boyd, P. A., Chamberlain, P. *et al.* (1991) 'Severe limb abnormalities after chorionic villus sampling', *Lancet* 337: 762–3.

Glantz, L. (1982) 'Legal aspects of disclosure: what constitutes 'confidential' information?' *Huntington Review of Neuropsychiatric Disorders* 1(2): 8–10.

Gusella, J. F., Wexler, N. S., Conneally, P. M. *et al.* (1983) 'A polymorphic DNA marker genetically linked to Huntington's disease', *Nature* 306: 234–8.

Harper, P. S. (ed.) (1991a) *Huntington's Disease*, London: W. B. Saunders Co. Ltd.

—— (1991b) 'Predictive testing for Huntington's disease. A worldwide perspective' (abstract), Proceedings of the 8th International Congress of Human Genetics. *American Journal of Human Genetics*, 49 (4): supplement, 62.

—— (1992) 'Huntington's disease and the abuse of genetics', *American Journal of Human Genetics* 50: 460–4.

—— (1993a) 'Insurance and genetic testing', *Lancet* 341: 224–7.

—— (1993b) 'Clinical consequences of isolating the gene for Huntington's disease', *British Medical Journal* 307: 397–8.

Harper, P. S. and Clarke, A. (1990) 'Should we test children for "adult" genetic disease?' *Lancet* 335: 1205–6.

Harper, P. S., Morris, M. and Tyler, A. (1991) 'Predictive tests in Huntington's disease', in P. S. Harper (ed.) *Huntington's Disease*, London: W. B. Saunders Co. Ltd, pp. 373–413.

Hayden, M. R. (1991) 'Predictive testing for Huntington's disease: are we ready for widespread community implementation?' *American Journal of Medical Genetics* 40: 515–17.

Hayden, M. R., Robbins, C., Allard, D. *et al.* (1988) 'Improved predictive testing for Huntington's disease using three linked DNA markers', *American Journal of Human Genetics* 43: 689–94.

Huggins, M., Bloch, M., Kanani, S. *et al.* (1990) 'Ethical and legal dilemmas arising during predictive testing for adult-onset disease: the experience of Huntington's disease', *American Journal of Human Genetics* 47: 4–12.

Huggins, M., Bloch, M., Wiggins, S. *et al.* (1992) 'Predictive testing for Huntington's disease in Canada: adverse effects and unexpected results in those receiving a decreased risk', *American Journal of Medical Genetics* 42: 508–15.

Huntington, G. (1872) 'On chorea', *Medical and Surgical Reporter* 26: 317–21.

Huntington's Disease Collaborative Research Group (1993) 'A novel gene that is expanded and unstable in Huntington's disease chromosomes', *Cell* 72: 971–83.

Journal of Medical Genetics special issue on Huntington's disease (1993) *Journal of Medical Genetics* 30: 975–1042.

Klein, R. (1992) 'Warning signs from Oregon', *British Medical Journal* 304: 1457–8.

Lam, R., Bloch, M., Jones, B. D. *et al.* (1988) 'Psychiatric morbidity associated with early clinical diagnosis of Huntington's disease in a predictive testing program', *Journal of Clinical Psychiatry* 49: 444–7.

Lamport, A. T. (1987) 'Presymptomatic testing in Huntington's chorea: ethical and legal issues', *American Journal of Medical Genetics* 26: 307–14.

Lazarou, L., Meredith, A. L., Myring, J. M. *et al.* (1993) 'Huntington's disease predictive testing and the molecular genetics laboratory', *Clinical Genetics* 45: 150–6.

McGuffin, P. and Sargeant, M. (1989) 'Ethics and psychiatric genetics', *Current Opinion in Psychiatry* 2: 681–4.

MacMillan, J. C., Snell, R. G., Tyler, A. *et al.* (1993) 'Molecular analysis and clinical correlations of the Huntington's disease mutation', *Lancet* 342: 954–8.

Mason, J. K. and McCall Smith, R. A. (1991) *Law and Medical Ethics*, London: Butterworths.

Mastromauro, C., Myers, R. H. and Berkman, B. (1987) 'Attitudes towards predictive testing in Huntington's disease', *American Journal of Medical Genetics* 26: 271–82.

Meissen, G. J. and Berchek, R. L. (1988) 'Intentions to use predictive testing by those at risk for Huntington's disease: implications for prevention', *American Journal of Community Psychology* 16: 261–77.

Morris, M. J. (1991) 'Huntington's disease: presymptomatic testing', *Current Opinion in Neurological Neurosurgery* 31: 337–41.

Morris, M., Tyler, A. and Harper, P. S. (1988) 'Adoption and genetic prediction for Huntington's disease', *Lancet* ii: 1069–70.

Morris, M., Tyler, A., Lazarou, L. *et al.* (1989) 'Problems in genetic prediction for Huntington's disease', *Lancet*, ii: 601–3.

Murray, T. H. (1983) 'Warning: screening workers for genetic risk', *Hastings Center Report* 31: 5–8.

Nance, M. A., Leroy, B. S., Orr, H. T. *et al.* (1991) 'Protocol for genetic testing in Huntington's disease: three years of experience in Minnesota', *American Journal of Human Genetics* 40: 518–22.

The President's Commission (1983) *Screening and Counselling for Genetic Conditions*, Washington, D.C.: US Government Printing Office.

Quarrell, O. W. J., Bloch, M. and Hayden, M. R. (1989) 'Insurance and the presymptomatic diagnosis of Huntington's disease', *Journal of the American Medical Association* 262: 2384–5.

Quarrell, O. W. J., Meredith, A. L., Tyler, A. *et al.* (1987) 'Exclusion testing for Huntington's disease in pregnancy with a closely linked DNA marker', *Lancet* i: 1282–3.

Rogers, C. R. (1942) *Counselling and Psychotherapy*, New York: Houghton Mifflin Co.

Royal College of Physicians Committees on Ethical Issues in Medicine and Clinical Genetics (1991) *Ethical Issues in Clinical Genetics*, London: Royal College of Physicians.

Shaw, D. and Youngman, S. (1991) 'Molecular genetic approaches to Huntington's disease', in P.S. Harper (ed.) *Huntington's Disease*, London: W. B. Saunders Co. Ltd, pp. 317–36.

Simpson, S. A. and Harding, A. E. (1993) 'Predictive testing for Huntington's disease: after the gene', *Journal of Medical Genetics* 30: 1036–8.

Snell, R. G., MacMillan, J. C., Cheadle, J. *et al.* (1993) 'Expansion of a specific trinucleotide repeat sequence in Huntington's disease. The molecular basis of phenotypic variation', *Nature Genetics* 4: 393–7.

Tibben, A., Vegter-van der Vlis, M., Skraastad, M. I. *et al.* (1992) 'DNA testing for Huntington's disease in the Netherlands: a retrospective study on psychosocial effects', *American Journal of Medical Genetics* 44: 94–9.

Turner, D. R. and Willoughby, J. O. (1990) 'Ethical issues in Huntington's disease presymptomatic testing', *Australian and New Zealand Journal of Medicine* 20: 545–6.

Tyler, A. (1988) 'Adoption in relation to presymptomatic testing for Huntington's disease', *Adoption and Fostering* 12: 57.

Tyler, A., Ball, D. and Crauford, D., on behalf of the United Kingdom Huntington's Disease Prediction Consortium (1992) 'Presymptomatic testing for Huntington's disease in the United Kingdom', *British Medical Journal* 304: 1593–6.

Tyler, A. and Harper, P. S. (1983) 'Attitudes of subjects at-risk and their relatives towards genetic counselling in Huntington's chorea', *Journal of Medical Genetics* 20: 179–88.

Tyler, A. and Morris, M. (1990) 'National symposium on problems of presymptomatic testing for Huntington's disease, Cardiff', *Journal of Medical Ethics* 16: 41–2.

Tyler, A., Morris, M., Lazarou, L. *et al.* (1992) 'Presymptomatic testing for Huntington's disease in Wales 1987–1990', *British Journal of Psychiatry* 161: 481–8.

Tyler, A., Quarrell, O. W. J., Lazarou, L. *et al.* (1990) 'Exclusion testing in pregnancy for Huntington's disease', *Journal of Medical Genetics* 27: 488–95.

Weatherall, D. J. (1991) *The New Genetics and Clinical Practice*, Oxford: Oxford University Press.

Wertz, D. C. and Fletcher, J. C. (1989) *Ethics and Human Genetics. A Cross-cultural Perspective*, Berlin: Springer.

Wexler, N. (1992) 'The Tiresias complex: Huntington's disease as a paradigm of testing for late-onset disorders', *FASEB Journal* 6: 2820–25.

World Federation of Neurology Research Group on Huntington's Disease (1989) 'Ethical Issues Policy Statement on Huntington's disease molecular genetics predictive test', *Journal of Neurological Science* 94: 327–32.

—— (1990) 'Ethical Issues Policy Statement on Huntington's disease molecular genetics predictive test, *Journal of Medical Genetics* 27: 34–8.

—— (1993) 'Presymptomatic testing for Huntington's disease: a worldwide survey', *Journal of Medical Genetics* 30: 1020–2.

Zolese, G. and Blacker, C. V. R. (1992) 'The psychological complications of therapeutic abortion', *British Journal of Psychiatry* 160: 742–9.

APPENDIX
RESEARCH SAMPLES FROM FAMILIES WITH GENETIC DISEASES: A PROPOSED CODE OF CONDUCT

Peter S. Harper

Abstract

Research on samples from families with genetic disease underlies many of the major advances that are occurring in medical genetics. But ethical and practical problems may arise when samples from relatives who are healthy but at risk are included in such studies. In particular, new molecular tests for specific gene mutations may result in the detection of a genetic defect in relatives who had neither expected this possibility nor given specific consent to such testing. Family members at risk should not be included in such studies unless strictly necessary, and in such cases specific consent should be obtained and information should be given about the implications of an abnormal result of a test. This is particularly important when stored samples from previous studies without such implications are being reused and is also relevant to the genetic testing of samples taken primarily for epidemiological studies of disorders when only a small proportion of cases is thought to be genetic in origin. There is a need for guidelines to protect both subjects and investigators in a field which is spreading rapidly and involving many clinical and laboratory research workers previously unfamiliar with genetic testing.

Over the past decade developments in molecular genetics have allowed the mapping and isolation of a large number of genes for serious human disorders; DNA analysis of specific mutations or of linked markers now gives the possibility of presymptomatic and prenatal diagnosis, of detection of healthy heterozygous carriers, and, in some instances, of inferring the severity of the disease from the nature of the mutation detected. Much of the research leading to these and other important advances has entailed the study of families with specific inherited disorders; samples from these families have provided an essential resource and will continue to do so.

Most samples taken for DNA analysis are of venous blood because of ease of sampling, minimal discomfort on the subject, and the large number of analyses possible on a single sample. Transformed cell lines are often established on particularly important samples, but more often the isolated DNA is stored at −20 or −70°C, providing a resource that can be used repeatedly without having to cause disturbance or discomfort by taking further samples.

Many research workers, both clinicians and laboratory scientists, maintain large collections of blood samples from patients with genetic disorders and their relatives. So far they have given little thought to the dangers of this practice as opposed to the advantages. Until recently I was as unaware of the potential pitfalls as most others but recent experience in providing a service of molecular diagnosis and prediction for several disorders, in particular a programme of presymptomatic testing for Huntington's disease, has shown that the dangers of misuse of research samples are real and likely to increase as more disease genes are isolated.

Indeed I am conscious that my awareness of most of the errors and problems described here is a direct result of having encountered them myself by not paying adequate attention to the points now recommended. This paper outlines some of the main problems and makes some suggestions for avoiding them. After discussion and modification they might form the basis of a code of conduct that could help both investigators and families with genetic diseases.

As most of the points raised here are self-evident it is perhaps surprising that they do not seem to have been specifically raised in print, especially as other ethical issues in genetics have received extensive debate and publicity. Thus the ethics of gene therapy has been the subject of a special report,[1] as has the research use of fetal material[2] and human fertilization and embryology.[3] By contrast the use of research samples for genetic tests receives no mention in the recent Medical Research Council booklet on responsibility in investigations on human participants[4] or in the Royal College of Physicians' report on ethical issues in medical genetics;[5] the United States bibliography on ethical, legal and social implications of the human genome project[6] contains no entry (among a total of around 2,400) that seems related to the subject.

What type of samples cause problems?

It is important to distinguish between the different categories of samples stored as the potential for problems and for misuse varies widely between them. Service DNA banks, where samples are deposited specifically for service use, are likely to be a problem only when research and service activities are carried out in the same laboratory and when a clear distinction is not made between the two categories.[7] Anonymous or strictly coded samples forming part of epidemiological studies are likewise not an issue, unless the worker proposes to break the code that protects an individual patient's identity. The principal concern is with identifiable samples taken from members of individual families for research purposes.

Within this group one can again distinguish between those affected with the disorder and those apparently unaffected but at risk. It is in this last group that most of the problems lie. Samples from affected patients are unlikely to cause difficulties unless they are taken from patients whose disorder has not previously been recognized as having a genetic basis (see below).

What problems can arise?

Most molecular studies of families with genetic diseases initially entail a genetic linkage approach by relying on a comparison of marker genotypes between affected and unaffected subjects to establish linkage with a particular marker. Once the gene is isolated, a comparative approach is again important to establish that any change identified in the gene is in fact specific to affected subjects and not a harmless polymorphism or other coincidental change.

Inevitably such an approach will from time to time detect the genetic defect (or high-risk marker) in a subject considered to be unaffected but who in fact may be very mildly affected in a variable disorder (for example, myotonic dystrophy) or who may develop the condition later in a disorder that is strongly age-dependent (for example, Huntington's disease). In yet other disorders a proportion of known carriers of the gene never develop the disease (for example, dominantly inherited retinitis pigmentosa, familial amyloidosis), so the subject detected may fall into this category.

The problem of unexpected detection of genetic defects is only important in disorders of relatively late onset or variable phenotype such as those mentioned above; commonly these are autosomal dominant in inheritance. For disorders of consistently early onset or static nature (for example, achondroplasia) such a case would not be likely to arise.

What are the adverse effects of unexpected detection?

The diagnosis of any serious genetic disorder is commonly accompanied by psychological upset, relating not only to the potential clinical effects of the disease but also to the genetic consequences.[8] The importance of careful preparation, counselling and support has been shown in genetic prediction for Huntington's disease, when adverse effects have in general been minimized by such measures.[9,10] The unexpected detection of such a defect in a subject who has not specifically asked for this does not permit such a process.

A number of more specific problems may be created for the person concerned. These include implications for life and health insurance[11] or for employment (if the finding is disclosed), and the genetic consequences for children, born or unborn, may have serious repercussions on marriage and family relationships. Uncertainty about the outcome may be a very real problem when the consequences of a disorder or a specific mutation are variable or incompletely known.

Problems of consent

Many of the problems mentioned above are aggravated or even created by uncertainties relating to consent. When the taking of a blood sample has been the only procedure, written consent may not have been obtained and it may be uncertain what consent was given for. Even written consent may be so limited or non-specific as to be of little use. When samples are stored, successive phases of research may use the same sample, starting with attempts to localize a gene and continuing through its isolation to the study of mutations. Implications for the use of samples may exist at this later stage that were not present or even thought of when the sample was originally taken. This raises the question as to how different the work has to be before a separate and specific consent is sought from the person who provided the sample.

As approval from an ethical review committee has to be obtained before a research project can proceed, it might be thought that this process would ensure that suitable consent was indeed obtained. Members of ethical committees, however, are often not experts in genetics and are likely to be more concerned with the dangers and discomfort of procedures or treatments than with the consequences of genetic information. Thus, a project entailing a simple venepuncture may pass review easily in comparison with an invasive measure without full consideration being given to the serious potential effects of detection of a genetic defect.

A particular difficulty that can arise when an abnormality is found is whether or not the person is expecting to receive a result from the sample taken. As the outcome of any research project is necessarily uncertain it is preferable to make it clear to any healthy member of a family from the outset that no result will be forthcoming either for themselves or for their doctor or medical record. This should resolve any later uncertainty. The situation may be different for samples from subjects affected by a known genetic disorder, when specific information such as type or nature of a mutation may be helpful and valuable.

Problems for the investigator

A problem is most often first recognized by the research worker when a sample from a person at risk but considered healthy is analysed and shows the specific gene defect expected only in affected subjects. What, if anything, should be done? Should the information be given to the person who provided the sample and, if so, how? Should their doctor be informed or the information be recorded in the person's medical record? Or should the research laboratory and clinical research worker keep the information to themselves or even destroy it?

Depending on the nature of the disease and the attitude of the investigator this question may receive varying answers. Many research workers feel strongly that they should do everything possible to help those who take part in research and that it is wrong to withhold information that could be important. This may especially be the case when the clinical research worker is also concerned in providing services.

The lack of clarity regarding consent, however, will often mean that the expectations and likely reactions of the subject will be uncertain or unknown and the process by which the information came to light will itself make any associated preparation and counselling difficult. The alternative of not disclosing the information but keeping the result in the laboratory may seem easier initially but also poses difficulties.

It may prove very hard to keep the information completely contained; later workers may not realize that it had not been disclosed while, if the research worker also has clinical contact with the family, the possession of such knowledge may produce an unacceptable dilemma, something not altered even if the information or identifying details are destroyed. The legal situation regarding non-disclosure of relevant results of research is also questionable.

The reason why it is usually impossible to resolve this dilemma satisfactorily is that the true origin of the problem lies further back – that is, the sample should not have been tested in the first place, at least not without specific permission and a clear understanding of the implications of the testing. Once the test has been done and an abnormal result obtained the problem has been created; any subsequent measures are more in the nature of damage limitation than a true solution.

In fact the use of samples from healthy but at-risk members of a family is often unnecessary for molecular genetic research. Such samples may commonly confuse genetic linkage analysis. That they are taken at all often implies lack of thought; relatives may often volunteer to provide a sample feeling that it must be of help or a family may simply be sampled *en masse* at a home visit. The serious consequences of such sampling may be apparent only much later. In a non-progressive disorder the discovery of a mutation thought to be pathogenetic in a proportion of healthy relatives may be of value in showing that the gene is not fully penetrant, but the genetic implications still necessitate information being given on this possibility before such samples are tested.

Genetic research if the affected subject is not known to have an inherited disorder

The discovery of relevant mutations in samples from subjects not known to have inherited disorders is likely to increase sharply as specific genes in common non-mendelian conditions become identified. Already genetic subgroups are being identified in disorders previously not considered as genetic; important examples include mutations in the gene for β amyloid protein in Alzheimer's disease,[12] prion mutations in Jakob-Creutzfeldt dementia,[13] and p53 mutations in multiple cancer syndromes.[14] Although initially detected in rare families showing mendelian inheritance, these mutations are now being searched for and detected in series of cases without an obvious family history.

The discovery of such a mutation poses grave consequences for relatives as well as for individual subjects by raising the question of whether the possibility of a genetic basis of the disorder being discovered, along with its consequences, was discussed and consented to at the time the sample was taken. It may occasionally be argued that a finding of this nature should not be withheld from relatives who may be at genetic risk as a result. Such a conclusion would seem to make it even more necessary for information to be given in advance that such an outcome might be possible. If the study has reused samples taken originally for non-genetic research additional consent would seem to be essential.

A tentative code of conduct

The problems involving research samples from families with genetic disorders are real and increasing; if not recognized and avoided they are likely to harm both the individual subjects detected and possibly the investigator. Can guidelines be suggested that will prevent problems arising and, at the same time, avoid unnecessary bureaucracy for those undertaking research? The following suggestions are made as a basis for further discussion.

(1) Family members 'at risk' should not be sampled unless this is strictly necessary for the research, especially in late-onset or variable disorders. This applies particularly to children. When unaffected subjects are included in a study the proposal should justify this and should include a clear plan as to what will be done in the event of a genotypic abnormality being detected.

(2) When consent is given for sampling by such a person it should specifically be made clear that the person's risk will not normally be modified and that no result in relation to this should be expected; also that no such result will be sent to their doctor or placed in their medical record unless this has been specifically requested.

(3) If the sample is to be stored and used for future tests new consent should be obtained if the implications for the person at risk resulting from the new research are considerably different – for example, if mutations are to be looked for rather than a general linkage analysis.

(4) If the possibility of identifying defects in people at risk is foreseen and inevitable then such samples should be coded or made anonymous for the purpose of these tests unless the person concerned has specifically requested that relevant information should be disclosed and has received information that allows the implications to be fully understood.

(5) If a person at risk giving a research sample later requests presymptomatic testing or other genetic services, a new sample should be taken and the request handled in the same way as it would be for any other person making this request as a service.

(6) When a test that may show a specific genetic defect is proposed on people affected by a disorder not previously known to be genetic, the possible genetic implications should be made clear and new consent obtained if previously taken samples are being restudied.

(7) Ethical committees should pay at least as much attention to the

consequences of a sample being taken as to the risks attached to the sampling procedure.

Conclusion

The power of the developments in molecular genetics is such that it is no longer adequate to rely on implied or general consent if genetic analysis is to be carried out on samples from family members at risk of a genetic disorder. The implications of finding an unexpected abnormality in a healthy relative are potentially too serious to make it wise to use samples except in a carefully controlled way: if such an abnormal result is likely to be obtained, investigators should attempt to ensure anonymity of the sample so as to protect both the person at risk and themselves.

The steps suggested here will inevitably entail some extra efforts in terms of consent and explanations at the time of sampling, but the adverse consequences of not following this course are likely in the long term greatly to outweigh the work involved. The adoption of a code of conduct in relation to genetic research of this type should not only help to avoid specific problems of the type described but also help to maintain trust between families and research workers. That trust has been the basis of much of the successful research so far and must be maintained in the future if genetic advances are to be continued and used to help families with serious inherited disorders.

Notes

1 *Committe on the Ethics of Gene Therapy. Report*, London: HMSO, 1992.
2 *Review of the Guidance on the Research Use of Fetuses and Fetal Material. Report*, London: HMSO, 1989.
3 Committee of Inquiry into Human Fertilisation and Embryology. *Report*, London: HMSO, 1984.
4 Medical Research Council, *Responsibility in Investigations on Human Participants and Material and on Personal Information*, London: Medical Research Council, 1992.
5 Royal College of Physicians, *Ethical Issues in Clinical Genetics*, London: Royal College of Physicians, 1991.
6 United States Department of Energy, *Bibliography: Ethical, Legal and Social Implications of the Human Genome Project*, Washington DC: US Department of Energy, 1992.
7 Yates, J. R. W., Malcolm, S., Read, A. P., 'Guidelines for DNA banking', *Journal of Medical Genetics* 1989 26: 245–50.
8 Firth, M. A., 'Diagnosis of Duchenne muscular dystrophy: experience of parents of sufferers', *BMJ* 1983 286: 700–1.
9 Brandt, J., Quaid, K., Folstein, S. E., Garber, P., Maestri, N. E., Abbott, M. H., *et al*. 'Presymptomatic diagnosis of delayed-onset disease with

linked DNA markers: the experience in Huntington's disease', *JAMA* 1989 261: 3108–15.

10 Morris, M. J., Tyler, A., Lazarou, L., Meredith, L., Harper, P. S., 'Problems in genetic prediction for Huntington's disease', *Lancet* 1989 ii:601–3.

11 Harper, P. S., 'Genetic testing and insurance', *Journal of the Royal College of Physicians, London* 1992 26: 184–7.

12 Yankner, B.A. and Mesulan, M. M., 'β-amyloid and the pathogenesis of Alzheimer's disease', *New England Journal of Medicine* 1991 325: 1849–57.

13 Prusiner S. B., 'Molecular biology of prion disease', *Science* 1991 252: 1515–22.

14 Srivastava, S., Zou, Z., Pirollo, K., Blattner, W., Chang, E. H., 'Germline transmission of a mutated p53 gene in a cancer-prone family with Li-Fraumeni syndrome', *Nature* 1990 348: 747–9.

Chapter 4

Ethical issues in newborn screening for Duchenne muscular dystrophy

The question of informed consent

Evelyn Parsons and Don Bradley

> Genetic research and screening for genetic disorders have the potential for doing great amounts of good and great amounts of harm. The way in which human societies deliberately move into this arena will be shaped as much by social forces as by concerns for the general public health.
>
> (Duster 1990)

INTRODUCTION

Screening is the identification, in an apparently healthy population, of those people who are at risk for a specific disorder. Screening, however, is not a single entity and genetic screening is no exception. It can be carried out at different times during the life course and programmes can be directed either towards a total population or to specific, at-risk groups. The opening quotation raises the issue of what forces shape a decision, by a particular society, at any one point in time, to introduce a screening programme.

There are two opposing views on the role and development of genetics and genetic screening. To some, modern medical genetics is only the old eugenics movement reborn; for them, a change of name does not herald a change of ethos (Yoxen 1982; Duster 1990). Rose, Lewontin and Kamin (1984) challenge the very foundations of biological determinism that locates the causes of social phenomena in the genetic make-up of the individual. Together with Duster (1990), they argue that many things run in families, including wealth, crime and occupational choice, and that the deterministic perspective is being used as a powerful weapon to legitimate inequalities in society. They recognize that there is a complex interactive relationship between the development of scientific theory and social order and that one needs to be aware of the role of social, cultural and political forces in structuring science and scientific medicine. In a society where disease is portrayed in terms of personal responsibility and external malevolence, genetic screening is seen as the inevitable answer to the diminution of the species. The natural outcome of such a response, it is argued, is the labelling and stigmatization of those with a discrediting or discreditable attribute (Goffman 1968). To caste screening in terms of altruism fails to recognize that within society there is a normative standard that states that the healthy should survive and the less than healthy should never even be born. No screening programme arrives at its point of inception devoid of a social, cultural and political agenda.

In contrast, there is the positive approach to human genetics which sees scientific advance as giving human beings greater control over their lives. Mapping the human genome, although not totally independent of personal gain, is essentially an altruistic exercise that should reduce human suffering. Screening, in this scenario, offers to increase human knowledge and make a substantial impact on the burden of disease. Whether it is a prenatal screening by ultrasound, newborn screening or carrier screening, the information gained empowers individuals to make decisions and shape an informed future for themselves. Acceptance of modern biomedicine and its advances is important in terms of the overall stability of society. Society needs individuals who take responsible and rational decisions in the light of scientific information. Science and scientific medicine have offered explanations for life and death that have largely superseded previous religious and philosophical paradigms. In the 1990s, to prefer values to hard, 'scientific' facts is to go against the very foundations of modern society. To ignore the offer of screening could be construed as a failure to act as a responsible citizen, and to question the ethics of screening, aimed at making society healthier, sounds, if not perverse, certainly unreasonable. There is a need, however, to explore the moral discourse that surrounds screening. On what principles can genetic screening be justified? Two theoretical models of responsibility in medicine will be explored and subsequently discussed in the context of newborn screening for a genetic disease, Duchenne muscular dystrophy (DMD).

MORAL RESPONSIBILITY IN MEDICINE: BENEFICENCE OR AUTONOMY?

The physician is the servant of the art.

(Hippocrates: *Epidemics* 1 xi 1, 165)

Should the physician be servant of the 'art' or servant of the client? Beauchamp and McCullough (1984) explore this issue in terms of two competing models of moral responsibility in medicine: beneficence and autonomy. The beneficence model understands the patient's best interest exclusively from the medical perspective. Medicine is seen as the sole source of scientific knowledge and skill which, when applied to the human condition, can alleviate disease. This model is rooted in the writings of Hippocrates, whose oath characterizes clinicians as a group of committed men (women were excluded from medicine at that time in Greece), set apart from and above the rest of society, whose duty and obligation was to help, or at least to 'do no harm' (Hippocrates, quoted in Beauchamp and McCullough 1984). It requires the physician, as the expert, to benefit the patient by balancing good over harm, with no regard to self-interest. Katz (1977) refers to this perspective as 'paternalism', where the physician assumes authority to manage the information disclosed on the grounds of beneficence.

In contrast to beneficence, the autonomy model places the patient at the centre, with the clinician respecting their values and beliefs. The final arbiter is the patient, who takes authority over their own medical future. The beneficence model sees the clinician operating discretion and possibly limiting disclosure and information if, in their judgement, that is in the best interests of their patient. The autonomy model, on the other hand, calls for the patient to be treated as an individual with the right to make their decisions on the basis of full information given by the expert; the clinician's responsibility is to inform, the patient's to decide. Katz (1977) refers to a potential 'conflict between two visions': the autonomous person versus the medical expert, full disclosure versus limited information at the physician's discretion. As Beauchamp and McCulloch (1984) argue, to follow the autonomy model and emphasize only the patient's right to information overlooks clinical realities. A possible solution is offered by Kant's formula for enjoining respect for persons: one should 'so act to use humanity, both in your own person and in the person of every other, always at the same time as an end, never simply as a means' (Kant 1964). Childress (1982) argues that it is possible to act beneficently towards a person by respecting their autonomy and at the same time refrain from undermining their capacity to act freely.

It is the practical application of these two apparently conflicting philosophical frameworks that will be explored in the context of newborn screening for DMD

POPULATION SCREENING: TRADITIONAL PRINCIPLES

The introduction of any new scientific or medical technique has always been paralleled by ethical concerns that are debated in legal, medical and other institutional arenas. Committees are often appointed to make recommendations on what they consider to be in the best interests of society (Warnock 1985; Royal College of Physicians 1991; Clothier 1992). There is a constant tension between the protection of the individual against premature scientific experimentation and the advancement of knowledge which needs human co-operation.

Screening is no exception; out of years of experience certain principles have come to be widely accepted as essential in any screening programme. It is argued that the acceptance of these principles safeguards individuals from unscrupulous scientific intrusion. Wilson and Junger (1968) proposed four principles that should be applied to a screening programme. First, the screening test should be simple, cheap and easy to perform on small, readily collected samples. Second, the test should be oversensitive, so that no cases are missed; there may be a number of false positives but there should be no false negatives. Third, the facilities should be available for the prompt study of all suspect cases by qualified experts. Fourth, there should be an effective treatment for the disorder once it has been identified. Clearly a number of existing prenatal screening programmes do not conform to these principles; the only available treatment is the termination of an affected or 'high-risk' fetus. In assessing the morality of any genetic screening programme, there is a need to ascertain not only the reliability of the test but also the degree of burden imposed by the acquisition of knowledge. What benefit does the lay community gain from the information, especially in the absence of a cure?

Newborn screening, which started in the 1960s, has been far less controversial than prenatal or carrier screening since its aim was treatment. In 1990, however, newborn screening for DMD, an untreatable disorder, was introduced in Wales. It is some of the ethical issues highlighted by this programme that are explored in this chapter.

DUCHENNE MUSCULAR DYSTROPHY (DMD)

DMD is a genetic disease which, in two out of three cases, is transmitted on the X chromosome to male offspring of female carriers; in the other cases, the gene mutation happens as a sporadic event and the mother is not a carrier. The disease manifestation is usually confined to males because females who have inherited the defective gene also have a second, normal X chromosome, which prevents the development of the disease. Muscle wasting is one of the devastating symptoms of this lethal disease. Affected boys are normal at birth and usually only begin to show signs of the disease from about the age of 2. The first indications are general developmental and motor delay; as walking becomes established, they show signs of clumsiness, with a tendency to fall over. From the age of 4 or 5 years, boys develop a typical waddling gait and from this point there is a steady deterioration with more than 90 per cent in a wheelchair by the age of 11. Some boys do survive into their twenties but the average age of death is nearer 17, generally caused by respiratory infection or heart failure.

Although the gene for DMD was isolated in 1987 (Koenig *et al.* 1987) and the gene's normal protein product, dystrophin, described the same year (Hoffman *et al.* 1987), at the time of writing there is still no treatment or cure for the disease. Joyce (1990) talks of the 'uncomfortable window that may extend over decades, when we can diagnose but not treat'.

THE ADVENT OF THE 'DNA GAZE'

Two centuries ago medicine was radically altered with the introduction of the 'clinical gaze' (Foucault 1973); this century has seen yet another, potentially more significant revolution: the 'DNA gaze'. The advent of recombinant DNA technology in the late 1970s means that it is now possible to look at aspects of an individual's genetic make-up, to define the 'normal' genotype and thus the likelihood of impending disease. Scientists are able to diagnose, on the basis of DNA analysis, disease not yet visible to the clinical eye. Genotypical identification of disease has become chronologically divorced from its phenotypical manifestation. The power of the 'DNA gaze' raises significant ethical issues; Lappe (1984, 1987) talks of clinicians becoming 'modern-day Cassandras', presymptomatically predicting diseases that are largely untreatable.

NEWBORN SCREENING FOR DUCHENNE MUSCULAR DYSTROPHY

Newborn screening for DMD became feasible, and was piloted in 1975, with the development of an assay sensitive enough to measure CK in the small heelprick blood samples collected on filter paper for PKU screening (Zellweger and Antonik 1975). The first screening programme for DMD was introduced in Lyon, France, in June 1975 (Planchu et al. 1987), soon followed by a voluntary programme in Breitnau, West Germany, in March 1977 (Scheuerbrandt and Mortier 1983). Since then other centres have established screening programmes: Manitoba (Jacobs et al. 1989), Pittsburgh and Antwerp. The two main arguments made for screening were the ability to prevent the birth of further affected boys in a family, together with evidence from parents with affected boys that they would rather have had an earlier diagnosis. Firth et al. (1983) found that 90 per cent of parents with an affected boy were in favour of newborn screening. Earlier, Beckermann et al. (1980) reported that 87 per cent of parents wished they had known sooner that their son had muscular dystrophy. More recently Smith et al. (1990), in an attitudinal survey of new mothers, found that over 90 per cent were in favour of screening for DMD.

During the 1980s advances began to be made in understanding the molecular biology of DMD, but these were not seen as sufficient to warrant the introduction of testing in the UK, since the majority of reproductive decisions were still being made on the basis of fetal sexing or uncertain risks (Parsons and Atkinson 1992, 1993; Parsons and Clarke 1993). By 1990, however, it was argued that sufficient progress had been made in terms of prenatal diagnosis (Clarke 1990) that screening was more acceptable. Several arguments were used to support the trial. First, it would enable families with an index case, or their extended family, to make choices in future pregnancies. It should be stressed here that the Welsh initiative was not established either on the principle of disease prevention, because of the eugenic overtones, or on the basis of cost–benefit analysis (ibid.). Second, it would identify a cohort of presymptomatic boys for when treatment does become available. Both Emery (1991) and Dubowitz (1991) call for a re-evaluation of newborn screening on the grounds that a potential form of treatment will soon be available. Third, it enables families to plan for the future on a practical level (Firth *et al.* 1983). Fourth, it enables families to meet specialist health professionals and take advantage of early institutional support. Fifth, families avoid that prolonged period of uncertainty common in the traditional pattern of diagnosis. Both Firth *et al.* (1983) and Parsons (1990) found that it often took more than two years for a diagnosis of DMD to be confirmed and that this delay can cause a great deal of distress. Smith *et al.* (1989a) reported that, despite efforts to encourage the earlier detection of new cases, diagnosis remained unsatisfactorily late with a mean age at diagnosis of 4.9 years. Sixth, the research programme in Wales that screened non-walking boys at 18 months concluded that a population-based screening programme of this type was unsatisfactory because of logistical difficulties at the community health-care level (Smith *et al.* 1989b). Finally, screening avoids misunderstandings by parents, friends or teachers about any developmental delays that the boy may manifest. Parents, unaware of their son's problem, have often retrospectively regretted negative attributions they have made.

However, there were a number of arguments against the programme, the main one being the absence of treatment. There was also concern that the presymptomatic diagnosis of a lethal condition would disturb maternal bonding and threaten family stability. Research evidence on the presymptomatic diagnosis in Huntington's disease (Craufurd *et al.* 1989; Tyler *et al.* 1992) indicates that a large number of people, when they have the opportunity to confirm their own genetic status, decline to do so. Would the same situation arise when parents have the choice to confirm a presymptomatic diagnosis of DMD in their son? Another caution raised was that, whilst there has been a considerable refining of reproductive risk through the application of molecular genetics, there are still some families who are uninformative, i.e. they cannot be given definitive statements of reproductive risk. In these families, whilst they could exercise some choice in future pregnancies, it would be a choice made on the basis of risk rather than certainty.

Screening for DMD is a good example of the tension between the power of the technological imperative and the protection of the individual. A particular test may be feasible, but is it in the best interests of the lay community for it to be introduced? When is it right for the scientist to translate research into public practice?

Measurement of CK as an indicator of DMD has been possible since 1975, but does presymptomatic knowledge of the disease, and an awareness of potential carrier risk in female family members, outweigh the potential trauma of such an early disclosure? At what point should the scientific community offer a test? Should they wait until there is a cure, or definitive carrier and prenatal tests, before they move to screening, or should they take their final steps to certainty together with the lay community?

Screening for DMD can best be described as 'walking on soft ground'. If you screen, there may be families who experience excessive trauma. If you do not offer screening, how do you face the family who have a second or even third boy before the first has been diagnosed, knowing that it was possible to make them aware of the risks? Is it right to offer choice in future pregnancies when that choice, for some families, involves decisions in the face of uncertainty? Aware of these tensions and that the programme did not meet the generally accepted principles of screening, three safeguards were built in. First, the programme was designed to operate on an 'opt-in' basis: the decision to have the test was made by the family on the basis of information they received. (The ethical dilemma of screening for an untreatable disease was resolved by adopting an autonomous model; the health professional responsible to inform, the parents to decide.) Second, the programme, together with the usual clinical, biochemical and genetic research, was to be socially evaluated for its three-year term. The ongoing nature of this social evaluation is unique to the Welsh programme. We aim to determine whether families and health professionals want the test introduced on a permanent basis whilst there is still no cure or treatment, whether presymptomatic diagnosis affects maternal bonding or family stability and whether the distress of the early diagnosis is any greater than that following the traditional clinical diagnosis. The third safeguard built into the programme was an informal agreement between the three principal researchers that, if there were significant threats to either family stability or the mother–baby relationship, the programme would be discontinued. The programme proceeded therefore on the basis of informed consent, ongoing social evaluation, and the promise that the programme would end if excessive trauma was generated. Clearly neither the second nor the third safeguards gave families, entering the programme during 1990–3, any protection as they became part of the research. The only safeguard they had was their ability to opt out of screening by making an informed choice to refuse the test. What is the nature of the informed consent in this newborn screening programme?

INFORMED CONSENT

The concept of informed consent has gained increasing importance over the past forty years. There is doubt in some writers' minds whether that comes from a greater concern to protect the patient from doctors, or the medical profession from legal liability. Whatever the motivation, the reality is that the language of human rights has now entered the arena of health care. Two key influences, Faulder (1985) argues, are the consumerist movement and the growth of feminism, both of which have raised lay expectations that autonomy should be the dominant paradigm in medical moral discourse. There is a new language which incorporates concepts of patients' rights and patients' autonomy. Faulder describes informed consent as being about 'the right to control our own destinies and to determine our own ends as far as humanly possible . . . . it is about the right of individuals to preserve their integrity'.

There are three elements in the concept of consent. First, choice: is there an awareness that refusal is possible? Second, has the choice been made without undue pressure? Third, did the individual understand what was being asked? What makes consent 'informed'? It is important that the individual knows the facts and that there is an understanding of the relevant issues. Faulder (1985) says that for informed consent there must be adequate disclosure met by adequate understanding and the ability freely to give or refuse consent.

Gillett (1989) proposes a model for informed consent which takes account of both the patient's and health professional's role. For him there are three stages in giving informed consent. First, accurate and adequate information must be effectively communicated by the health professional. The level of effectiveness can be influenced by the time available to explain the procedure, the language that the health professionals use and their level of knowledge. Communication problems may lie not only with the health professional: the message may be clearly given but the person being informed may be unable to absorb the details; they may be distracted by other issues that they consider to be more relevant. Second, a reasoned decision must be taken without coercion; the individual must be free to make a decision for their own reasons. One needs to recognize not only the use of direct persuasion but also the effects of more subtle indirect influences structuring how choices are made. Finally, a valid consent must be given.

INFORMED CONSENT IN SCREENING FOR DMD: PRINCIPLES IN PRACTICE

Screening on the basis of informed consent is central to the newborn screening programme for DMD in Wales, but how real is that consent? How informed is it? For Gillett (1989) the first element is the giving of accurate and adequate information. In Wales, families receive information in two ways. There is an information leaflet (available in a number of languages) that is given to mothers either prenatally or a few days after a baby boy is born, the expectation being that they will discuss the decision with their partner before the midwife calls to take the heelprick sample. The leaflet is headed by the question: 'A New Test For Baby Boys: Do You Want It?' It explains that DMD is a progressive muscular disease that affects boys, that no symptoms are evident at birth but that their muscles get progressively weaker over the years until, at about the age of 10, they become unable to walk. Three reasons are given for having the test: help in future pregnancies, ability to plan for the future, and the offer of early support. There are also details on how the results will be given and some information on what would happen if the test proved to be positive. It is emphasized that it is a screening test and that there could be other reasons for a positive result on the first occasion. The final sentence says: 'If you have any other questions about the tests then please ask your midwife or the person who gave you this leaflet.' Verbal communication is the second source of information for the family. Primary health-care workers need detailed knowledge, not only about the disease but also the testing procedure.

There is evidence that the manner in which a test is offered significantly influences its uptake. Beck et al. (1974) found that when advocates were informed and motivated the uptake of voluntary carrier testing for Tay-Sachs disease was higher. The uptake of carrier testing in cystic fibrosis was only 10 per cent when the offer was made in writing but rose to 87 per cent when offered verbally with enthusiasm (Watson et al. 1991). The effect of negative and positive framing of test offers has also been explored (Marteau 1989; Meadows et al. 1990) and translating this to the offer of newborn screening for DMD, it is quite easy to speculate potential scenarios where the offer could be framed very differently:

- You do want all the tests don't you?
- You don't want the Duchenne test do you?
- You do want the new Duchenne test don't you?
- Have you thought about the new test? What have you decided to do?

The offer of the heelprick test is part of a midwife's everyday routine. Drawing from the work of Freidson (1970) and Bloor (1978), one can see a parallel between the midwife and the clinician in the routinization of that offer and the development of a 'personal mythology'. There may be a body of specialist knowledge in midwifery but there is also an 'art' in the way it is communicated, which is influenced by the midwives' definition of the situation and prior experience of the testing and its outcome. All midwives may be offering the same test but the way that offer is made becomes midwife-specific. Modell, Kuliev and Wagner (1991) recognize that there is still a lot to learn about the social aspects of neonatal screening, in particular the way information is given to families – something that is being addressed in the Welsh programme.

There are two indications from the Welsh experience that there is variability in midwifery practice. First, although the overall refusal rate has remained relatively constant at about 5 per cent, there is a large variation between districts. Second, interesting feedback is coming, both from families who have accepted and from those who have refused the test, on their perceptions of how the test was offered.

By October 1993 there had been twenty-one positive DMD screening tests. Of these families, three were sure that they had not seen the information leaflet and had no recollection that their baby had been screened at all. There is evidence that practice in terms of both the quantity and the quality of information on which families base their informed consent is highly variable. This issue was recognized early in the programme and has been addressed in terms of educational programmes developed specifically for the primary health-care team. Although it will be impossible totally to eliminate every personal variation in communication, there is a need for health professionals working with families to be supported by a systematic body of specialist knowledge.

Information needs not only to be effectively communicated; it also needs to be received and understood by the person or persons concerned. The immediate postnatal period is a time when significant redefinitions are taking place. It is a period of physical and psychological adjustment, where new information is constantly being incorporated into a mother's existing stock of knowledge. It is possible, perhaps even likely, that details of a screening programme are not ranked highly in terms of relevance, at a time when sleep is at a premium and sanity depends on meeting the stringent demands of a new baby.

The second condition that Gillett (1989) lays down for informed consent is that a reasoned decision should be taken without coercion. It would be naive to accept that any offer of population screening was neutral and value-free. When that offer is made by a respected health professional and is part of an overall screening package that is widely accepted, there is clearly social pressure at both a micro and a macro level. The coercion at the micro level is perhaps easier to detect than the subtle pressures at the macro or structural level. Clarke (1991), in his discussion on the nature of genetic counselling, contends that the offer of a test implies a recommendation to accept. Voysey (1975) talks about the expectations in society of what constitutes responsible parenthood and one such expectation is that parents 'should' do the 'best' for their children. In talking to a number of mothers, the reason they gave for having the test was: 'We have all the tests'; 'We have everything done then we know he's all right.' There is the underlying assumption that if a test is available then it must be in the baby's best interests. This hidden agenda is also constructed on the basis that the test is being offered by 'experts' and they would not make such an offer if it was not 'good' and 'right'. Tijmstra (1990) argues that one significant influence in the ready acceptance of screening is that people want to avoid future feelings of regret regarding decisions they have made: 'I do not want to blame myself later for not having tried everything I could.' This process of 'anticipated decision regret' endows screening with a peculiar imperative character. People are also influenced by the response of others: non-participation in a screening programme appears to need explanation. Rothman (1987) and Farrant (1985), writing about the offer of prenatal testing, argue that it is harder to refuse a test than 'go with the tide'.

The practice of informed consent may not always meet the philosophical ideal. The Report from the Royal College of Physicians recognizes that very issue: 'In large scale programmes it may be virtually impossible to make sure that all individuals tested understand the issues and implications sufficiently to give fully informed consent' (Royal College of Physicians 1991).

That should not prevent every effort being made to ensure that conditions are optimized to facilitate informed consent. Quoting from Beecher, Faulder (1985) argues that a client's greatest safeguard is the presence of a skilful, informed, intelligent, honest, responsible, compassionate health professional. That certainly is the aim in the Welsh programme, so that health professionals have the information and are aware of the intervening pressures that might prevent a family from making an informed decision.

INFORMED CONSENT: THE ROUTE FROM SCREENING TO DIAGNOSIS

It would be naive to assume that informed consent is a single event; that, once given at the initial heelprick, it need not be invoked again. In the Welsh programme it was recognized that, at every stage from the screening test to the final confirmation of diagnosis, families need to be made aware of the options available to them. Do they want to proceed with a venous blood sample to confirm the elevated CK level? Do they want the laboratory to search for a deletion in the gene by DNA analysis to confirm muscular dystrophy? Do they want their son to have a muscle biopsy as the final diagnostic step? It is a potential myth in medical genetics that everyone wants confirmation of their genetic status, whether it be in terms of carrier potential or pre-symptomatic diagnosis. The numbers involved in the newborn screening programme are only small but there is some indication that choice is being exercised. By November 1993 there were twelve confirmed positive cases; three of these families had decided not to proceed with a muscle biopsy to confirm the diagnosis before the onset of clinical symptoms. In two of these cases no gene deletion had been found on DNA analysis and so, although there was every indication of muscular dystrophy, they chose to live with uncertainty and risk.

In addition to the choice on DNA studies and muscle biopsy, the family is asked whether they want to have genetic counselling. This gives them the opportunity to meet a geneticist to discuss the inheritance pattern of the disease and its implications for them and their extended family in future pregnancies. It is this process of 'genetic arborization', the move from a single index case to a whole family network, that raises a number of significant ethical issues. Is there a potential conflict between the autonomy of one family member and another? Whose rights should be predominant and should the clinician act beneficently and decide whose rights should prevail? Autonomy has become the increasingly accepted philosophy in western medicine; it underpins the screening programme and yet genetics calls for the potential sublimation of individual rights for the good of the whole. What are the implications for, and the moral obligations placed on, the wider extended family? This issue is discussed in the Royal College of Physicians Report (1991), where it is recognized that, although there is a general acceptance that individuals have strong moral rights to autonomy and confidentiality, there could be reasons for considering, in the context of genetics, these *prima facie* rights becoming secondary. It could be argued that this is necessary to prevent disease and, in the light of conflicting rights of others, to obtain genetic information. The report concludes that established principles in medical ethics should not be presumed to apply in the context of clinical genetics. West (1988) argues that, as a general principle, all members of a family should have the right of access to information that is relevant to them about a genetic disease and its inheritance pattern. He places the duty with the doctor to persuade 'reluctant' clients to communicate with other members of their family and when this approach fails, 'the doctor must decide whether the need to know outweighs the duty of confidentiality to the index patient'. He moves from an autonomous perspective towards potential beneficence. Gillon (1988), replying to West, warns that with every erosion in medical confidentiality, in the so-called interests of others, the principle itself becomes even more suspect and 'decrepit'. She calls for a 'rigorous scrutiny' of the ethical issues surrounding genetic counselling and confidentiality.

CONCLUSION

Screening for DMD in the newborn has given the opportunity to explore, in practice, a screening programme that is based on the interrelated principles of autonomy and informed consent. Has there been evidence of the tension that Katz (1977) and Beauchamp and McCulloch (1984) predicted between theory and practice? Does a model of family autonomy and informed consent take into account the realities of everyday life and individual response to the potential diagnosis of a lethal genetic disease?

During the course of the programme two incidents illustrate the potential tensions that can exist between theory and practice. First, the original information leaflet, on which families based their informed consent, gave details of the poor prognosis in DMD, including the fact that the boys faced an early death. A number of families specifically mentioned how upset they had been by that particular piece of information; they felt they could cope with muscle wasting and the spectre of a wheelchair, but not with the thought of losing their son so young. The leaflet had been written so as to respect the principle of autonomy and the need to maximize lay understanding of the issues involved. It was argued that to make an informed choice families needed to have details of the prognosis. We had acted in terms of the autonomy principle but families were asking us to be beneficent. They wanted to be shielded initially from some of the facts and expected us to operate a degree of paternalism.

Another area where there was evidence of tension between principle and practice was over the question of how much detail the family should be given about why a second blood sample was required. Three of the fifteen families who had a positive screening test said they would rather the primary health-care team had not told them initially which of the screening tests was being queried. One mother said, 'I wish he [the doctor] had told me, well, a white lie'. A father said that they (the health team) could have told the family that the original blood sample had gone missing. What both were saying was that, until the result of the second test was available, they would rather the doctor and health visitor had acted beneficently and used their discretion by limiting the disclosure. They wanted the health professionals to take a decision not to treat them as autonomous individuals, but to limit the information in their best interests.

It would seem that principles are constantly under siege in the face of everyday reality. Are principles absolute and is it possible to define the point at which an eroded principle is no longer a principle at all? The pure principle of (family) autonomy has been brought into question by the very group it was introduced to protect. Is it right to introduce a programme on the ethical principle of informed consent and negotiate that basis in the light of practical experience? Faulder, in arguing that 'A study is ethical or not at its inception' (1985), fails to take account of the complex relationship between principle and practice. The reality is that neither is absolute, nor are they mutually exclusive: underlying principles influence practice and practical applications modify perceptions of principle. Out of the dialogue emerges a newly negotiated order that is being continuously reconstructed in response to changes in reality. One is not witnessing erosion of principles, but rather their renegotiation.

ACKNOWLEDGEMENTS

This work was supported by the Muscular Dystrophy Group of Great Britain.

REFERENCES

Beauchamp, T. L. and McCullough, L. B. (1984) *Medical Ethics – the Moral Responsibilities of Physicians*, New Jersey: Prentice Hall.

Beck, E., Blaichman, S., Scriver, C. R. *et al.* (1974) 'Advocacy and compliance in genetic screening', *New England Journal of Medicine* 291: 1166–70.

Beckermann, R., Robert, J. M., Zellweger, H. *et al.* (1980) 'Neonatal screening for muscular dystrophy', in H. Bickel, R. Guthrie, and G. Hammersen (eds) *Neonatal Screening for Inborn Errors of Metabolism*, Berlin: Springer-Verlag.

Bloor, M. (1978) 'On the routinised nature of work in people-processing agencies: the case of adenotonsillectomy assessments in ENT outpatient clinics', in A. Davis (ed.) *Relationships Between Doctors and Patients*, Farnborough: Saxon.

Bradley, D. M., Parsons, E. P. and Clarke, A. J. (1993) 'Preliminary experience with newborn screening for Duchenne muscular dystrophy in Wales', *British Medical Journal* 306: 357–60.

Childress, J. F. (1982) *Who Should Decide? Paternalism in Health Care*, New York: Oxford University Press.

Clarke, A. (1990) 'Genetics, ethics and audit', *Lancet* 335: 1145–7.

—— (1991) 'Is non-directive genetic counselling possible?' *Lancet* 338: 998–1001.

Clothier, C. M. (1992) *Report by the Commission on the Ethics of Gene Therapy*, London: HMSO Cm. 1788.

Craufurd, D., Dodge, A., Kerzin-Storrar, L. *et al.* (1989) 'Uptake of presymptomatic predictive testing for Huntington's disease', *Lancet* ii: 603–5.

Dubowitz, V. (1991) 'Remarks on neonatal screening for Duchenne muscular dystrophy', in *Neuro Muscular Disease News Bulletin*, Baarn: European Alliance of Muscular Dystrophy Associations, March: 17.

Duster, T. (1990) *Backdoor to Eugenics*, New York: Routledge.

Emery, A. (1991) 'Remarks on neonatal screening for Duchenne muscular dystrophy', in *Neuro Muscular Disease News Bulletin*, Baarn: European Alliance of Muscular Dystrophy Associations, March: 16–17.

Farrant, W. (1985) 'Who's for amniocentesis? The politics of prenatal screening', in H. Homans (ed.) *Sexual Politics of Reproduction*, Vermont: Gower.

Faulder, C. (1985) *Whose Body is it? The Troubling Issue of Informed Consent*, London: Virago.

Firth, M., Gardner-Medwin, D., Hosking, G. *et al.* (1983) 'Interviews with parents of boys suffering from Duchenne muscular dystrophy', *Developmental Medicine and Child Neurology* 25: 466–71.

Foucault, M. (1973) *The Birth of the Clinic: Archaeology of Medical*

Perception, trans. A. M. Sheridan Smith, London: Tavistock.

Freidson, E. (1970) *Profession of Medicine: A Study of the Sociology of Applied Knowledge*, New York: Harper Row.

Gillett, G. R. (1989) 'Informed consent and moral integrity', *Journal of Medical Ethics* 15: 117–23.

Gillon, R. (1988) 'Genetic counselling, confidentiality and the medical interest of relatives', *Journal of Medical Ethics* 14: 171–2.

Goffman, E. (1968) *Stigma: Notes on the Management of Spoiled Identity*, Harmondsworth: Penguin.

Hoffman, E. P., Brown, R. H. and Kunkel, L. M. (1987) 'Dystrophin, the protein product of the Duchenne muscular dystrophy locus', *Cell* 51: 919–28.

Jacobs, H. K., Wrogemann, K., Greenberg, C. R. *et al.* (1989) 'Neonatal screening for Duchenne muscular dystrophy – the Canadian experience', in B. J. Schmidt (ed.) *Current Trends in Infant Screening*, Amsterdam: Elsevier.

Joyce, C. (1990) 'Physician heal thy genes', *New Scientist* 15 September: 53–6.

Kant, I. (1964) *Groundwork on the Metaphysics of Morals*, trans. H. J. Paton, New York: Harper Row.

Katz, J. (1977) 'Informed consent: a fairy tale? Law's vision', *University of Pittsburgh Law Review* 39 (Winter):139.

Koenig, M, Hoffman, E. P., Bertelson, C. J. *et al.* (1987) 'Complete cloning of the Duchenne muscular dystrophy (DMD) cDNA and preliminary organization of the DMD gene in normal and affected individuals', *Cell* 50: 509–17.

Lappe, M. (1984) 'The predictive power of the new genetics', in *The Hastings Center Report*, October: 18–21.

—— (1987) 'The limits of genetic enquiry', in *The Hastings Center Report*, August: 5–10.

Marteau, T. (1989) 'Framing of information: its influence upon decisions of doctors and patients', *British Journal of Psychology* 28: 89–94.

Meadows, J., Jenkinson, S., Catalan, J. *et al.* (1990) 'Voluntary HIV testing in the antenatal clinic: differing uptake rates for individual counselling midwives', *AIDS Care* 2: 229–33.

Modell, B., Kuliev, A. M. and Wagner, M. (1991) *Community Genetic Services in Europe*, Denmark: WHO Regional Publications, European Series no. 38.

Parsons, E. P. (1990) 'Living with Duchenne muscular dystrophy: women's understandings of disability and risk', Ph.D. thesis, University of Wales.

Parsons, E. P. and Atkinson, P. A. (1992) 'Lay construction of genetic risk', *Sociology of Health and Illness* 14: 437–55.

—— (1993) 'Genetic risk and reproduction', *Sociological Reviews* 41(4): 679–706.

Parsons, E. P. and Clarke, A. J. (1993) 'Genetic risk: women's understandings of carrier risks in Duchenne muscular dystrophy', *Journal of Medical Genetics* 30: 562–6.

Plauchu, H., Dorche, C., Carrier, H. *et al.* (1987) 'Systematic neonatal screening for Duchenne muscular dystrophy: results of a ten year study in Lyon, France', in B. L. Therrell (ed.) *Advances In Neonatal Screening*, Amsterdam: Excerpta Medica.

Rose, S., Lewontin, R. C. and Kamin, L. (1984) *Not in our Genes: Biology, Ideology and Human Nature*, London: Penguin.

Rothman, B. K. (1987) *The Tentative Pregnancy: Prenatal Diagnosis and the Future of Motherhood*, New York: Penguin.

Royal College of Physicians (1991) College Report: 'Ethical issues in clinical genetics', *Journal of the Royal College of Physicians of London* 25: 284–8.

Scheuerbrandt, G. and Mortier, W. (1983) 'Voluntary newborn screening for Duchenne muscular dystrophy, a nationwide pilot programme in West Germany', in H. Naruse and M. Irie (eds) *Neonatal Screening*, Amsterdam: Excerpta Medica.

Smith, R. A., Sibert, J. R., Wallace, S. *et al.* (1989a) 'Early diagnosis and secondary prevention of Duchenne muscular dystrophy', *Archives of Diseases in Childhood* 64: 787–90.

Smith, R. A., Rogers, M., Bradley, D. M. *et al.* (1989b) 'Screening for Duchenne muscular dystrophy', *Archives of Diseases in Childhood* 64: 1017–21.

Smith, R. A., Williams, D. K., Sibert, J. R. *et al.* (1990) 'Attitudes of mothers to neonatal screening for Duchenne muscular dystrophy', *British Medical Journal* 300: 1112.

Tijmstra, T. (1990) 'The psychological and social implications of serum cholesterol screening', *International Journal of Risk and Safety in Medicine* 1: 29–44.

Tyler, A., Morris, M., Lazarou, L. *et al.* (1992) 'Presymptomatic testing for Huntington's disease in Wales 1987–1990', *British Journal of Psychiatry* 161: 481–8.

Voysey, M. (1975) *A Constant Burden: The Reconstitution of Family Life*, London: Routledge & Kegan Paul.

Warnock, M. (1985) *A Question of Life: The Warnock Report on Human Fertilisation and Embryology*, Oxford: Blackwell.

Watson, E., Mayall, E., Chapple, J. *et al.* (1991) 'Carrier screening for cystic fibrosis', *British Medical Journal* 303: 405–7.

West, R. (1988) 'Ethical aspects of genetic disease and genetic counselling', *Journal of Medical Ethics* 14: 194–7.

Wilson, J. M. G. and Junger, G. (1968) *Principles and Practics of Screening for Disease*, Geneva: WHO.

Yoxen, E. J. (1982) 'Constructing genetic disease', in P. Wright and A. Treacher (eds) *The Problem of Medical Knowledge: Examining the Social Construction of Medicine*, Edinburgh: Edinburgh University Press.

Zellweger, H. and Antonik, A. (1975) 'Newborn screening for Duchenne muscular dystrophy', *Pediatrics* 55: 30–4.

Chapter 5

Termination of a second-trimester pregnancy for fetal abnormality

Psychosocial aspects

Margaretha White-van Mourik

INTRODUCTION

When couples embark on a pregnancy they hope for a 'normal' child, yet 2 per cent will have an abnormal outcome. In the past, if fate gave you a defective child, you accepted it as well as you could and learned to live with the consequent, perpetual grief. Parents who were aware of a genetic problem within their family may have avoided having any children because their fear of having an abnormal child outweighed the desire for offspring. They subsequently suffered the sadness of not realizing their desired family. Developments in obstetrics, biochemistry and cytology, concurrent with the introduction in Britain of laws allowing abortion for fetal abnormality, have opened the way to antenatal screening and prenatal diagnosis. These combined advances now provide couples with choice.

In this chapter we will examine what happens to couples when an 'Act of God' is transformed into an act of their own choosing, and what practical, ethical, spiritual, emotional and social issues are involved in trying to live with the decision to terminate a pregnancy for fetal abnormality. We will explore how the medical community and society can reduce the emotional burden of this choice.

IDENTIFICATION WITH THE FETUS

Western cultures have still not decided officially on the status of the human embryo (Reilly 1979; Dunstan 1988). Some other cultures have traditionally had personification of the fetus before birth (Cranley 1981a). The relationship with the fetus starts after the awareness of conception, and subsequent to delivery it continues in a modified way. The Ojibwa Indian mother speaks to her fetus during pregnancy and teaches its soul the ways of animals and elements, thus preparing it for its future development. The Siriona of East Bolivia perform the same bereavement ritual for a miscarried fetus as for a deceased adult.

Cranley (1981b), reporting on the relationship of parents with their 'unborn', stated that there was a wealth of interaction between the mother and her fetus. She observed that both father and mother developed bonding behaviour towards the fetus. She perceived that this phenomenon displayed an involvement with the fetus, in which the fetus is experienced as a future child.

Although the infant–mother relationship develops gradually, quickening (maternal awareness of the fetal movements in the fourteenth to twentieth week of pregnancy) was often seen as a milestone (Bibring *et al*. 1961; Hollerbach 1979). New developments in diagnostic techniques have been shown to induce an earlier and more intense involvement with the fetus (Reading *et al*. 1981; Fletcher and Evans 1983; Blumberg 1984). Fetal life is now audible (fetal heart sounds) and visible (ultrasonography) from 8 to 10 weeks and these techniques present the mother with undeniable evidence of fetal life (Lumley 1980). It is not unusual for the first ultrasound picture to be saved as the first photograph of the child.

FETAL LOSS, GRIEF AND MOURNING

With the increased parental awareness of the fetus as an independent identity it is not surprising that the loss of a wanted and planned pregnancy is experienced as the loss of a child. Many women who abort spontaneously experience anguish, loneliness and depression following the realization of pregnancy loss (Pasnau and Farah 1977; Borg and Lasker 1982). Where there was ambivalence towards the pregnancy there could be guilt feelings. A sense of physical inadequacy and responsiblity for the loss is experienced by many.

The response to fetal loss is appropriately viewed as a form of bereavement (Lloyd and Laurence 1985). Grieving is not a patho-logical symptom but a normal, and even necessary, reaction after fetal loss (Pedder 1982). Shock, numbness and disbelief may give way to anger, protest, guilt, despair and pining. The duration of the reaction depends on the success with which the individual does 'grief work', which chiefly entails the acceptance of the feelings of intense distress. Avoiding these feelings and denying what has happened may lead to 'morbid grief', which is either a delayed reaction precipitated by specific circumstances perhaps years later, or a distorted reaction which may be difficult to recognize as the original grief. This unresolved grief may in turn have an adverse effect on health (Stroebe and Stroebe 1987).

It is often assumed that the longer the period of gestation, the closer the bonding to the fetus and therefore the greater the feelings of bereavement after pregnancy loss. However, just as not all births of live healthy babies result in immediate and ideal attachment, so women with first- or second-trimester pregnancy loss must not be assumed to have a less severe reaction to bereavement. More important criteria are the significance of the pregnancy to the parents, their previous experience of loss and adaptation to it, their personalities, and their perception of social support.

TERMINATION OF PREGNANCY FOR FETAL ABNORMALITY

With expanding technology lengthening the list of adverse conditions which can be recognized in the fetus comes a greater awareness that there is now some element of choice in the avoidance of genetic disease and congenital malformations. Prenatal diagnosis is available for many couples with a family history of genetic disease, enabling them to dare to consider further pregnancies. Antenatal maternal serum screening is offered to an increasing number of pregnant women. With the availability of these techniques there is the option of terminating the pregnancy when an affected fetus is diagnosed. The emotional implications of screening and prenatal diagnosis are many and complex, but this chapter will concentrate on the couples who were subjected to the acute trauma imparted by the discovery of fetal defect and who chose the option of termination of pregnancy.

The realization of an unfavourable result triggers an immediate grief response that may be characterized by disbelief, shock and anger (Blumberg 1984; Blumberg *et al.* 1975; Donnai *et al.* 1981; Alder and Kushnick 1982). Hopes and expectations are dashed by the revelation of the fetal abnormality. The medico-legal necessity of a quick decision either to continue or terminate the pregnancy adds to the burden of the already distressed couple. Previous abstract attitudes towards abortion appeared to provide little guidance for couples trapped in this moral dilemma. The parents' understanding of the specific defect affecting the fetus is a significant determinant of their course of decision and action (Blumberg 1984; Korenromp *et al.* 1992).

THE PSYCHOSOCIAL SEQUELAE OF A TERMINATION OF PREGNANCY FOR FETAL ABNORMALITY

In contrast to the mostly positive reactions of women after an abortion for psychosocial indications (Doane and Quigley 1981; Adler *et al.* 1990), many authors (Blumberg *et al.* 1975; Donnai *et al.* 1981; Leschot *et al.* 1982; Becker *et al.* 1984; Thomassen-Brepols 1985; Lloyd and Laurence 1985; Black 1989; Frets *et al.* 1990; White-van Mourik *et al.* 1992; Korenromp *et al.* 1992) have observed the opposite following a termination of pregnancy for fetal abnormality. Only Jones *et al.* (1984) did not show such negative sequelae, but they stressed the low response rate of 39 per cent and the probability that coping problems were the main reasons for non-participation.

When the findings in the literature are collated, the reasons for the increased distress emerge. The majority of women who agreed to antenatal screening or prenatal diagnosis had planned and/or welcomed the pregnancy. All were in the second trimester of their pregnancy and those who agreed to screening had often not seriously considered an abnormal result. The intervention had thus the psychological meaning of the loss of a wanted child. Loss implies mourning; yet coping and grieving were complicated by other problems which needed attention, such as the loss of biological, moral and social competence and the associated loss of self-esteem. Conflicting emotions were subsequently elicited by two conflicting images: the image of the wished-for, fantasized baby and the image of the damaged or handicapped child (Thomassen-Brepols 1985).

THE SHORT-TERM ASPECTS OF THE SEQUELAE

The first reaction reported by most couples immediately after the termination of pregnancy procedure was a feeling of relief that it was over. Many felt numbed by the diagnosis and the agonizing decisions that had been made in the previous few days. For some this numbness continued during their stay as in-patients; others became painfully aware of their loss during their time in hospital. As many women are cared for in postnatal wards, this awareness was reinforced by hearing babies cry, yet seeing their own empty cot. Especially painful were questions regarding the baby's well-being from fellow patients and well-meaning auxiliary staff. Low self-esteem was reinforced by leaving the hospital with empty arms. One woman illustrated this by mentioning:

> My loss became real when I was told I could go home. From then until I left 2 hours later I saw no-one. I walked out of the ward with my husband and no-one spoke to us, yet when I got to the exit a couple and their baby were leaving with four nurses or midwives to see them off. I felt so guilty and such a failure.

Low self-esteem was further reinforced for some on return home. Studies reported that as many as 52 per cent of couples were not contacted by any member of the primary care team (GP, midwife, health-visitor), nor were they invited to the surgery or visited at home; yet 60 per cent of the women in studies experienced breast engorgement and lactation lasting at least five days (Lloyd and Laurence 1985; White-van Mourik *et al.* 1990). One woman said: 'I felt that the medical profession had lost interest in me. The faulty fetus was terminated, so that was the end of the problem. But for me my problems were just starting.'

The realization of an unfavourable result triggered an immediate grief response and this was frequently characterized by disbelief, shock and anger. It was in this frame of mind that couples had to make decisions about their fetus. It is therefore not unusual for some newly bereaved parents to start to experience feelings of doubt shortly after the termination of pregnancy. In a recent study (White-van Mourik *et al.* 1992) 48 per cent of the women admitted that they felt ambivalent about their decision. This was often linked to a lack of understanding of the fetal defect. There were fears that the medical professionals might have made a mistake, and that they were disapproved of for the act of terminating the pregnancy. Mothers whose fetal abnormality had been identified by maternal serum screening had frequently only a vague comprehension of the fetal condition for which they had been offered the intervention. Doubts were particularly common in very young women (16–20 years), those belonging to a lower socio-economic group, and those in whom the severity of the defect was uncertain. Most women who were identified by routine ultrasonography did not perceive the burden of choice as a consequence of their decision. This was in contrast to 40 per cent of women who were identified as at risk through the maternal serum screening programme and who felt that they had not fully considered the implications of accepting the test. Doubts in these groups were significantly lessened if, at a post-termination consultation, time was taken to explain the condition of the fetus, the nature of the anomaly or illness, and the likely prognosis. Two years after the intervention, even where there had been initial doubts, the vast majority of couples felt at peace with their decision (Thomassen-Brepols 1985; White-van Mourik *et al*. 1992).

SUBJECTIVE PERCEPTION OF EMOTIONAL AND SOMATIC REACTIONS IN THE FIRST SIX MONTHS AFTER THE TERMINATION OF PREGNANCY

It is common for a feeling of deep sadness to be experienced by both partners after the termination of pregnancy. Depression, anger, fear, guilt and failure were the other most frequently mentioned strong emotions. The anger was often a reaction to the feeling of help-lessness for not having been able to protect their child from harm. The feeling of responsibility for this new life was mentioned by some men, but was expressed principally by women. Feelings of guilt could be focused on various aspects: towards the child, because a decision was made that it should not live, towards a previous child with a similar defect and towards one's partner. The differences in the feelings expressed by men and women are illustrated in figure 5.1 When expressing their feelings about fear, couples stressed the possibility of recurrence of the abnormality and the idea of having to repeat the whole decision-making process. Having to face the consequences of that choice was, and for some remained, terrifying.

Some women complained of prolonged numbness, panic spells and palpitations but only men admitted to feeling withdrawn and being excluded (White-van Mourik *et al*. 1992; Korenromp *et al*. 1992). One male partner typically explained: 'I did not want to talk about it or dwell on the event. It was too upsetting. I just wanted to be left alone to get on with my own life.' In our society, reproduction and reproductive failure are still frequently perceived as the woman's purview. One husband explained:

Everyone asked how my wife felt but nobody seemed to consider that I had feelings too. Even when things went wrong, the obstetrician explained all about it to my wife and her mother and by the time I came home from work (they did not want to worry me)

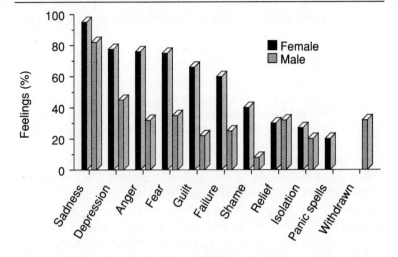

Figure 5.1 Emotional feelings after a termination for fetal abnormality.
Differences between men and women

they had more or less decided to terminate my baby. I felt so angry
and redundant, but could not show it as my wife was upset and
needed me.

As well as coping with strong feelings many couples report
somatic symptoms. Of these, listlessness, loss of concentration,
irritability and crying are mentioned most frequently. Male partners
found that a lack of concentration in the first few months led to
mistakes at work and to unexpected failures in exams.

Nightmares commonly have one or more of three elements.
Replay: in which the termination procedure is repeated night
after night, and sometimes continues intermittently for up to a year
after the termination of pregnancy. *Persecution*: in which the
parent runs away to prevent pursuers from taking the baby. *Blame*:
in which the baby, or family members, would appear and accuse the
parent of murder.

Despite these dissonant feelings and complaints, many couples
feel reluctant to bring them up in discussion with health professionals, family or friends for fear of being judged mentally
unstable or weak. This reticence may be overcome by carefully
formulated questions asked as part of the routine post-termination
protocol.

LONG-TERM PSYCHOSOCIAL ASPECTS OF SEQUELAE

Two years after the termination of pregnancy, most couples reported that they had regained equilibrium. For some this happened less than six months after the intervention; others took longer. However, most continued to experience sadness about the loss of the baby and to fear recurrence of the condition in a subsequent pregnancy. The feeling of continuing relief was especially mentioned by those families familiar with a distressing handicap or genetic disease.

In studies (Thomassen-Brepols 1985; White-van Mourik *et al.* 1992) about 20 per cent of women continued to feel angry, guilty, a failure, irritable and tearful (see figure 5.2). They felt that these strong emotions had a disruptive impact on their lives and relationships. Men appeared to come to terms with their loss more quickly than their spouses (figure 5.3). The same analysis was made by Martinson *et al.* (1980), who observed that after the loss of a child, fathers were twice as likely as mothers to report that the most intensive part of grieving was over in a few weeks. However, their response may have reflected the social expectations of the father 'to take it like a man'. Men appear to have a greater need to keep their grief private (De Frain *et al.* 1982) and this may even give their partners the impression that they are not affected by the loss, yet it was often the male partners who were more apprehensive about the idea of a further pregnancy.

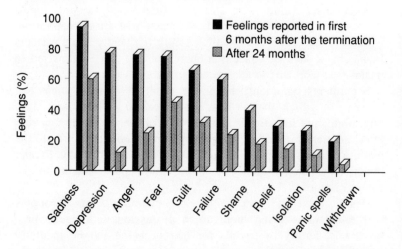

Figure 5.2 Emotional feelings in women 6 and 24 months after a termination for fetal abnormality

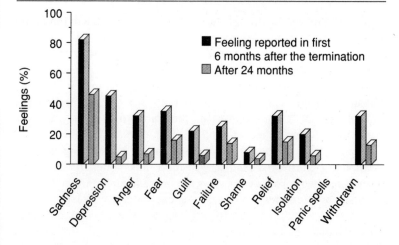

Figure 5.3 Emotional feelings in men 6 and 24 months after a termination for fetal abnormality

CONSEQUENCES OF THE TERMINATION FOR THE MARITAL RELATIONSHIP

The majority of partners report an initial closeness after the termination of pregnancy. Many find that the procedure and the deep emotions after the intervention have brought a new dimension to the relationship. Where there had been a close relationship before the intervention, partners generally tried to be understanding and supportive. Where difficulties were experienced, these were reported to be most pronounced after three to six months and may be due to lack of communication, irritation and an intolerance of the different coping mechanisms used in coming to terms with the bereavement.

Sexual problems arose where the partners experienced different needs and were unable to communicate them. The woman might have difficulties separating the sexual act from pregnancy and conception, while the man might want to reinforce emotional closeness; or vice versa. In rare cases, sexual difficulties had continued over the two years post-termination without help being sought.

SOCIAL SUPPORT AFTER THE TERMINATION OF PREGNANCY

In time of stress and uncertainty, the majority of people turn to their close friends and relatives for support. Understanding, good listening and thoughtfulness were felt to be the most important aspects of this support. Bereaved parents need to feel that others are sensitive to their anguish and share their feeling of loss. It was the relationships that meant the most to the couple which produced most friction; friends and relatives are often unsure how to help. In other situations the grieving couple may indicate what help is needed, but in the case of a termination for fetal abnormality they too are bewildered. Couples report conflicting feelings: of feeling grateful and angry, supported and isolated, rationally recognizing the prevention of the birth of a handicapped child and emotionally mourning the wanted baby. These conflicts were instrumental in the reluctance to instigate discussion which was evident in many couples.

The general public prefer to avoid the subjects of genetic inheritance, handicap and abortion, especially when they come 'too close to home'. This means that couples who already find it difficult to talk about their intervention are actively discouraged from doing so. When expressing grief and loss they were sometimes reminded by supporters that they had been lucky to have had the choice. This further created feelings of guilt and failure. Other supporters kept a well-intentioned silence that was readily misinterpreted: it was frequently assumed by outsiders that a strong grief reaction was linked to regretting the termination, and silence was employed to prevent guilt in the couple. As discussed earlier, two years of follow-up showed that most grieved but on reflection few regretted the termination. As time passes, women find it painful when those around them, especially their spouses, seem totally unaware of the expected date of delivery and the anniversary of the termination.

MORAL IMPLICATIONS

Grieving after a termination for fetal abnormality is complicated by a loss of moral self-esteem, because there is an awareness of personal contribution to the pregnancy loss. Unlike miscarriage or stillbirth, the loss was not unavoidable but had been chosen. There is a confrontation with one's own morality in making decisions about life and death. Even the knowledge that the fetus would have died anyway does not take away the overwhelming sense of responsibility for this new life. The decision to terminate the pregnancy frequently conflicted with previously held beliefs about right and wrong. This ethical conflict and the moral pain of having to choose either against life or for possible suffering was strongly illustrated by the fact that many couples were preoccupied with searching for purpose or reason and had experienced spiritual disturbance (Thomassen-Brepols 1985; White-van Mourik *et al.* 1992).

SUPPORT FROM THE MEDICAL COMMUNITY

Hospital staff were often reported to be kind and caring but few hospitals appeared to have a protocol concerning the discharge and follow-up procedures after the termination of pregnancy. This meant that it was not uncommon for the woman to turn up in the surgery of her family doctor, only to be asked how the pregnancy was progressing. This was extremely painful for the bereaved women and embarrassing for their GPs who had not been informed. Even where there was kindness, ambivalence towards the termination of pregnancy was shown in subtle ways. Some hospitals, for instance, refused parents access to a memorial book. This book is kept to acknowledge babies lost after late miscarriage, stillbirth or neonatal death. Hospitals were unable to give convincing explanations for this.

There is reluctance in both men and women to report emotional disturbances or somatic complaints to the family doctor for fear of being put on tranquillizers or anti-depressants or even being admitted to a psychiatric hospital. Empathy, good listening and an understanding of the subjective qualities of the experience were highly appreciated by the couple when members of the primary and obstetric care team gave them. Equally important was clear, factual information about preconception care and recurrence risk for future pregnancies.

REPRODUCTIVE BEHAVIOUR AFTER A TERMINATION FOR FETAL ABNORMALITY

One of the factors which affects couples after a termination for fetal abnormality is loss of biological self-esteem. Like fetal loss, the production of a handicapped child is still, if at times subconsciously, perceived to be reproductive failure. Feelings of shame and failure were frequently reinforced by the family and in-laws, who would fervently declare that this abnormality could not come from their side of the family. This exaggerated the bereaved parents' loss of self-value, yet, as observed in the literature about grief response (Thomassen-Brepols 1985), a feeling of self-value is an important ingredient in the coping strategy. Further complicating the issue is an increased incidence of fetal abnormality in subsequent pregnancies.

Most couples have a planned family size but the procreative wish may be amended by circumstances. In the past, couples at risk of genetic disease were often deterred from planning further pregnancies (Emery *et al.* 1972, 1973; Reynolds *et al.* 1974; Klein and Wyss 1977). Many authors reported changed reproductive behaviour after the introduction of prenatal diagnosis in that couples dared to try to achieve their planned family (Modell *et al.* 1984; Kabach *et al.* 1984; Wyss-Hutin 1979; Modell and Bulyzhenkov 1988; Evers-Kiebooms *et al.* 1988). However, the decision-making process was perceived to be more burdensome by the couples who were deciding to have children using the option of prenatal diagnosis than it was by those for whom prenatal diagnosis was not available (Frets *et al.* 1990). The literature about the sequelae of a termination for fetal abnormality provides anecdotal information about couples refraining from further pregnancy. Only two studies examined the reproductive behaviour of couples after a termination for fetal abnormality (Thomassen-Brepols 1985; White-van Mourik 1989). In the Thomassen-Brepols study, where 40 per cent of the women were 38 years and over, 49 per cent opted for further pregnancies, but 42 per cent experienced a reproductive conflict in that the desired family size had not been realized, but the couple did not dare to try for further children. In White-van Mourik (1989), where the mean maternal age was 27 years and only 6 per cent of the women were over 38 years of age, 82 per cent tried to achieve their wished-for family composition, and 14 per cent experienced a reproductive conflict.

These two studies confirmed Lippmann-Hand and Fraser's view (1979) that neither the objective interpretation of the recurrence risk, nor single factors such as religious conviction, negative feeling about the termination procedure or lack of support post-intervention, necessarily deterred couples from further reproduction. The deciding factors in the reproductive conflict after a termination for fetal abnormality are maternal age, an unexpected diagnosis, the presence of children in the family, and a subtle combination of factors. Frets made similar observation in genetic counsellees (Frets *et al.* 1990).

The reason that the risk of procreational conflict is largest amongst women of advanced maternal age is that for them time is running out with the approaching end of fertility. Not only did this group have to contend with the losses described in the sequelae of termination for abnormality, but they frequently experienced disapproval for their desire for further pregnancies from their spouse, relatives and friends, especially if they had other, older children. Another group which wanted more children but often decided against further pregnancies was of women who had received an unexpected diagnosis, i.e. one different from the one for which they may have requested prenatal diagnosis (Leschot *et al.* 1982; Thomassen-Brepols 1985). Previous knowledge of fetal abnormality was not only helpful during the decision-making process, but also in attempts to come to terms with the termination of pregnancy; thus a surprise diagnosis reinforced the loss of biological competence and decreased the feeling of self-value. Help could be offered to couples with such a conflict by providing focused counselling. In this the counsellor focuses on the counsellee's feelings concerning the reproductive decision, accepts apparently irrational considerations (because these feelings indicate the influence of unconscious motives) and understands the role which guilt plays in the decision (Frets, Los *et al.* 1990).

All women who subsequently became pregnant in the Thomassen-Brepols (1985) and White-van Mourik (1989) studies chose prenatal diagnosis.

INTERVENTION PROGRAMMES

No care, however thoughtful and thorough, can take away the pain of loss; neither can reassuring remarks take away moral anguish. Resolution of grief does not mean forgetting the event, as many women who lost babies decades ago could testify. Support can be provided by recognizing that the turmoil of feelings after a termination of pregnancy may be disabling but is not usually pathological, and by helping couples who have difficulties unravelling their ambivalence.

The only examples of intervention in this field are the perinatal mortality programmes, which started to gain popularity in the mid-1980s (Forrest *et al.* 1981, 1982; Kirkley-Best and Kellner 1982; Bourne and Lewis 1984; Kirk 1984; Kellner *et al.* 1984). These programmes were instigated with a greater awareness of psychological problems of families after a stillbirth or neonatal death. These programmes allowed, and then encouraged, bereavement processes to run their course until there was a resolution of grief. An immediate pregnancy to counteract the grieving process is discouraged. An important strategy is to encourage parents to hold and see their dead baby so that farewells can be said and thus provide an end to a process that started with the discovery and confirmation of the abnormal pregnancy. The reality of the farewell facilitates the grieving process which made resolution possible. In the White-van Mourik (1989) study, the women who most deeply regretted not seeing their fetus were those who were too frightened or too tired to request a viewing after the termination of pregnancy procedure. They would have welcomed a picture of the fetus on file. It is indeed not uncommon for women to ring the hospital a decade after the intervention to request a picture of the fetus.

Although Forrest *et al.* (1982) and the other authors mentioned that the duration of bereavement reactions was appreciably shortened by support and counselling, the possibility of iatrogenic effects (poor outcome due to intervention) was rarely discussed and their occurrence in psychosocial intervention has not yet been reported. Self-help groups have been seen as invaluable in supporting women by reducing isolation (Vachon *et al.* 1980). Their role in public relations and their help in the education of professionals has done much to raise public awareness of the problems.

ETHICAL CONSIDERATIONS RAISED REGARDING THE SEQUELAE OF A TERMINATION FOR FETAL ABNORMALITY

The issue brought up most frequently by the couple, after the termination, was that of confusion concerning their status. Directions may have been given regarding tests, the condition of the fetus, the admission to hospital, and the termination procedure. This may not have been done very well but at least there was a system. However, when the termination was completed all became vague. Medical and social responsibility frequently seemed to have come to an end. The choices had been offered and the couples themselves had made the decisions. As has been discussed, for many couples and especially for those unfamiliar with the diagnosed fetal abnormality, the long process of realization, grieving and resolution was just starting. Unfortunately, few hospitals have a protocol for after-care or long-term follow-up. Few couples are given the information about the psychosocial sequelae of the intervention or are helped to explore the coping strategies for coming to terms with the decision. Barbara Katz Rothman (1989) observed that:

> These women are victims of a social system that fails to take collective responsibility for the needs of its members, and leaves

individual women to make impossible choices. We are spared collective responsibility, because we individualise the problem. We make it the woman's own. She chooses, and so we owe her nothing. Whatever the cost, she has chosen. It is her problem not ours.

In view of this, surely it should be an integral part of all antenatal screening programmes and diagnostic services, not only to provide choice but to help couples to learn to live with this choice?

Many times in the past new directions in screening and prenatal diagnosis have been funded for their scientific development while funding for research into the psychosocial consequences has been neglected.

COUPLES' PERCEPTION OF GOOD MANAGEMENT

When couples were asked for their recommendations on good management, three themes clearly emerged: recognition, information and hope.

Recognition was described in several ways: as the confirmation of the couples' status as parents by medical staff, relatives and friends, as perception and comprehension of the grief, as an insight into the fact that apparent choice is often perceived as no choice at all but as the only action feasible under the circumstances, as an understanding of the fear of social disapproval and the subsequent reticence in asking for help when required, as perception of the turmoil of ambivalent feelings, and the time it may take to come to terms with the event. Recognition prevents trivialization and the use of platitudes.

Information and communication were found to be of enormous value in coming to terms with the termination of pregnancy for fetal abnormality. Explanations using appropriate language about the fetal abnormality, the termination of pregnancy procedure, and preparation for the physical, psychosocial, short- and long-term sequelae were considered essential. Better and continuing communication minimized the feeling of being out of control and reduced misunderstanding.

Hope for another pregnancy was felt to be of great importance to those wishing to achieve their planned family. A successful subsequent pregnancy counterbalanced the loss of biological self-esteem and to some extent restored a sense of social competence. Couples attached great importance to discussions about the implications of the fetal abnormality for further pregnancies, prenatal diagnosis, and preconception health care.

PRACTICAL CONSIDERATIONS FOR PROFESSIONALS

Within the context of continuing medical care, professionals have a responsibility to understand this new kind of grief and to recognize the signs that may indicate a need for further counselling or professional mental health intervention. In view of society's ambivalence towards abortion and to issues concerning handicap, the couples' reticence and lowered self-esteem should be recognized as they may be reluctant to initiate discussion and ask for help. Better communication and preparation for the sequelae were highly recommended.

Discussions before prenatal diagnosis should include preparation for the possibility of an unexpected result, especially for one where the prognosis may be unclear (e.g. discovery of a sex chromosome aneuploidy following amniocentesis for high risk of Down syndrome).

After the discovery of the abnormality, uncertainties about the consequences, prognosis, and life expectancy of the fetus should ideally be minimized. Referrals to relevant support groups may be helpful, and some couples may need extra counselling during the decision-making time.

After the decision to terminate the pregnancy, preparations should include not only a discussion on the termination procedure and analgesics but further information should be given on the importance of seeing the fetus, the possibility of a religious blessing, and whether a cremation or a burial is appropriate. Having tangible memories and a greater feeling of involvement can be extremely valuable in coping. The short-term psychosocial sequelae to a termination of pregnancy should be discussed, emphasizing the feelings of ambivalence experienced by many couples.

On leaving hospital couples should be given adequate information on the physical sequelae, the short-term psychosocial sequelae, and an explanation about the follow-up procedures..

The follow-up visit should be no more than three months after the termination of pregnancy. It provides an opportunity to discuss the fetal post-mortem. Subsequent to this an appointment for genetic counselling is often appropriate. Couples may want to discuss further pregnancies and, considering the grieving process, the undesirability of a new pregnancy soon after the termination should be explored. A discussion on general preconception care is usually appreciated. A psychosocial assessment should be made in order to determine the optimum aftercare for each individual couple. A standard protocol designed to counteract the couples' reticence would facilitate better short- and long-term care.

Research and development into new prenatal procedures and screening programmes must include studies into the psychosocial consequences so that provision for information, care and counselling can be made concurrently with implementation of these procedures. Finally, regional audit of communication, provision of information and criteria of service will ensure that standards are being upheld.

REFERENCES

Adler, B. and Kushnick, T. (1982) 'Genetic counselling in prenatally diagnosed trisomy 18 and 21', *Paediatrics* 69: 94–9.

Adler, N. E., Henry, P. D., Major. B. *et al.* (1990) 'Psychological responses after abortion', *Science* 248: 41–4.

Becker, J., Glinski, L. and Laxova, R. (1984) 'Long-term emotional impact of second-trimester pregnancy termination after detection of fetal abnormality', *American Journal of Human Genetics* 36: 122s.

Bibring, B. L., Dwyers, T. S. , Huntington, D. S. and Valenstein, A. F. (1961) 'Study of psychological processes in pregnancy and of earliest mother–child relationship', *Psycho-analytical Study of the Child* 16: 9–24.

Bibring, B. L. and Valenstein, A. F. (1967) 'The psychological aspects of pregnancy', *Clinical Obstetrics and Gynecology* 19: 357–71.

Black, R. B. (1989) 'A 1 and 6 month follow-up of prenatal diagnosis patients who lost pregnancies', *Prenatal Diagnosis* 9: 795–804.

Blumberg, B. D. (1984) 'The emotional implications of prenatal diagnosis', in A. E. H. Emery and I. M. Pullen (eds) *Psychological Aspects of Genetic Counselling*, London: Academic Press, pp. 202–17.

Blumberg, B. D., Golbus, M. C. and Hanson, K. (1975) 'The psychological sequelae of abortion performed for a genetic indication', *American Journal of Obstetrics and Gynecology* 122: 799–808.

Borg, S. and Lasker, J. (1982) *When Pregnancy Fails: Coping with Miscarriage, Stillbirth and Infant Death*, London: Routledge & Kegan Paul.

Bourne, S. and Lewis, E. (1984) 'Pregnancy after stillbirth or neonatal death: psychological risk and management', *Lancet* ii: 31–3.

Brown, W. (1982) 'Early loss and depression', in C. Parkes and J. Stevenson-Hide (eds) *The Place of Attachment in Human Behaviour*, New York: Basic Books, pp. 283–6.

Cao, A., Cossu, P., Monni, G. *et al.* (1987) 'Chorionic villus sampling and acceptance rate of prenatal diagnosis', *Prenatal Diagnosis* 7: 531–3.

Cao, A., Rossatelli, P., Galnello, R. *et al.* (1989) 'The prevention of thalassaemia in Sardinia', *Clinical Genetics* 36: 277–85.

Cranley, M. S. (1981a) 'Roots of attachment: The relationship of parents with their unborn', in R. P. Lederman, B. S. Raff and P. Caroll (eds) *Perinatal Parental Behaviour: Nursing Research and Implications for the Newborn Health*, New York: Alan R Liss, pp. 59–83.

—— (1981b) 'Development of a tool for measurement of maternal attachment during pregnancy', *Nursing Research* 30: 281–4.

De Frain, J., Taylor, J. and Ernst, L. (1982) *Coping with Sudden Infant Death*, Lexington, Mass.: Lexington Books.

Doane, B. K. and Quigley, B. G. (1981) 'Psychiatric aspects of therapeutic abortion', *Canadian Medical Association Journal* 125: 427–32.

Donnai, P., Charles, N. and Harris, R. (1981) 'Attitudes of patients after genetic termination of pregnancy', *British Medical Journal* 282: 621–2.

Dunstan, G. R. (1988) 'Screening for fetal and genetic abnormality: social and ethical issues', *Journal of Medical Genetics* 25: 290–3.

Emery, A. E. H., Watt, M. S. and Clark, E. R. (1972) 'The effects of genetic counselling in Duchenne muscular dystrophy', *Clinical Genetics* 3: 147–50.

—— (1973) 'Social effects of genetic counselling', *British Medical Journal* i: 724–6.

Evers-Kieboom, G.,, Denayer, L., Cassiman, J. J. *et al.* (1988) 'Family-planning decisions after the birth of a cystic fibrosis child: impact of prenatal diagnosis', *Scandinavian Journal of Gastroenterology* (Supplement) 143: 38–46.

Fletcher, J. C. and Evans, M. I. (1983) 'Maternal bonding in early fetal ultrasound examinations', *New England Journal of Medicine* 308: 392–3.

Forrest, G. C., Claridge, R. and Baum, J. D. (1981) 'The practical management of perinatal death', *British Medical Journal* 282: 31–2.

Forrest, G. C., Standish, E. and Baum, J. D. (1982) 'Support after perinatal death: a study of support and counselling perinatal bereavement', *British Medical Journal* 285: 1475–9.

Frets, P. G., Duivenvoorden, H. J., Verhage, F. *et al.* (1990) 'Model identifying the reproductive decision after genetic counseling', *American Journal of Medical Genetics* 35: 503–9.

—— (1991) 'Analysis of problems in making the reproductive decision after genetic counselling', *Journal of Medical Genetics* 28 (3): 194–200.

Frets, P. G., Los, F. J., Sachs, E. S. *et al.* (1990) 'Psychological counselling of couples experiencing a pregnancy termination after amniocentesis', *Journal of Psychosomatic Obstetrics and Gynecology* 11 (Special Issue 1): 53–9.

Hollerbach, P. E. (1979) 'Reproductive attitudes and the genetic counsellee', in Y. E. Hsia, K. Hirschorn, R. L. Silverberg *et al.* (eds) *Counselling in Genetics*, New York: Allan Liss, pp. 155–222.

Jones, O. W., Penn, N. E., Schuchter, S. *et al.* (1984) 'Parental response to midtrimester therapeutic abortion following amniocentesis', *Prenatal Diagnosis* 4: 249–56.

Kaback, M., Zippin, D., Boyd, P. *et al.* (1984) 'Attitudes towards prenatal diagnosis of cystic fibrosis among parents of affected children', in D. Lawson (ed.) *Cystic Fibrosis: Horizons*, New York: John Wiley & Sons, pp. 6–28.

Kellner, K. R., Donelly, W. H. and Gould, S. D. (1984) 'Parental behaviour after perinatal death: lack of predictive demography and obstetric variables', *Obstetrics and Gynecology* 63: 809–14.

Kirk, E. P. (1984) 'Psychological effects and management of perinatal loss', *American Journal of Obstetrics and Gynecology* 149: 46–51.

Kirkly-Best, E. and Kellner, K. R. (1982) 'The forgotten grief, a review of the psychology of stillbirth', *American Journal of Orthopsychiatry* 52: 420–9.

Klein, D. and Wyss, D. (1977) 'Retrospective and follow-up study of approximately 1,000 genetic consultations', *Journal de Génétique Humain* 25: 4–57.

Korenromp, M. J., Iedema-Kuiper, H. R., van Spijker, H. G. *et al.* (1992) 'Termination of pregnancy on genetic grounds: coping with grieving', *Journal of Psychosomatic Obstetrics and Gynecology* 13: 93–105.

Leschot, N. J., Verjaal, M. and Treffers, P. E. (1982) 'Therapeutic abortion on genetic indication: a detailed follow-up study of 20 patients', *Journal of Psychosometric Obstetrics and Gynecology* 1: 47–56.

Lippman-Hands, A. and Fraser, F. C. (1979) 'Genetic counselling: the provision and perception of information', *American Journal of Medical Genetics* 3: 113–27.

Lloyd, J. and Laurence, K. M. (1985) 'Sequelae and support after termination of pregnancy for fetal malformation', *British Medical Journal* 290: 907–9.

Lumley, J. (1980) 'The image of the fetus in the first trimester', *Birth Family Journal* 7: 5–14.

Martinson, I., Modow, D. and Henry, W. (1980) *Home Care for the Child with Cancer*, final report (Grant no. Ca19490)., US Department of Health and Human Services, Washington D.C.: National Cancer Institute.

Modell, B. and Bulyzhenkov, V. (1988) 'Distribution and control of some genetic disorders', *World Health Statistics* Q 41: 209–18.

Modell, B., Petrou, M., Ward, R. H. *et al.* (1984) 'Effect of fetal diagnostic testing on birth-rate of thalassaemia major in Britain', *Lancet* ii: 1383–6.

Pasnau, R. and Farah, J. (1977) 'Loss and mourning after abortion', in C. Hollingworth and R. Pasnau (eds) *The Family In Mourning*, New York: Grune & Stratton.

Pedder, J. R. (1982) 'Failure to mourn, and melancholia', *British Journal of Psychiatry* 141: 329–37.

Reading, A., Sledgemere, C. M., Campbell, S. *et al.* (1981) 'Psychological effects on the mother, of real-time ultrasound in antenatal clinics', *British Journal of Radiology* 54: 546.

Reilly, P. (1979) 'Genetic counselling: a legal perspective', in Y. E. Hsia, K. Hirschorn, R. L. Silverberg *et al.* (eds) *Counselling in Genetics*, New York: Alan Liss, pp. 311–28.

Reynolds, B. D., Puck, M. H. and Robinson, A. (1974) 'Genetic counselling: an appraisal', *Clinical Genetics* 5: 177–8.

Rothman, B. K. (1988) *The Tentative Pregnancy*, London: Pandora.

Stroebe, W. and Stroebe, M. (1987) *Bereavement and Health: The Psychological and Physical Consequences*, Cambridge: Cambridge University Press, especially pp. 168–223.

Thomassen-Brepols, L. J. (1985) 'Psychosociale aspecten van prenatale diagnostiek' (Psycho-social aspects of prenatal diagnosis), Ph.D. thesis, Erasmus University, Rotterdam.

Vachon, M. L. S., Lyall, W. A. L., Rogers, J. *et al.* (1980) 'A controlled study of selfhelp intervention for widows', *American Journal of Psychiatry* 137: 380–4.

White-van Mourik, M. C. A. (1989) 'The psychosocial sequelae of a termination of pregnancy for fetal abnormality', M.Sc thesis, University of Glasgow.

White-van Mourik, M. C. A., Connor, J. M., and Ferguson-Smith, M. A. (1990) 'Patient care before and after termination of pregnancy for neural tube defect', *Prenatal Diagnosis*, 10: 497–505.

—— (1992) 'The psychosocial sequelae of a second-trimester termination of pregnancy for fetal abnormality', *Prenatal Diagnosis* 12: 189–204.

Wyss-Hutin, D. (1979) 'Les conséquences du conseil génétique', *Journal de Génétique Humain* 27 (Supplement 1): 53–96.

Chapter 6

Lessons from a dark and distant past

Benno Müller-Hill

ABSTRACT

Genetic counselling bridges the interface between genetics and society. Thus a science, human genetics, meets and merges with the beliefs and demands of society. History provides frightening examples of the danger inherent in this process. Two will be discussed: (1) judgement of and measures against race mixing and (2) the policy of sterilization for carriers of supposed inherited mental disorders. There seems now to be general agreement that a genetic counsellor is not a scientific agent of the state whose job is to execute its decrees. But there seems to be less agreement whether a genetic counsellor should be nothing but a scientific expert and advertiser of the market.

INTRODUCTION

The daily burden of a genetic counsellor is heavy: she[1] has to follow the latest results of a fast developing field. The advent of the Human Genome Project (See *Human Genome News*, a monthly publication sponsored by the US Department of Energy and the National Institute of Health since 1989) guarantees that the conceptual and technical developments will be faster here than in any other medical field. And she does not operate in a social vacuum. It has not yet been determined how legislation on the use of genetic information will affect insurers, employers and the state itself. She has to teach the client or patient both the scientific truth and the social reality and – possibly – the different values held by herself and others.

All this sounds too much to deal with. When I present here a chapter on the history of the field I can already hear the reaction:

1 The counsellor may, of course, also be male.

'Forget it!' And I will not hide the fact that I am not an MD, that I have never done any genetic counselling myself and – the final blow – that I am not a professional historian of science but a molecular biologist who has worked only peripherally on problems of human genetics (Kang *et al.* 1987). My only credentials for this article are a book (Müller-Hill 1988) and some articles (Müller-Hill 1987, 1991a, 1991b) on the history of human genetics in Germany in 1933–45.

The borders between science and beliefs were and are still today ill-defined in human genetics. It may pay to define science as a sum of knowledge which has predictive power. This sum of knowledge is available to all scientists not just some of them. For example, the maps of the four chromosomes of the fruit-fly *Drosophila melanogaster* can be used to accommodate more genes, but they will never change fundamentally or become irrelevant. All geneticists will read a DNA sequence on a gel in essentially the same way and all of them will discuss the number of open reading frames coded by such a piece of DNA in the same manner. These are examples of hard science. Thus somebody who deliberately, like Lysenko (1949), denies this network of knowledge stands outside science. The German human geneticists active during the Third Reich accepted Mendelism. They stood within science (Müller-Hill 1988; Proctor, 1988; Weindling 1989).

All human geneticists will agree upon the molecular defect in sickle-cell anaemia but there will often be disagreement where the relevant phenotypes are supposed mental defects. Here the human geneticists have to rely upon the results of psychiatry, psychology, ethnology and so on. In these fields one finds, of course, temporary agreement among the experts to a greater or lesser degree, but after some years the agreement may shift totally. Another field in which the agreement among scientists has shifted over time is the study of race, and judgements about 'racial mixing'.

The treatments or measures proposed by human geneticists also change with time. There was a time when sterilization was considered *the* treatment of choice; now it is abortion. I will discuss here the history of this issue as it has unfolded in Germany and Sweden. The role of the patient has also changed: the patient has turned into a client. This is more appropriate. The clients no longer have to accept the decisions of the counsellor; now they buy advice to help them make the best choice from what is available. Thus, the genetic counsellor no longer decides the fate of a patient: she teaches a client. Or to put it differently: she advertises the various options available in the market. But in advertising, what is truth?

THE CASE OF RACE MIXING

The notion of different races existed at least a century prior to the rediscovery of Mendel's work in 1900. At that time the community of European and US American white scientists (Kevles 1985) shared the same low opinion of all black people. They almost all agreed that black people were unable to do abstract thinking. The only question was how profound this inability actually was. The genocide of black ethnic groups was regarded by many as normal and inevitable.

Under these conditions it is not surprising that a young German assistant professor of anatomy, Eugen Fischer, who was deeply interested in human Mendelian genetics, applied successfully for a grant in 1908 to study a small community of the offspring of white settlers and black women in one of the German African colonies – now Namibia. He studied both the physical and psychological characteristics of the members of this community. He came to the conclusion that Mendel's laws were operating for *all* phenotypes he analysed. The black–white hybrids (he called them 'bastards') were thus in their intelligence somewhere between the high white and the low black level (Fischer 1913).

At the time when Fischer began his work, intermarriage between black women and white German settlers was against the law. The particular legal situation was thus in principle similar to the one then prevailing in several southern states of the USA. In Namibia the general situation was certainly worse: the German colonial policy was genocidal (Swan 1991). When Germany lost its colonies a few years later during the First World War, the whole problem became almost academic for the German human geneticists. However, the French used colonial soldiers to occupy the western part of Germany. Thus about 600 coloured children were born in Germany during those years. They were all illegally sterilized in 1937–8 after being analysed by Eugen Fischer and his colleagues (Müller-Hill 1988).

Eugen Fischer became the first director of a new institute of the *Kaiser Wilhelm-Gesellschaft* (now *Max Planck-Gesellschaft*) founded in 1927 to promote human genetics and eugenics. He and his institute had an excellent international reputation. He was president of the International Congress of Genetics held in Berlin in the same year. In 1929 he was asked by C. B. Davenport (Cold Spring Harbor) to become chairman of the committee on racial crosses (mixing) of the international Federation of Eugenic Organisations. His institute received a grant from the Rockefeller Foundation in 1932 for the work on twins done by his subdirector Otmar von Verschuer. He was elected rector of Berlin University in 1933 just before the Nazis came to power. In his rectorial speech he praised the law which led to the expulsion of Jewish professors and other civil servants as a scientific necessity. He did the same when the Nuremberg laws were announced which prohibited German–Jewish intermarriage and sexual intercourse. He was certainly not alone in defending the Nuremberg laws as arising from scientific necessity. German geneticists also compared the Nuremberg laws with the various American laws prohibiting black–white intermarriage and pointed out that the Nuremberg laws were rather lenient in comparison.

It was then and only then that the race concept held by the international community of geneticists was seen to be untenable. One could possibly argue against intermarriage of blacks and whites but it was more than difficult to defend the Nuremberg laws to Jewish colleagues. When – finally – in 1945 Nazism and its defenders fell, it became generally impossible to defend prohibitions of interracial marriage. This shift in opinion was not a shift in knowledge caused by new scientific results, but rather a shift brought about by political, social and cultural factors (Teich 1990).

STERILIZATION IN GERMANY

Sterilization was regarded as the negative measure of choice in eugenics or race hygiene. Its proponents pointed out that the operations are easy to carry out in both males and females and that the operation does not interfere with the sexual life of the person operated on. I will not attempt to give here a full historical panorama (see, for example, Kevles 1985; Trombley 1988). Instead I will concentrate on two countries, Germany (Bock 1986) and Sweden (Broberg and Tyden 1991; Lindquist 1991).

The German eugenicists (or, as the anti-Semites among them called themselves, the race hygienicists) pushed for a law legalizing sterilization long before the Nazis came to power. There was no chance of such a law legalizing involuntary sterilization before or during the Weimar Republic. Only the Nazis advocated that. The proposed law therefore allowed only voluntary sterilization for a defined group of persons including the schizophrenics and the feeble-minded. The realists among the German eugenicists pushed for the law as a first step. A few of them actually believed in the necessity of the patient's free choice; most others did not. When the Nazis came to power they immediately passed a law allowing sterilization in the exact words of the draft of the Weimar Republic but with two major changes: they allowed involuntary, coercive sterilization and included alcoholism as one of the conditions (Gütt *et al.* 1934). All private doctors who noted one of the listed defects in one of their patients had to notify officially the nearest MD active in the state-run health-care system (Schrader 1936). This oficial had then to bring the case before the court. The court decision was made by two MDs and one judge. An appeal was possible. What looked to the outside as a safe and just procedure was in fact for most victims a sham. Neither the victims nor their lawyers were allowed to see the detailed diagnosis. Often the victims only learned in court that they were to be sterilized. The exact number of patients sterilized is known for the first three years, 1934–6 (62,463; 71,760; 64,646), and one can assume that the numbers did not change substantially until the beginning of the war. Thus during those years about 0.1 per cent of the German population was sterilized per year. The misery of these 350,000 persons which was produced by coercive genetic counselling should not be underestimated or forgotten.

The community of German human geneticists also supported the sterilization policies as a means of stopping the spread of racially undesirable genes. Three different human groups were envisaged:

1 All coloured people. As stated before, all half-coloured Germans were illegally sterilized in 1937/8. The human geneticists helped in defining the criteria for selecting the victims.
2 Most Gypsies. The Gypsies living in Germany were regarded as the descendants of an originally pure Indo-Germanic tribe who, after coming to Europe, had intermarried with the lowest criminal strata of all European countries. According to this view most Gypsies were not pure Gypsies but *Mischlinge* who had to be sterilized because of their non-Gypsy genes. This policy was actively supported by the community of German human geneticists.
3 When the total annihilation of the Jews became the policy in 1941/2, discussion about the possible sterilization of all *Juden-Mischlinge* who had at least one Jewish grandparent began. Eugen Fischer was present as an honorary guest at a conference held on March 26–8 1941 in Frankfurt where an official speaker asked for the sterilization of all quarter-Jews. Fischer's collaborator and successor von Verschuer reported on the conference in his journal (Müller-Hill 1988). The relevant bureaucracy soon understood

that the realization of the project was impossible for purely practical reasons: during the war all hospital beds were needed, the officials who would be needed were busy in the war effort, etc. These measures were therefore never implemented.

It has to be pointed out here that the criteria which defined partly coloured people, half-Gypsies or quarter-Jews were morally revolting but logically consistent. I would like to discuss this in the typical case of a part-Jew: it was only after 1800 in Germany that a substantial number of Jews left their religion to be baptized and to intermarry with non-Jewish Christian Germans. Thus a Jew was defined as the descendant of persons who had not been baptized in 1800. If a person defined by such church documents found himself pure Jewish or half-Jewish in 1940, the only legal way to avoid deportation and likely death was to claim that the legal (Jewish) father was not the biological father. Hundreds of such cases kept the German human geneticists busy. The clients who asked for help hoped, of course, that they could bribe the human geneticists in one way or another to falsify their paternity and to save their lives. The human geneticists knew that telling the truth meant suffering and possible or certain death for the client, but that lying too often would undermine their scientific reputation. The Austrian human geneticists seem to have been totally corrupt; the German ones sided with science and inhumanity. One may thus say that the German geneticists prostituted genetics: they were procurers who sold the most intimate knowledge of their patients and clients to torturers and murderers. The documentation can be found in von Verschuer's textbook of human genetics, which was published in 1941; it is worth noting that von Verschuer never had the slightest problem in his academic career in Germany after the war.

STERILIZATION IN SWEDEN

One may argue that Germany is so untypical that it is not a pertinent example. So let's look at an impeccable European democracy: Sweden (Broberg and Tyden 1991; Lindquist 1991). In the first half of this century the Swedish government was run by social democrats. Yet Sweden was the first European country to found – in 1922 – an Institute for Race Biology at the University of Uppsala. Its director, Herman Lundborg, had close connections with the German (human) geneticists and he sympathized later with the German Nazis. He retired around the time the Nazis took power in Germany. His successor, Gunnar Dahlberg, paved the way (partly a semantic one) from the old race hygiene or eugenics to modern medical genetics.

A law legalizing sterilization in Sweden was passed in 1934 and its scope was broadened in 1941. Between 1935 and 1975, when the law was revoked, 62,888 persons, almost all of them women, were sterilized in Sweden (Broberg and Tyden 1991). The highest number (2,351) was sterilized in 1949. Many of the sterilized were *tattare*, the Swedish name for part-Gypsies. When sterilization began in 1935, it was almost always for eugenic reasons; when it ended in 1975, it was almost entirely for medical reasons. The turning point in the reasoning was the year 1948.

During the years when more then 1,000 persons per year were sterilized (from 1942 to 1975) the incidence of Swedish sterilization was between 15 and 30 per cent of that in Nazi Germany. And this happened under a law which did not allow sterilization against a person's will! How was this possible? The victims were badly informed and mildly coerced. Lindquist's book (1991) contains interviews with several victims. They tell how they were tricked into the operation-room and how sterilization mutilated them for life.

In Lindquist's book one of the doctors who advocated sterilization is interviewed by the author (pp. 28–31). He remembers 'the time was like that. All of us thought like that. . . . We dreamed we could improve human body and soul. . . . That's how the geneticist saw it then and some of them see it still today.'

DIRECTIVE VERSUS NON-DIRECTIVE COUNSELLING TODAY

I have tried to show that belief in the various dogmas of psychiatry, psychology, social theory, etc. led – and not only in Germany – to a treatment of patients and clients which in retrospect seems incredibly brutal and pointless. It becomes clear that directive counselling was regarded most suspiciously after the defeat of Germany and was therefore abandoned first in the USA and later in Germany too. To the best of my knowledge directive counselling is still practised only in the former eastern bloc countries. But that is a different story.

Non-directive counselling leaves the decision to the patient or client. Here the counsellor just explains all the options, as honestly as she can. The counsellor is no longer responsible for the decisions and acts of the patient or client. The genetic diagnosis poses in general no problems on the technical side. It is straightforward. The existential not the medical risks pose the problem. Is it sufficient for the counsellor just to mention them? Or should she actively try to diminish them when possible?

It is to be expected that the diagnostic power of medical genetics will increase dramatically as more and more of the human genome becomes known. I am not thinking so much about extremely rare diseases but on the contrary about common ones. So far – at least in Europe – employers and insurers have by and large resisted the temptation to get genetic information about employees or clients and to arrange contracts according to risk estimates. But times are changing (Billings *et al.* in press). Can the genetic counsellor remain neutral in this development? Can she maintain that all she does is to make available (or even promote) the cheapest solution in an objective manner?

The enthusiasm of those who argue in this way is understandable. In a world in which the market and nothing but the market sets the standard, their activities are impeccable. They just sell the truth. They are also supported by philosophy. Truth is the highest value for most philosophers. Even the great Kant argued that truth is so important that you have to give the murderer the address of your friend, if he asks for it (1797). I would like to point out here that the German human geneticists did just that under the Nazis.

So what is to be done? Non-directive counselling was a step forward beyond the terrible rigidity of directive counselling. Yet it seems just one of several additional necessary steps. Let me call the next step 'Hippocratic non-directive counselling'. I would like to recall that the eighth commandment does not say 'Thou shalt tell the truth' but 'Thou shalt not bear false witness'. This implies that the counsellor has to see that justice is not lost in the process of counselling. Justice seems to me to be lost where there is no help for the weak but when they are just left to be destroyed by the forces of the market.

REFERENCES

Billings, P. R., Kohn, M. A., de Cuevas, M. *et al.* (1992) 'Discrimination as a consequence of genetic testing', *American Journal of Human Genetics* 50: 476–82.

Bock, G. (1986) *Zwangssterilisation im Nationalsozialismus.* Opladen: Westdeutscher Verlag.

Broberg, G. and Tyden, M. (1991) *Oönskade i Folkhemmet. Rashygien i och Sterilisering i Sverige*, Stockholm: Gidlunds.

Fischer, E. (1913) *Die Rehoboter Bastarde und das Bastardi-sierungs-problem beim Menschen*, Jena: Verlag von Gustav Fischer.

Gütt, A., Rüdin, E. and Ruttke, F. (1934) *Gesetz zur Verhütung erbkranken Nachwuchses vom 14. Juli 1934*, Munich: J. F. Lehmanns Verlag.

Kang, J., Lemaire, H.-G., Unterbeck, A. *et al.* (1987) 'The precursor of Alzheimer's disease amyloid A4 protein resembles a cell surface receptor', *Nature* 325: 733–6.

Kant, I. (1797) Über ein vermeintliches Recht aus Menschenliebe zu lügen', *Berlinische Blätter* 1: 301–4. Reprinted in *Werkausgabe* VIII (1977), Frankfurt a. M.: Suhrkamp Verlag, pp. 637–43.

Kevles, D. (1985) *In the Name of Eugenics. Genetics and the Use of Human Heredity*, New York: Alfred A. Knopf and (1986) Harmondsworth: Penguin.

Lindquist, B. (1991) *Förädlade Svenskar – Drömmen om at Skapa en Bättre Mäniska*, Hässleholm: Alfabeta Bokförlag.

Lysenko, T. D. (1949) 'On the situation in biological science', in *The Situation in Biological Science*, Moscow: Proceedings of the Lenin Academy of Agricultural Sciences of the USSR, Foreign Language Publishing House, pp. 11–50.

Müller-Hill, B. (1987) 'Genetics after Auschwitz', *Holocaust and Genocide Studies* 2: 3–20.

—— (1988) *Murderous Science, Elimination by Scientific Selection of Jews, Gypsies and Others, Germany 1933–1945*, Oxford: Oxford University Press.

—— (1991a) 'Psychiatry in the Nazi era', in S. Bloch and P. Chodoff (eds) *Psychiatric Ethics* vol. 2, Oxford and New York: Oxford University Press, pp. 461–72.

—— (1991b) 'Bioscience in totalitarian regimes: the lesson to be learned from Nazi Germany', in D. J. Roy, B. E. Wynne and R. W. Olds (eds) *Bioscience and Society*, Schering Foundation Workshop 1, London: John Wiley & Sons, pp. 67–76.

Proctor, R. O. (1988) *Racial Hygiene. Medicine under the Nazis*, Cambridge, Mass.: Harvard University Press.

Schrader, E. (1936) 'Die psychologische Einstellung des Arztes zum Untersuchten bei erbbiologischer Begutachtung', *Der Erbarzt* 3: 85–7.

Swan, J. (1991) 'The final solution in South West Africa', *The Quarterly Journal of Military History* 3: 36–55.

Teich, M. (1990) 'The unmastered past of human genetics', in M. Teich and R. Porter (eds) *Fin de Siècle and its Legacy*, Cambridge: Cambridge University Press, pp. 296–324.

Trombley, S. (1988) *The Right to Reproduce: A History of Coercive Sterilization*, London: Weidenfeld & Nicolson.

Verschuer, O. v. (1941) *Leitfaden der Rassenhygiene*, Leipzig: Georg Thieme Verlag.

Weindling, P. (1989) *Health, Race and German Politics between National Unification and Nazism 1870–1945*, Cambridge: Cambridge University Press.

Chapter 7

Prenatal genetic testing and screening

Constructing needs and reinforcing inequities

*Abby Lippman**

ABSTRACT

This chapter considers the influence and implications of the application of genetic technologies to definitions of disease and to the treatment of illness. The concept of 'geneticization' is introduced to emphasize the dominant discourse in today's stories of health and disease and the social construction of biological phenomenon is described. The reassurance, choice and control supposedly provided by prenatal genetic testing and screening are critically examined, and their role in constructing the need for such technology is addressed. Using the stories told about prenatal diagnosis as a focus, the consequences of a genetic perspective for and on women and their health care needs are explored.

INTRODUCTION

During the past two decades, numerous techniques have been developed that allow geneticists to assess the physical status of the fetus during a woman's pregnancy. The variety of prenatal diagnostic techniques[1] and detectable/diagnosable fetal conditions continues to expand. These screening and testing procedures are already the most widespread application of genetic technology to humans.

This chapter, part of an ongoing project, explores the genetic stories[2] told about health and disease today, the storytellers and the

---

* Prenatal diagnosis, the focus of much of this chapter, is troublesome for all women, users and critics alike. In no way do I intend my remarks about it to reflect on women who have considered or undergone testing; criticism of the technologies is not to be read as criticisms of them. Women considering childbearing today face agonizing issues I was fortunate enough not to have to confront, and I can only admire their resilience and strength.

circumstances in which these stories are told. In this chapter, I first discuss how disease categories and biomedical practices are constructed within their cultural context, and provide some technical information regarding prenatal diagnosis. I then examine the stories constructed about genetic testing and screening; the particular assumptions upon which they are grounded;[3] and the necessarily problematic nature of applications of these genetic technologies with respect to perceptions of pregnancy and the healthcare needs of women considering childbearing. I demonstrate how the approach implicit in the use of genetic technology is as much a cultural and social activity as it is scientific. Specifically, I examine why prenatal diagnosis is made available, discussing some of the rationales usually presented for its use, and explore how a 'need' for prenatal diagnosis is currently constructed. I then consider how existing health, health care beliefs and North American social stratifications situate prenatal technologies and how these activities may them selves influence health and health care inequities.

HEALTH AND DISEASE AND THE STORIES TOLD ABOUT THEM

In today's western world, biomedical and political systems largely define health and disease, as well as normality and abnormality.[4] They also determine the individuals to whom each term will be applied. Westerrn biomedicine does not just describe a pre-existing biological reality, but is grounded in particular social and cultural assumptions.[5] No strictly objective and value-free view of the biological world exists. Any attempt to explain or order it will be shaped by the historical and cultural setting within which it occurs.[6]

Although there is a biological reality to disease, biological processes take on particular forms in different human groups and in different periods of time.[7] Disorders and disabilities are not merely physiological or physical conditions with fixed contours. Rather, they are social products with variable shapes and distributions. Defining and studying these categories and the people assigned to them is necessarily subjective, reflecting how those with power at any particular historical time construct them as problems.

In studying the distribution of health and disease, any one of the factors influencing their occurrence (social and physical environments, economic conditions, heredity, personal behaviours, health services, etc.) may be chosen for attention and the investment of resources. This choice and its subsequent expression in public policies and private practices reflect the assumptions, vested interests and ideologies of the investigators and those funding them.[8] Because 'disease is socially mutable' and medical responses are 'maleable',[9] there is abundant raw material from which to create metaphors and stories describing health and disease. The same observations may be taken as evidence to construct very different hypotheses or stories.[10]

Today's stories about health and disease, both in professional journals[11] and in mass circulation magazines,[12] are increasingly told in the language of genetics. Using the metaphor of blueprints,[13] with genes and DNA fragments presented as a set of instructions, the dominant discourse describing the human condition is reductionist, emphasizing genetic determination. It promotes scientific control of the body, individualizes health problems and situates individuals increasingly according to their genes. Through this discourse, which is beginning seriously to threaten other narratives, clinical and research geneticists and their colleagues are conditioning how we view, name and propose to manage a whole host of disorders and disabilities. Though it is only one conceptual model, 'genetics' is increasingly identified as *the* way to reveal and explain health and disease, normality and abnormality. Baird, for example, sees the 'major determinants' of disease as internal genetic factors.[14]

This conditioning directs how intellectual and financial resources are applied to resolve health problems.[15] More critically, it profoundly influences our values and attitudes. To capture this process, I use the term 'geneticization'.[16] Although most neologisms confuse rather than clarify, enlarging our lexicon to interpret human genetics is appropriate. A new canon deserves a new vocabulary.

Geneticization refers to an ongoing process by which differences between individuals are reduced to their DNA codes, with most disorders, behaviours and physiological variations defined, at least in part, as genetic in origin. It refers as well to the process by which interventions employing genetic technologies are adopted to manage problems of health. Through this process, human biology is incorrectly equated with human genetics,[17] implying that the latter acts alone to make us each the organism she or he is.

Duster captures much of this in describing how prevailing social concerns of our age are leading us to see things through a genetic 'prism'.[18] 'Geneticization' goes further, however, and poses genetics as the source of illumination itself, not merely one of the ways in which it might be refracted.

Prenatal diagnosis, already designated as a 'ritual' of pregnancy, at least for white, middle-class women in North America, is the most widespread application of genetic technology to humans today.[19] It provides a central activity around which to explore geneticization and the health stories told in its language.

PRENATAL DIAGNOSIS: A TECHNICAL AND A SOCIAL CONSTRUCTION

Of all applied genetic activities, prenatal diagnosis is probably most familiar to the general population and is also the most frequently used. Prenatal diagnosis refers to all the technologies currently in use or under development to determine the physi(ologi)cal condition of a fetus before birth. Until recently, prenatal diagnosis usually meant amniocentesis,[20] a second-trimester procedure routinely available for women over a certain age (usually 35 years in North America),[21] for Down syndrome detection. Amniocentesis is also used in selected circumstances where the identification of specific fetal genetic disorders is possible.[22] Now, in addition to amniocentesis, there are chorionic villus sampling (CVS)[23] tests that screen maternal blood samples to detect a fetus with a neural tube defect or Down syndrome, and ultrasound screening.[24] Despite professional guidelines to the contrary,[25] ultrasound screening is performed routinely in North America on almost every pregnant woman appearing for prenatal care early enough in pregnancy. And although ultrasound is not usually labelled as 'prenatal diagnosis', it not only belongs under this rubric but was, I suggest, the first form of prenatal diagnosis for which informed consent is not obtained.[26]

Expansion of prenatal diagnosis techniques, ever-widening lists of identifiable conditions and susceptibilities, changes in the timing of testing and the populations in which testing is occurring, and expanding professional definitions of what should be diagnosed *in utero*, attest to this technology's role in the process of geneticization.[27] But these operational characteristics alone circumscribe only some aspects of prenatal diagnosis. Prenatal diagnosis as a social activity is becoming an element in our culture and this aspect, which has had minimal attention, will be examined in depth.

Prenatal diagnosis and the discourse of reassurance

Contemporary stories about prenatal diagnosis contain several themes, but these generally reflect one of two somewhat different models.[28] In the 'public health' model, prenatal diagnosis is presented as a way to reduce the frequency of selected birth defects.[29] In the other, which I will call the 'reproductive autonomy' model, prenatal diagnosis is presented as a means of giving women information to expand their reproductive choices.[30] Unfortunately, neither model fully captures the essence of prenatal diagnosis. In addition, neither acknowledges the internal tension, revealed in the coexistence of quite contradictory constructions of testing that may be equally valid: (1) as an assembly-line approach to the products of conception, separating out those products we wish to develop from those we wish to discontinue;[31] (2) as a way to give women control over their pregnancies, respecting (increasing) their autonomy to choose the kinds of children they will bear,[32] or (3) as a means of reassuring women that enhances their experience of pregnancy.[33]

The dominant theme throughout the biomedical literature, as well as some feminist commentary, emphasizes the last two of these constructions.[34] A major variation on this theme suggests, further, that through the use of prenatal diagnosis women can avoid the family distress and suffering associated with the unpredicted birth of babies with genetic disorders or congenital malformations, thus preventing disability while enhancing the experience of pregnancy.[35] Not unlike the approach used to justify caesarean sections,[36] prenatal diagnosis is constructed as a way of avoiding 'disaster'.

The language of control, choice and reassurance certainly makes prenatal diagnosis appear attractive. But while this discourse may be successful as a marketing strategy,[37] it relates a limited and highly selected story about prenatal diagnosis. Notwithstanding that even the most critical would probably agree prenatal diagnosis *can be* selectively reassuring[38] (for the vast majority of women who will learn that the fetus does not have Down syndrome or some other serious diagnosable disorder), this story alone is too simplistic. It does not take account of why reassurance is sought, how risk groups are generated and how eligibility for obtaining this kind of reassurance is determined. Whatever else, prenatal diagnosis *is* a means of separating fetuses we wish to develop from those we wish to discontinue. Prenatal diagnosis does approach children as consumer objects subject to quality control.

This is implicit in the general assumption that induced abortion will follow the diagnosis of fetal abnormality.[39] This assumption is reinforced by the rapid acceptance of CVS, which allows prenatal diagnosis to be carried out earlier and earlier in pregnancy when termination of a fetus found to be 'affected' is taken for granted as less problematic.[40] The generally unquestioned assumption that pre-implantation diagnosis is better than prenatal diagnosis also undermines a monotonic reassurance rhetoric.[41] With pre-implantation (embryo) diagnosis, the selection objective is clear: only those embryos thought to be 'normal' will be transferred and allowed to continue to develop.[42] Thus, embryo destruction is equated with induced abortion.[43] In perhaps the most blatant example, Brambati and colleagues have proposed the combined use of *in vitro* fertilization, gamete intrafallopian transfer, chorionic villus sampling and fetal reduction to 'avoid pregnancy termination among high risk couples' [*sic*], and have stated that the 'fetus was reduced' when describing a situation in which this scenario actually occurred.[44]

Thus, while no single storyline is inherently true or false, the reassurance discourse appears to mask essential features of genetic testing and screening that are troubling. Reassurance – for pregnant women or for geneticists[45] – notwithstanding, the story is more complex. Prenatal diagnosis necessarily involves systematic and systemic selection of fetuses, most frequently on genetic grounds.[46] Though the word 'eugenics' is scrupulously avoided in most biomedical reports about prenatal diagnosis, except when it is strongly disclaimed as a motive for intervention, this is disingenuous.[47] Prenatal diagnosis presupposes that certain fetal conditions are intrinsically not bearable. Increasing diagnostic capability means that such conditions, as well as a host of variations that can be detected *in utero*, are proliferating, necessarily broadening the range of what is not 'bearable' and restricting concepts of what is 'normal'. It is, perhaps, not unreasonable to ask if the 'imperfect' will become anything we can diagnose.[48]

While the notion of reassurance has been successfully employed to justify prenatal testing and screening as responses to the problems of childhood disability, we need to question both the sufficiency and the necessity of its linkage to prenatal diagnosis. At best, reassurance is an acquired, not an inherent, characteristic of prenatal diagnosis. Even if testing provides 'reassurance', it is of a particular and limited kind. For example, although the fetus can be shown not to have Down syndrome, most disabilities manifest themselves only after birth. Further, it is not the (only) way to achieve a global objective of 'reassuring' pregnant women. Indeed, it may even be counter-productive. This becomes clear if one reconstructs the notion of reassurance. Assuming it is an acceptable objective of prenatal care, are there ways to reassure pregnant women desiring 'healthy' children that do not lead to genetic testing and control?

Data from the United States Women, Infants and Children Program leave little doubt that 'low-technology' approaches providing essential nutritional, social and other supportive services to pregnant women will reduce the low birth weight and prematurity responsible for most infant mortality and morbidity today.[49] Providing an adequate diet to the unacceptably large number of pregnant women living below the poverty line would clearly 'reassure' them that their babies were developing as well as the babies of wealthier women. Similarly, allocation of funds for home visitors, respite care and domestic alterations would 'reassure' women that the resources required to help them manage their special needs were readily available without financial cost, should their child be born with a health problem. It would also be 'reassuring' to know that effective medication and simplified treatment regimes were available or being developed for prevalent disorders. Reassurances such as these may be all that many pregnant women want. Not only would these alternative approaches provide 'reassurance' with respect to (and *for*) fetal disability, they would diminish a woman's feeling of personal responsibility for a child's health, rather than 'exacerbate' it as does prenatal diagnosis.[50]

Genes may contribute to the distribution of low birth weight and prematurity in North America, and some investigators will probably seek their location and the order of their DNA base sequences on the human gene map. The social and economic inequalities among women with which they are associated,[51] however, are already well 'mapped'; the 'location' of women who are at increased risk is well known; the 'sequences' of events leading to the excessively and unnecessarily high rates of these problems have been well described. From this perspective, *gene* mapping and sequencing may be irrelevant as a source of reassurance in view of the most pressing needs of pregnant women. Even if genes were shown to be related to these problems, it must be remembered that the individuals to whom reassurance will be provided, as well as the concerns chosen for alleviation, rest on social, political and economic decisions by those in power. Such choices require continued analysis and challenge.

Constructing the 'need' for prenatal diagnosis

While reassurance has been constructed to justify health professionals' offers of prenatal diagnosis, genetic testing and screening have also been presented in the same biomedical literature as responses to the 'needs' of pregnant women. They are seen as something they 'choose'. What does it mean, however, to 'need' prenatal diagnosis, to 'choose' to be tested?[52] Once again, a closer look at what appear to be obvious terms may illuminate some otherwise hidden aspects of geneticization and the prenatal diagnosis stories told in its voice.

We must first identify the concept of need as itself a problem and acknowledge that needs do not have intrinsic reality. Rather, needs are socially constructed and culture-bound, grounded in current history, dependent on context and, therefore, not universal.

With respect to prenatal diagnosis, 'need' seems to have been conceptualized predominantly in terms of changes in capabilities for fetal diagnoses: women only come to 'need' prenatal diagnosis after the test for some disorder has been developed. Moreover, the disorders to be sought are chosen exclusively by geneticists.[53] In addition, posing a 'need' for testing to reduce the probability that a woman will give birth to a child with some detectable characteristic rests on assumptions about the value of information, about which characteristics are or are not of value and about which risks should or should not be taken. These assumptions reflect almost exclusively a white, middle-class perspective.[54]

This conceptualization of need is propelled by several features of contemporary childbearing.[55] First, given North American culture, where major responsibility for family health care in general, for the fetus she carries and for the child she bears, is still allocated to a woman,[56] it is generally assumed that she must do all that is recommended or available to foster her child's health. At its extreme, this represents the pregnant woman as obliged to produce a healthy child. Prenatal diagnosis, as it is usually presented, falls into this category of behaviours recommended to pregnant women who would exercise their responsibilities as caregivers.[57] Consequently, to the extent that she is expected generally to do everything possible for the fetus/child, a woman may come to 'need' prenatal diagnosis, and take testing for granted. Moreover, since an expert usually offers testing, and careseekers are habituated to follow through with tests ordered by physicians,[58] it is hardly surprising that they will perceive a need to be tested.[59] With prenatal diagnosis presented as a 'way to avoid birth defects', to refuse testing, or perceive no need for it, becomes more difficult than to proceed with it.[60] This technology perversely creates a burden of not doing enough, a burden incurred when the technology is *not* used.[61]

A second feature, related to the first, is that women generally, and pregnant women specifically, are bombarded with behavioural directives[62] that are at least as likely to foster a sense of incompetence as to nourish a feeling of control.[63] It is therefore not surprising that a search for proof of competence is translated into a 'need' for testing; external verification takes precedence over the pregnant woman's sense of herself. Evidence that the fetus is developing as expected may provide some women with a sense that all is under control (although this suggestion has not been studied empirically to the best of my understanding). Personal experience is set aside in favour of external and measured evidence.[64] Moreover, given that a pregnant woman is more and more frequently reduced to a 'uterine environment',[65] and looked upon as herself presenting dangers to the fetus (especially if she eats improperly, smokes, drinks alcoholic beverages, takes medications, etc.), being tested becomes an early warning system to identify whether this 'environment' is adequate. Women who share these suspicions and doubt that they can have a healthy baby without professional aid are likely to subject themselves to tests that are offered.[66]

Third, prenatal diagnosis will necessarily be perceived as a 'need' in a context, such as ours, that automatically labels pregnant women 35 years and over a 'high-risk' group.[67] Although this risk labelling is, itself, socially rather than biologically determined,[68] women informed that they are 'at risk' may find it hard to refuse prenatal diagnosis or other measures that are advertised to be risk-reducing. Once again, however, this 'need' does not exist apart from the current context that created it by categorizing homogeneously those of 35 and older who are pregnant as 'at risk'. Mere identification of oneself as a member of a 'high risk' group may influence the interpretation of an absolute risk figure[69] and the acceptance of a test. In this light, the additional screening and testing possibilities generated by genome projects are likely to expand greatly the ranks of those deemed 'needy'.[70] As the number of factors or people labelled as risks or at risk increases, so, too, will offers of intervention.[71]

Fourth, as prenatal diagnosis becomes more and more routine for women 35 years and older in North America, the risks it seems to avoid (the birth of a child with Down syndrome) appear to be more ominous,[72] although the frequency of Down syndrome has not changed. This, too, may have a framing effect, generating a 'need' for prenatal testing among women in this age group. Interestingly, however, this perception may inadvertently influence both the implementation and the efficiency of proposed screening programmes designed to supplement risk estimates based on maternal age with information from maternal blood samples.[73] Having been socialized during the past fifteen to twenty years to view age 35 and over as the entry card to prenatal diagnosis, and convinced that once past this birthday they are 'at risk', how will women beyond this age respond when blood test results remove them statistically from those in 'need' of prenatal diagnosis? Will there be lingering doubts, and their sequelae, or will it be as easy to remove a risk label as it has been to affix one? What about the younger women who will have become prematurely aged (that is, eligible 'by age' for prenatal diagnosis though not yet 35)? As the title of a recent book phrases it, are pregnancy screening and fetal diagnosis *Calming or Harming?*[74] We neither have the data necessary to answer this question, nor do we give priority to studies that would be informative.[75] Instead, we proceed as if calming were a foregone conclusion. Programmatic changes such as these, no less than those subsequent to developments in genomics, underline how risk groups and needs are generated and constructed.

Fifth, on the collective level, prenatal diagnosis is generally presented as a response to the public health 'need' to reduce unacceptably high levels of perinatal mortality and morbidity associated with perceived increases in 'genetic' disorders. This reduction is of a special kind, in that prenatal diagnosis does not *prevent* the disease, as is usually claimed.[76] Yet, even this 'need', ostensibly based on 'hard' data demonstrating the size of the problems, is constructed. For example, geneticists say 'their' kinds of diseases are increasing as the prevalence of infectious diseases decreases, making genetic intervention seem appropriate. But others construe the same data as evidence of an increase in the 'new morbidity' of paediatrics (developmental delays, learning difficulties, chronic disease, emotional and behavioural problems, etc.), the problems of concern in *their* speciality.[77] Clearly, what one counts, emphasizes and treats as 'evidence'[78] depends on what one seeks as well as on the background beliefs generating the search. The numbers are then tallied, justifying a 'need' to do something.[79]

Moreover, unacceptably high rates of morbidity generate all sorts of 'needs'.[80] Reducing these solely to biomedical problems hides the range of potential responses that might be considered.

Viewing needs and demands as cultural creations within a social context leads to doubts that assumptions of 'free choice' with respect to the actual use of prenatal diagnosis are appropriate. It also clarifies why it is not fruitful to think that there may be a conflict between women who want prenatal diagnosis and critics who do not want them to have it. Not only does this polarization misinterpret the critics' position, but it fails to recognize, for example, that prenatal diagnosis cannot really be a choice when other alternatives are not available,[81] or that accepting testing as 'needed' may be a way for a woman to justify going through what is a problematic experience for her. Society does not truly accept children with disabilities or provide assistance for their nurturance. Thus, a woman may see no realistic alternative to diagnosing and aborting a fetus likely to be affected.

Parallel to the creation of a woman's 'need' for prenatal diagnosis is the development of health professionals' 'need' for technological solutions to problems of malformation. Thus, geneticists increasingly choose to use and develop prenatal diagnosis to deal with problems of malformation excluding, if not precluding, consideration of other approaches. They 'need' to employ these technologies, and in doing so they establish professional norms about how much is needed. Individual decisions about when a woman needs testing accumulate, and rapidly establish new standards for the profession.[82] The routine use of ultrasound to monitor all pregnancies is probably the most obvious example. Regardless of the driving forces for dependency on this technology, the result is the construction of a particular 'need': the basic 'need' to know the gestational age of the fetus; the additional 'need' to demonstrate that the pregnancy is progressing 'normally'. And the 'needs' grow.

'Needs' for prenatal diagnosis are being created simultaneously with refinements and extensions of testing techniques themselves.[83] In popular discourse – and with geneticists generally silent witnesses – genetic variations are being increasingly defined not just as problems, but, I suggest, as problems for which there is, or will be, a medical/technical solution. With but slight slippage these 'problems' come to be seen as *requiring* a medical solution. This again hides the extent to which even 'genetic' disease is a social/psychological experience as much as it is a biomedical one.[84] This process is likely to accelerate as gene mapping enlarges the numbers of individuals declared eligible for genetic testing and screening. Given the extent of human variation, the possiblities for constructing 'needs' are enormous.

Prenatal diagnosis and the social control of abortion and pregnancy

The third element in the prenatal discourse that I will consider here stems from the often told story that testing is an option that increases women's reproductive choices and control. This claim has had much attention in the literature and I will examine it only with respect to how some features of prenatal diagnosis do increase control, but allocate it to someone other than a pregnant woman herself. This is most apparent in the context of abortion.[85]

Without doubt, prenatal diagnosis has (re)defined the grounds for abortion[86] – who is justified in having a pregnancy terminated and why – and is a clear expression of the social control[87] inherent in this most powerful example of geneticization. Geneticists and their obstetrician colleagues are deciding which fetuses are healthy, what healthy means and who should be born, thus gaining power over decisions to continue or terminate pregnancies that pregnant women themselves may not always be permitted to make.

To the extent that specialists' knowledge determines who uses prenatal diagnosis and for what reasons, geneticists determine conditions that will be marginalized, objects of treatment or grounds for abortion.[88] Prenatal diagnosis is thus revealed as a biopolitical as well as a biomedical activity.[89] For example, an abortion may only be 'legal' in some countries if the fetus has some recognized disorder,[90] and the justifying disorder only becomes 'recognizable' because geneticists first decide to screen for it. Fuhrmann suggests that in Europe, in fact, geneticists significantly influenced legislators establishing limits within which abortion would be at all permissible, by arguing that access to abortion be maintained through a gestational age that reflected when results from amniocentesis might be available.[91] One wonders where limits might have been placed had first-trimester chorionic villus sampling been available *before* amniocentesis? Would they have been more restrictive?

Other potential participants in what should be an intensely personal matter for 'control' include insurance companies and governments.[92] If either funds genetic screening programmes or covers the cost of treatment for conditions diagnosable *in utero*, they may claim a say in determining which tests are carried out and what action the

results entail.[93] Recently circulated reports about a health main-
tenance organization planning to withdraw medical coverage for a
woman who could have avoided the birth of a child with cystic
fibrosis if she had 'chosen' to abort the pregnancy after the prenatal
diagnosis was made, gives substance to concerns about changes in
the locus of control.[94] While this kind of abuse of power grabs
headlines – and gets discounted as something regulations can
prevent – there are more subtle forms of control that achieve the
same ends and actually result from seemingly benevolent regulations and public policies. For example, newborn screening for
Phenylketonuria (PKU) is carried out in the United States with
universal approval. However, in only four states are health insurers
required to cover the cost of the special foods children with PKU
need.[95] What choices/control does a woman have in this context?
What are her options if prenatal diagnosis for PKU is offered? It
would not be unreasonable to believe that a pregnant woman who
learns that the fetus has the genes for PKU and does not see this as a
reason for abortion may feel compelled to terminate her pregnancy
because she could not herself finance the special diet her child would
require after birth. Such pressures (explicit and implicit) exerted on
a woman to abort a pregnancy following the prenatal diagnosis of
some problem that makes her unable to keep a pregnancy she wants
reveal another way in which social control over abortion may be
genetically based.

Policy decisions establish control, too, in the guise of guidelines
for seemingly straightforward features of prenatal screening and
testing programmes. For example, it has been shown that parents'
decisions about pregnancy termination for the same chromosome
abnormality are influenced by whether or not fetal anomalies are
visualized on ultrasound.[96] Even *who* does the counselling associated with prenatal diagnosis can influence what a woman does after
learning of a fetal chromosome abnormality;[97] rates of induced
abortion are higher when obstetricians relate the results of testing
than when geneticists do.[98] Similarly, the interval between prenatal
diagnosis counselling and testing is of consequence. This is demonstrated clearly in the reported association between the rates of
amniocentesis utilization and the interval between counselling and
testing: the shorter the interval, the greater the use.[99] Pressure from
state policies establishing when (as well as how)[100] genetic counselling will be provided to screening programme participants may be
covert, but this does not prevent it from being controlling. In sum,

prenatal testing and screening may provide control. But for whom? To what ends? For whose benefit?

THE CONTEXT OF GENETICIZATION

I now turn from the specific stories being told about prenatal diagnosis to the circumstances in which they are being told, in an attempt to show the interactions between content and context. The links are numerous and the required analysis substantial. I shall concentrate here on the existence of the connections rather than on their critique. My overall thesis is that characteristics (political, economic, social) of the North American society in which prenatal diagnostic technologies have been developed determine how these techniques will influence how we define individual health, health care and the health care system. The same technology will have different consequences in different societies, so that exploring the characteristics of the system in which it is introduced is important.[101] The critical characteristics derive from current stratifications of North American society and the inequities with which they are associated.[102] These influence (and are influenced by) the use of prenatal technology in ways that laws, regulations or even ethical codes for screening and testing alone do not – and probably cannot – address.

Is the 'playing field' level?

Access to, a perceived need for and the use of either health care providers or the health care system vary markedly between people. The outcomes of these encounters (or of their non-occurrence) also are quite variable. A person with certain signs, characteristics or features may be referred to different people/services/systems for help.[103] Variations in the perspective and nature of the 'help', along with variations in people's approach to and use of these different services, mean that disease and illness are labelled and socialized differentially according to where one becomes situated.[104] The definition of and help offered for the same 'sickness' or characteristic will vary according to an individual's economic and social power. This variability distributes inequities in health problems and their resolution.

Moreover, since health-related naming and helping activities occur in a cultural/political context where restraints on options vary with a person's place in the society, 'life choices',[105] presented as ways to manage or avert health problems, will not be randomly distributed.[106] This certainly includes a 'choice' of asking for or accepting information obtainable through genetic screening tests. Again, societal differences, no less than individual psychological ones, underlie these differential behaviours.

Life circumstances, broadly defined, establish an individual's place in society. They act, therefore, as powerful restraints on health options from identification of a problem to approaches, by the individual or others, to its resolution, and they influence possible options, expectations and responses.[107] These dynamics establish the inequities, the contours/terrain of the society (the so-called 'playing field'), that will modulate the impact of genetic screening and testing just as the latter may themselves landscape the 'playing field' and its inequities. To illustrate this, I shall consider in very broad terms how two stratifications – gender and class – shape and are shaped by genetic testing and screening.[108] Although these are inseparably linked, I shall arbitrarily isolate each one to clarify the discussion.

Gender

Prenatal testing and screening represent techniques applied to women. How, when, why and by whom they are applied will be conditioned by prevailing attitudes about women, their bodies and their roles. Because the world in which genetic and other reproductive technologies are developing is gendered, it would be naive to think that these technologies can escape gendered use.[109] In this world, women are disadvantaged, generally powerless, and frequently socialized to follow authority and acquiesce in certain norms surrounding maternity and motherhood.[110] Furthermore, because a child's disability is viewed as a private problem for the family, the gendered attribution of responsibilities for family health to women obliges them to deal with it alone, whether by avoiding, reducing or managing disability. Prenatal diagnosis in such a context can hardly be 'neutral'.

Perhaps the most dramatic consequence of gender stratification for prenatal diagnosis is the (potential) use of genetic screening and testing to identify and select fetuses on the basis of their sex alone. Being female is of less value than being male, and the fetuses that are least valued are those most likely to be aborted.[111] Though generally condemned by North American geneticists,[112] and commonly considered unlikely when 'selection' entails a second-trimester abortion, the availability of chorionic villus sampling resurrects the problem anew, as if the timing of abortion were the (only) problematic aspect.[113] Because this use of prenatal diagnosis as a tool *against* women has had much attention in the literature, with one commentator calling it 'previctimization',[114] it will not be considered further here other than to emphasize that 'sex selection' is problematic no matter when it is carried out, whether or not it requires some technological assistance, and that preconceptional selection differs from postconceptional selection only with respect to process, not principles.[115] However it is done, it can only reinforce gender-based inequities.

Another consequence, less immediately obvious, is how the current applications of prenatal diagnosis are subtly entangled with another long-standing problematic for women: ageing.[116] Not only has the availability of prenatal diagnosis and professionally imposed limits on access to testing created the 'social category'[117] of 'the older woman at risk', considered above,[118] but, not unlike cosmetic surgery or estrogen replacement regimens, testing has been presented as another way for women to circumvent features of ageing,[119] with prenatal diagnosis supposed a tool *for* women. The increasing probability of chromosomal non-disjunction associated with increases in a woman's age[120] can be managed, just as can other bodily changes associated with 'getting older'. The biological 'failure' causing Down syndrome can be controlled and 'older' women need not be 'less fit'[121] for childbearing, just as wrinkles of the skin or hot flushes can be controlled. 'Old enough' to warrant control is getting younger all the time.[122] When age, whether chronological or 'equivalent',[123] is used as a principal criterion for prenatal diagnosis, it appears to be essential for defining a woman (and women in general). Age-based strata come to be seen strictly as fixed 'facts' of life, camouflaging the extent of their social production.[124]

Existing gender (and age) strata mean that procreation-linked testing and screening cannot but be *of* major consequence to women (irrespective of any consequences it may have *for* them).[125] Thus, the *geneticization* of pregnancy is following a trajectory similar to – but perhaps even more alienating than – that described and analysed eloquently by others studying the medicalization of pregnancy.[126] Once again, those with greater power – physicians – control powerful technologies to monitor, regulate and even obliterate the female body when they situate a fetus in conflict with a pregnant woman in the provision of obstetric care.[127] With dramatic images obtained by ultrasound, a presentation of the pregnant woman as a fetal container,[128] a uterine environment,[129] perhaps even a 'fetal abuser'[130] gains force. Once again, an underlying ideological premise that women's inadequacy can threaten the success of reproduction justifies some technological intervention, and this time the 'inadequacy' is innate. Purposefully or not, pre-natal testing and screening reinforce stereotyped gender definitions of women and traditional values regarding their behaviour. It would be particularly unfortunate, therefore, if realistic and serious con-cerns about increasing threats to women's already fragile abortion rights were to silence no less realistic and serious concerns about the place of prenatal diagnosis in a gendered society.

Economic class

Morbidity patterns associated with all aspects of procreation (fer-tility, abortion, pregnancy or giving birth, for example) have repeatedly been shown to be influenced by a woman's economic circumstances.[131] As previously noted, these circumstances are created and result from general class- and power-based inequities that determine how illness is named and treated (by the individual or others).[132] A woman's social (political) status will also lead in-escapably to 'classist' effects in the use of genetic testing, screening and the resulting information. Most simply, varying circumstances (and psychological differences) cause individuals to react to offers of testing and screening unequally, and differentials in the use of genetic services have repeatedly been observed.[133] For example, from the time amniocentesis first became available, utilization rates of prenatal diagnosis among women of 35 and over have been associated with a women's socio-economic status: those with more education or wealth undergo amniocentesis more often than women with less schooling or income. This is true even in Canada, where there is no direct financial charge for testing.[134] Whatever the exact reason,[135] the potential consequences of this distribution are similar. One is the possibility of a substantial socially created alteration in the epidemiology of chromosomal disorders: Down syndrome, which heretofore was generally unrelated to socio-demographic factors might no longer be so in the future. To the extent that use of prenatal diagnosis is class-specific, and abortion of fetuses with trisomy 21 the general pattern, so, too, will be the prevalence of this condition among births. Similarly, with 'routine' prenatal care automatically including an ultrasound examination of a woman early in her pregnancy, children with neural tube defects may be born increasingly out of proportion to women whose circumstances prevent early prenatal care – the poor and the powerless.[136] Leaving aside important questions about the priority to assign to this or any other sophisticated prenatal genetic screening programme in a society that does not guarantee access to adequate prenatal care for all women, establishing such programmes on today's 'playing field' may be more likely to reinforce than to reduce existing inequalities in the distribution of health problems.[137] The failure to reduce inequalities in health among social groups during the past forty years, despite the proliferation of other biomedical developments during this interval,[138] strengthens this concern.

The conditions of this playing field also, and unfortunately, mean that posing 'access' as an *isolated* problem of prenatal diagnosis may result in failure to grapple fully with the issue of who is (or can get) tested. If access is defined merely as having sufficiently affordable and geographically available services, class-based inequities are likely to persist. Comparable availability does not automatically lead to equity, especially when individuals start off unequally. If nothing else, inequities in the distribution of information will keep the poor excluded in a class-stratified society.[139] 'Access' may not even be a meaningful feature when the allocation of resources and services is controlled by those who develop and employ them, rather than by those on whom they are used.

With respect to genetic screening, particularly those programmes likely to follow gene mapping, the 'bumps' in the playing field deriving from class strata based on occupation may be of special pertinence, especially for women. The unequal distribution of workplace hazards by type of activity and the continued existence of female employment ghettos, combined with persisting racial discrimination, mean that some women will be seen as 'more' eligible for certain genetic screening tests than others. To the extent that one finds what one is looking for, the identification of only certain groups of workers as 'susceptible' to some putative workplace hazard might be used as a supposedly scientific justification for workplace discrimination.[140] Occupational segregation, no less than racial or residential segregation, is entangled with differential perceptions of the acceptability and 'appropriate' applicability of genetic testing. Will testing level – or build up further – 'bumps'?

CONCLUSION

There is an unlimited number of ways to tell stories about health and disease, and an extensive vocabulary exists for telling them. Yet today, an increasing number of these stories are being told in the same way and with the same language: genetics, genes and genetic technologies. These genetic presentations of health, disease and ways to deal with them are grounded in the political and social context of the storytellers. My concern has been to decipher some of the stories about prenatal genetic screening and testing, and to reveal alternative constructions and interpretations to those already written.

Prenatal testing and screening, as has been repeated throughout this text, are most often presented as ways to decrease disease, to spare families the pain of having a disabled child, and to enhance women's choice. The best-selling stories about them speak of reassurance, choice and control. As has also been suggested, this discourse presents a child born with some disorder requiring medical or surgical care as (exhibiting) a 'failure'.[141] This failed pregnancy theme is reinforced in counselling provided to these families when counsellors emphasize how most fetuses with an abnormality abort spontaneously during pregnancy, are 'naturally selected', as it were, and how prenatal testing is merely an improvement on nature.

Just as there are several ways to construe reassurance, choice and control, the birth of a child with a structural malformation or other problem, 'genetic' or otherwise, can be presented in other than biomedical terms. Is the story claiming that the pregnancy has malfunctioned (by not spontaneously aborting),[142] resulting in a baby with a malformation, any 'truer' than the story suggesting that *society* has malfunctioned because it cannot accommodate the disabled in its midst?[143] Social conditions are as enabling or disabling as biological conditions. Why are biological variations that create differences between individuals seen as preventable or avoidable while social conditions that create similar distinctions are likely to be perceived as intractable givens?[144]

While 'many people don't believe society has an obligation to adjust to the disabled individual',[145] there is nothing inherent in malformation that makes this so. Consequently, arguing that social changes are 'needed' to enable those with malformations to have rich lives is not an inherently less appropriate approach. Actually, it may be more appropriate, since malformation, a biomedical phenomenon, requires a social translation to become a 'problem'. Expanding prenatal diagnostic services may circumvent but will not solve the 'problem' of birth defects; they focus on disability, not on society's discriminatory practices.[146] They can, at best, make only a limited contribution to help women have offspring free of disabilities, despite recent articles proposing prenatal diagnosis and abortion as ways to 'improve' infant mortality and morbidity statistics.[147] Thus, as socio-political decisions about the place of genetic testing and screening in the health care system are made, it will be important to consider how problems are named and constructed so that we don't mistakenly assume the story told in the loudest voice is the only one – or that the 'bestseller' is best.

Unarguably, illness and disability *are* 'hard' (difficult) issues,[148] and no one wants to add to the unnecessary suffering of any individual. But being 'hard' neither makes illness or disability totally negative experiences,[149] nor does it mean they must all be eliminated or otherwise managed exclusively within the medical system. Women's desire for children without disability warrants complete public and private support. The question is how to provide this support in a way that does no harm.

To date, support has been constructed to comprise genetic screening and testing. This construction is, in many ways, a result of the current system of health-care delivery in North America and the economic pressures on it. At a time when cost containment is a dominant theme and a primary goal of policy-makers, identifying those with, or susceptible to, some condition and preventing the occurrence of the anticipated condition seem to 'make sense'. It coincides, too, with the risk–benefit approach currently applied to most social and environmental problems.[150] It corresponds with middle-class attitudes towards planning, consumers' rights and quality. But while this approach seems to 'make sense', it does not suffice as a justification for the use of these technologies. Though it is more than twenty years since the first fetal diagnosis of Down syndrome by amniocentesis, we do not yet know the full impact of prenatal testing and screening on women's total health, power and social standing.

When amniocentesis was introduced, abortion subsequent to a diagnosis of fetal abnormality was presented as a temporary necessity until treatment for the detected condition could be devised.[151] Advocates assumed that this would soon be forthcoming. With time, however, the gap between characterization and treatment of disease has widened.[152] New information from efforts at gene mapping will certainly increase the ability to detect, diagnose and screen, but not to treat. A human gene map will identify variations in DNA patterns. Genes that 'cause' a specific disease, as well as those associated with increased susceptibility to specific disorders, will be found. Simultaneously, prenatal screening and testing are evolving in a context where a 'genetic approach' to public health is gaining great favour.[153] All the variations that will be mapped can become targets of prenatal testing. Which targets will be selected in the quest for improved public health? And who will determine that they have been reached? Given the extraordinary degree of genetic variability within groups of people, what does 'genetic health' actually mean – and does it matter?

For society, genetic approaches to health problems are fundamentally expensive, individualized and private. Giving them priority diminishes incentives to challenge the existing system that creates illness no less than do genes. With prenatal screening and testing in particular, the genetic approach seems to provide a 'quick fix' to what is posed as a biological problem, directing attention away from society's construction of a biological reality *as* a problem and leaving the 'conditions that create social disadvantage or handicap . . . largely unchallenged'.[154]

Justice in the domain of health care has several definitions, but only one is generally employed in contemporary choice-and-control stories of genetic screening and testing. In these stories, justice is defined by the extent to which testing and screening programmes are available and accessible to all women.[155] Distributive justice is the goal: fair treatment requires access for all.

This definition seems insufficient. Access involves more than availability, even broadly defined. Not all individuals can respond similarly even to universally 'available' services and, even if they can, unfairness and injustice may continue. Thus, perhaps we need to introduce other concepts of justice when thinking about prenatal testing and how these programmes contribute to, or diminish, fairness in health and health care for women (and others). Do they ensure good for the greatest number (social justice),[156] given all the causes of perinatal morbidity and mortality? Do they recognize and seek to correct past discrimination (corrective justice), given current and historically based inequities in health? Will they level the playing field for women, for the poor?

One approach to justice is not necessarily better than another. In fact, depending on the circumstances, each one might be seen as 'better'. We need to keep these multiple routes to fairness in mind as we determine those to whom we wish to be fair and that for which fairness will be sought. For instance, human relationality may be as worthy of guarantees and respect as human autonomy;[157] 'individual good' is not always synonymous with 'common good', though social responsibility need not become paternalism. There are choices to be made and the choices will reflect our values and ideology. How we choose our culture (by the routes we take) is no less problematic than how we choose our children, and consequences from both will be among our legacies.[158]

Addressing these choices will itself be 'hard', and will require us to recognize and grapple with disjunction[159] between goals and needs – perhaps even 'rights' – on the social and on the individual levels. What seems to be appropriate or best for the individual may not be so for the collectives to which we all belong.[160] We need urgently to address these contradictions now, using our energies to situate, understand and maybe even in some way resolve them, rather than keep them at the periphery of our vision. We must confront the possible need to choose between what is unfortunate and what is unfair in the distribution and reduction of risks to health and well-being. We must also acknowledge how our compassion for an individual's situation may harm women's health in general if address-ing private needs dislocates provisions required for the public or solidifies existing inequities in women's positions. This disjunction is not unique to genetic screening and testing,[161] but is certainly echoed with force in this area.

This disjunction will make dialogue about the place of prenatal diagnosis in women's health care especially difficult (and, on occa-sion, tense). However, this only underscores the need to avoid pre-mature closure of discussion and to avoid reducing it to sterile debates between 'pros' and 'cons'. The issue is *not* between experts pro-moting technology and Luddites trying to retard science. It is not between women who 'want' prenatal diagnosis and women who don't want 'them' to have it. It is not a dispute between advocates of prenatal diagnosis who are seen as defending women's already fragile rights to abortion and critics who are said to be fuelling 'right-to-life' supporters seeking to impose limits on women (and their choices).[162] All of these themes are being played out, but to focus on them is to create false polarities and to trivialize the possible advantages and disadvantages of these technologies when trying to deal with women's health concerns. Moreover, it incorrectly decontextualizes these technologies, severing their essential relatedness to time and place and isolating them from the broader health and social policy agenda of which they are a part.

Consequently, it is imperative that we continue to listen to the stories being told about prenatal testing and screening with a critical ear, situate them in time and place, question their assumptions, demystify their language and metaphors and determine whether, and to what extent, they can empower women. These technologies warrant social analysis.[163] Not to examine repeatedly the tales and their tellers will be to abdicate responsibility to the generations that present and future genetic screening and testing programmes will, or will not, allow to be born. A perspective that makes us responsible for the future effects of our current activities, the well-intentioned and the unintended, may stimulate the imaginative re-vision required so that we consider not just 'where in the world' we are going with the new genetics,[164] but where we want to go and whether we in fact want genetics to lead us there.

ACKNOWLEDGEMENTS

This chapter, and the larger project from which it derives, would have been impossible without the support (emotional and intellectual) of an especially generous and thoughtful number of friends and colleagues who have nurtured my work and ideas (and, not infrequently, me) during the past several years. Some of these individuals are personal friends; others I've either met only recently or know only through their writing because of our common interests in and concern about the impact on women of reproductive and genetic technologies. Among the latter, Peggy McDonough, Christine Overall, Rayna Rapp, Janice Raymond and Barbara Katz Rothman have been of particular influence. In many ways, this chapter represents a synthesis of much of what they and I have said or written on various occasions in our interconnecting and overlapping commentaries. I have tried to disentangle who said/wrote what first so as to give credit where it is due, but I fear I have not always been successful. This means that the initiator of some argument or the coiner of some phrase may not be appropriately acknowledged here. I request forgiveness for these citational lapses and count on those whose work I have unconsciously adopted and adapted without credit to point them out.

I extend special gratitude, too, to Louise Bouchard, Myriam

Marrache and Marc Renaud, colleagues at the University of Montreal who helped me think through some aspects of this project during its earliest stages in its – and their – mother tongue.

I have benefited in many ways from my friends Gwynne Basen, Margrit Eichler, Patricia Kaufert, Karen Messing and Louise Vandelac. Their insightful ideas and comments have given depth and breadth to my own thinking about the issues discussed here, and their constant support has kept me going. Friendship with these very special women has enriched my life enormously.

The same is true of Ruth Hubbard, who graciously and thoughtfully shared her wisdom and provided encouragement. She was first to introduce many of the issues and concerns I address and her presence is apparent throughout this text. Her proposal that I use the opportunity of this chapter to pull together several partial manuscripts I had been carrying around, on paper and in my head, was, moreover, just the stimulus needed to get me going at a time when this project was stalled and likely to remain so forever. But, while she is responsible for the process, any shortcomings in the product are mine alone.

There are others whom I would also like to thank: Marion Kaplan, the 'best friend' everyone should have who, with Irwin, was an extravagant donor of bed and board during my sojourn in New York; the staff at the Hastings Center for their hospitality and the occasion to get carried away in their library during my month there as a visiting international scholar in 1989; Ryk Edelstein and Bill Swetland, who made emergency house calls when my limited word-processing skills made manuscript drafts mysteriously disappear; Zeba Hashmi, who put up with multiple document conversions trying to harmonize her WP 5.0 with my 4.2 as we created the text and its multiple annotations; the Social Sciences and Humanities Research Council of Canada for providing funds to support research assistants for project-related studies that allowed me to meet and work with Fern Brunger, a graduate student who held my hand during my first steps in the world of critical medical anthropology, and provided clear evidence of how the best learning is a two-way street; the National Health Research Development Program of Health and Welfare Canada for a Scholar Award that provides my personal support; and finally, but perhaps most of all and with much love, Christopher and Jessica for being in my life.

NOTES

1 See notes 20–6 below and accompanying text for a discussion of these techniques.

2 In this chapter, the word 'stories' is not used to suggest that what is said is not true (this may or may not be the case). Rather it is used in a literary, not a legal, sense to capture the idea that how scientists present their observations and study results is no different from how novelists present *their* interpretations of the external world. 'Raw' material is shaped and interpreted to convey a message by both groups, with their constructions reflecting the prevailing social/cultural context. Further, to the degree that the same story is repeated and becomes accepted and used, it will itself begin to shape this context.

3 I attempt, in this way, to enter 'an old text from a new critical direction': A. Rich (1979) 'When we dead awaken', in *On Lies, Secrets and Silence* 35. I consider how stories about prenatal diagnosis both reflect and affect the social process of geneticization, how they emerge from existing cultural values at the same time as they interactively influence this very culture, altering our values, redefining our reality. See *infra*.nn. 101–40 and accompanying text. Using the biomedical and social science literature, and switching analogies, I want to creat a 'femmage', a 'sister concept' to the collage, wherein a composite describing these stories is created from multiple sources. See S. Price (1989) *Primitive Art in Civilized Places* 4 (quoting Meyer and Shapiro (1978) 'Waste not, want not: an inquiry into what women saved and assembled', *Heresies* 4: 66–9.

4 It should be emphasized that the priority given to matters of health is historically dependent and determined on a local level. These issues may not warrant political, economic or scientific attention in all places or at all times. A malady that is diagnosed and treated as a prevalent disease in one country may be diagnosed and treated completely differently in another country. See generally L. Payer (1988) *Medicine and Culture*.

5 See P. Wright and A. Treacher (eds) (1982) *The Problem of Medical Knowledge: Examining the Social Construction of Medicine* (hereinafter *The Problem of Medical Knowledge*); M. Lock and D. Gordon (1988) 'Relationship between society, culture, and biomedicine: introduction to the essays', in M. Lock and D. Gordon (eds) *Biomedicine Examined*, 11–18; Taussig, 'Reification and the consciousness of the patient', *Social Science and Medicine* 14: 3 (through reification, 'disease is recruited into serving the ideological needs of the social order'); Young, (1982) 'The anthropologies of illness and sickness', *Annual Review of Anthropology* 2: 257; Young (1981) 'When rational men fall sick: an inquiry into some assumptions made by medical anthropologists', *Culture Medicine and Psychology* 5: 317; see also Young (1982) 'Rational men and the explanatory model approach', *Culture, Medicine and Psychology* 6: 57 (containing Young's replies to comments directed towards 'When rational men fall sick').

6 See generally S. Tesh (1988) *Hidden Arguments: Political Ideology and Disease Prevention Policy* 3 ('there is an inextricable interrelationship

between facts and values, both in the search for the causes of disease and in the process of developing the best preventive policy').

7 See Laurell (1989) 'Social analysis of collective health in Latin America', *Social Science and Medicine* 28: 1183; M. Lock, 'Mind, matter and middle age: ideologies for the second sex', to be published in S. Lindenbaum and M. Lock (eds) *Analysis in Medical Anthropology.*

8 See L. Winner (1990) 'Is there any light under our bushel? Three modest proposals for S.T.S.', *Bulletin of Science, Technology and Society* 10: 12.

9 Woolhandler and Himmelstein (1989) 'Ideology in medical science: class in the clinic', *Social Science and Medicine* 28: 1205, 1206.

10 See generally H. Longino (1990) *Science as Social Knowledge: Values and Objectivity in Scientific Inquiry.*

11 E.g., Chui, Wong and Scriver (1991) 'The thalassemias and health care in Canada: a place for genetics in medicine', *Canadian Medical Association Journal* 144: 21; Koshland (1990) 'The rational approach to the irrational', *Science* 250: 189; Stead, Senner, Reddick and Lofgren (1990) 'Racial differences in susceptibility to infection by *Mycobacterium tuberculosis*', *New England Journal of Medicine* 322: 422, 426; Watson (1990) 'The Human Genome Project: past, present, and future', *Science* 248: 44.

12 E.g., Alexander (1989) 'The gene hunt', *Time*, 20 March 1989, 52; Beers (June 1990) 'The gene screen', *Vogue*, 236, 237; Montgomery (March 1990) 'The ultimate medicine', *Discover*, 60; Schmeck (1990) 'Battling the legacy of illness', *New York Times Good Health Magazine*, 28 April, 36.

13 See Council for Responsible Genetics (1990) 'Position paper on genetic discrimination', *Issues in Reproductive and Genetic Engineering* 3: 287 (criticizing the 'blueprint' notion); Newman (1988) 'Idealist biology', *Perspectives in Biology and Medicine* 31: 353, 361 (DNA is one component of a 'complex dynamical system', not a 'command center' that is impervious to environmental input); Rose (1984) 'Human perfectibility', *Lancet* ii: 1380–1 (emphasizing the effects of environment on DNA). See generally G. Lakoff and M. Johnson (1980) *Metaphors We Live By.*

14 Baird (1990) 'Genetics and health care: a paradigm shift', *Perspectives in Biology and Medicine* 33: 203–4.

15 See Lippman, A. (1991) 'Genetics and public health: means, goals and justices', *American Journal of Human Genetics* 48: 1201–2; A. Lippman, K. Messing and Mayer (1990) 'Is genome mapping the way to improve Canadians' health?' *Canadian Journal of Public Health* 81: 397, 398 (noting that 'undirected' studies of, for instance, 'environmental protection against genotoxicants or of nutritional supplementation during pregnancy', will suffer financially because funds are going to human genome mapping).

16 A. Lippman, 'La 'geneticiziation' da la vie' (unpublished manuscript presented at Seminaire, Lalonde-les-Maures, France, May 1990). A few years ago, in an article only recently rediscovered, Edlin described a process he called 'geneticizing' to refer to the tendency to label as 'genetic' diseases and disorders 'of possible polygenic-multifactorial

origin' for which there was, in fact, 'scant or no genetic evidence'. Edlin (1987) 'Inappropriate use of genetic terminology in medical research: a public health issue', *Perspectives in Biology and Medicine* 31: 47, 48. He argued that geneticizing led to premature categorization of diseases as genetic, and caused research funds to be allocated to genetic research to the detriment of other research. Ibid. at 48. I have deliberately chosen not to resurrect his term, since the processes I want to describe go beyond those that he emphasized. In this regard, too, the concept of geneticization goes beyond Yoxen's discussion of the 'construction' of genetic disease. Yoxen 'Constructing genetic diseases', in *The Problem of Medical Knowledge, supra* n. 5, at 144. Apparently, the term 'geneticism' was used even earlier in an essay by Sir Peter Medawar also to describe the inappropriate genetic labelling of variations between people. Medawar (1969) 'The genetic improvements of man', *Australasian Annals of Medicine* 18: 317, 319.

17 See R. Hubbard (1990) *The Politics of Women's Biology*, 52 (noting that in a less individualized society than ours, people might find many aspects of biology 'more interesting than heredity, genes and ... DNA'); Murphy (1979) 'The logic of medicine', *American Journal of Medicine* 66: 907, 908 (warning against a 'narrow concern with single genes' that 'destroys our vision of the human organism').

18 T. Duster (1990) *Backdoor to Eugenics*, 2. Duster defines the 'prism of heritability' as a 'way of perceiving traits and behaviors that attributes the major explanatory power to biological inheritance'. Ibid. at 164. In this definition, he is very close to Edlin's 'geneticizing'. See *supra* n. 16. However, only when Duster notes, but without detailed development of the theme, that labels will determine how we choose to respond to a problem, does he begin to incorporate all that I place under the rubric of geneticization. The concept of geneticization explicitly makes this an essential part of the process.

19 Rapp, R. (1988) 'The power of "positive" diagnosis: medical and maternal discourse on amniocentesis', in K. Michaelson (ed.) *Childbirth in America: Anthropological Perspectives* 103, 105. See generally R. Blatt (1988) *Prenatal Tests: What they are, their Benefits and Risks, and How to Decide Whether to Have them or Not.*

20 In amniocentesis, a hollow needle is inserted through a woman's abdomen and into the amniotic sac in order to remove a small sample of the fluid that surrounds the developing fetus. The procedure is usually preceded by an ultrasound examination to document the age of the fetus and its location so that an appropriate site for insertion of the amniocentesis needle can be chosen. The fluid that is removed – amniotic fluid – contains cells from the fetus that, if allowed to divide in the laboratory, can then be analysed. In particular, one can count the number of chromosomes in the cells, determine fetal sex and carry out biochemical and specific genetic analyses on these cells. Amniocentesis is performed at about sixteen to twenty weeks' gestation, the second trimester of pregnancy: before this time not enough fluid or enough cells are available. Once a fluid sample has been obtained, there is a further three- to four-week wait for the analyses to be completed and results to be

available, since it takes this long to grow a sufficient number of cells for study. Thus, if a fetus is found to be affected with the condition for which testing was done and the woman chooses to abort the pregnancy, the abortion is not induced until about the twentieth week, which is half-way through the pregnancy. See E. Nightingale and M. Goodman (1990) *Before Birth: Prenatal Testing for Genetic Disease*, 32–5. Recent technical developments that allow diagnoses to be made following amplification of the genetic material in a single cell can shorten considerably the time needed to obtain results. See *infra* n. 23 and accompanying text.

21   See *infra* n. 67 and accompanying text for a discussion of the social, rather than biological, bases for categorizing women over 35 as 'at risk'.

22   Over 150 'single gene' disorders can now be detected, and testing may be carried out for women who have a documented family history of one of these or who are otherwise known to be at increased risk. Testing is not carried out for these disorders without specific indications. See generally Antonarakis (1989) 'Diagnosis of genetic disorders at the DNA level', *New England Journal of Medicine* 320: 153 (reviewing recent progress in identifying single gene disorders).

23   In chorionic villus sampling (CVS), a small tube (catheter) is inserted through the vagina and cervix. It is then advanced, under ultrasound guidance, until it reaches the placenta, from which a small amount of tissue (chorionic villi) is removed. Some obstetricians now obtain a sample through a needle inserted into the abdomen instead. Any chromosomal or biochemical disorder can, in theory, be diagnosed with tissues obtained by CVS, because the cells of the fetus and placenta (which are formed from chorionic villi) are genetically the same. See Vekemans and Perry (1986) 'Cytogenic analysis of chorionic villi: a technical assessment', *Human Genetics* 72: 307. This procedure was first used successfully in China as early as 1975 to determine fetal sex. Tietung Hospital Department of Obstetrics and Gynaecology (1975) 'Fetal sex prediction by sex chromatin of chorionic villi cells during early pregnancy', *Chinese Medical Journal* 1: 117. CVS can be done as early as eight or nine weeks after a woman's last menstrual period and, while the results of tests carried out on the placental tissue can be available within hours, a two- or three-day waiting period is usually required. See Nightingale and Goodman, *Before Birth*, 35–6. If a woman chooses to abort the pregnancy following CVS, the abortion can be carried out in the first trimester. Finally, CVS does not appear more likely to cause a spontaneous abortion than amniocentesis. Canadian Collaborative CVS – Amniocentesis Clinical Trial Group (1989) 'Multi-centre randomised clinical trial of chorion villus sampling and amnio-centesis', *Lancet* i: 4.

24   During an ultrasound examination, high frequency sound waves are projected into the uterus; the sound waves that are reflected back are resolved visually to allow one to 'see' the fetus on a television-like display screen. A. Oakley (1984) *The Captured Womb: A History of the Medical Care of Pregnant Women*, 155–68.

25   See Nightingale and Goodman, *Before Birth*, 31–2. A consensus de-

velopment conference in the United States recently recommended reserving the use of ultrasound for pregnancies that may require it for specific medical reasons. Public Health Service, U.S. Department of Health and Human Services, Consensus Development Conference, *Diagnostic Ultrasound Imaging in Pregnancy*, 11 (National Institute of Health Publication no. 667). This recommendation is clearly not being followed and, at present, in many major North American teaching hospitals, almost all pregnant women are referred for two 'routine' ultrasound examinations – one before the twentieth week and one in the third trimester – for purposes of dating the pregnancy, even though the benefits of such a policy have not been established. Even more frequent scans are considered routine in France. As a specific tool for prenatal diagnosis, ultrasound can be used to identify certain malformations such as neural tube defects, cleft lip, or limb shortening in fetuses known to be at risk for one of these abnormalities. It can also be used to identify fetal sex. Most subtle malformations will not be identified when ultrasound is applied routinely on a non-diagnostic basis, however; the detailed examination that would be necessary requires more than the time that is usually allowed (or the machinery that is employed) when the primary goal is pregnancy dating. Nevertheless, some fetal problems can be diagnosed and their recognition may influence subsequent decisions about how pregnancy is managed.

26 See Chervenak, McCullough and Chervenak (1989) 'Prenatal informed consent for sonogram', *American Journal of Obstetrics and Gynecology* 161: 857, 860; Lippman (1986) 'Access to prenatal screening: who decides?' *Canadian J. Women L.* 1: 434. Chervenak and colleagues have recently called attention to the issue of informed consent for ultrasound, but their conclusions are troublesome. They consider the pregnant woman 'the patient's fiduciary', the 'patient' to them being the fetus. Chervenak, McCullough and Chervenak, *supra*, 858. This suggests that the consent process they propose will be coercive.

It is also worth noting that ultrasound is no longer the only genetic technology applied without prior consent. Screening for carriers of haemoglobin disorders, for example, is also done without the knowledge of the individuals being tested in certain jurisdictions. See Rowley, Loader, Sutera and Walden (1989) 'Do pregant women benefit from hemoglobinopathy carrier detection?' *Annals of the New York Academy of Sciences* 565: 152, 153. These authors noted that consent for sickle-cell and other haemoglobinopathies was not obtained because: 'Consent for screening was not routinely sought; providers agreed that obtaining timely informed consent required counseling approaching that to be provided to identified carriers and many providers declined to participate if they had to obtain it.' Rowley, *supra*, 153.

27 See generally 'Who decides?', 434.

28 Ibid.

29 See, e.g., Kolker (1989) 'Advances in prenatal diagnosis: social-psychological and policy issues', *International Journal of Technology Assessment Health Care* 5: 601; see also Dalgaard and Norby (1989) 'Autosomal dominant polycystic kidney disease in the 1980s' *Clinical*

Genetics 36: 320, 324 (placing importance on 'selective reproduction prevention').

30 See President's Commission for the Study of Ethical Problems in Medical and Biomedical and Behavioral Research, Screening and Counseling for Genetic Conditions (1983) *The Ethical, Social, and Legal Implications of Genetic Screening, Counseling, and Education Programs* 55 ('In sum, the fundamental value of genetic screening and counseling is their ability to enhance the opportunities for the individual to obtain information about their personal health and childbearing risks and to make autonomous and noncoerced choices based on that information.')

31 See B. Rothman (1989) *Recreating Motherhood: Ideology and Technology in a Patriarchal Society*, 21 (describing the 'commodification of life, towards treating people and parts of people . . . as commodities . . . . We work hard, some of us, at making the perfect product, what one of the doctors in the childbirth movement calls a "blue ribbon baby".'). See also Ewing (1990) 'Australian perspectives on embryo experimentation: an update', *Issues in Reproductive and Genetic Engineering* 3: 119; Rothman, 'The decision to have or not to have amniocentesis for prenatal diagnosis', in *Childbirth in America*, 92.

32 See Hill (1986) 'Your morality or mine? An inquiry into the ethics of human reproduction', *American Journal of Obstetrics and Gynecology* 154: 1173, 1178–80.

33 See generally Royal College of Physicians of London (1989) *Prenatal Diagnosis and Genetic Screening: Community and Service Implications*.

34 See, e.g., Women's Rights Litigation Clinic (1987) *Reproductive Laws for the 1990s: A Briefing Handbook*; 'Who decides?', 438.

35 P. McDonough (1990) 'Congenital disability and medical research: the development of amniocentesis', *Women and Health* 16: 137, 143–4. McDonough notes that three rationales for amniocentesis emerged from her survey: 'The procedure offered those at risk the possibility of "health" . . . . [it] provided parents with reassurance and avoided abortion . . . [and it] prevent[ed] disease and disability.' Ibid.

36 See, e.g., McClain (1983) 'Perceived risk and choice of childbirth service', *Social Science and Medicine* 17: 1857, 1862.

37 There is no evidence that control, autonomy and reassurance are actually enhanced and not merely assumed to occur. In fact, there have been very few in-depth studies in this area, and the conclusions of these investigations seem to vary with the orientation of the investigator. Studies reported in the social science and feminist literature suggest that prenatal diagnosis removes control; studies reported in the biomedical literature are interpreted to show how reassurance is provided. For an overview of these studies, see A. Lippman (1991) 'Research studies in applied human genetics: a quantitative analysis and critical review of recent (biomedical) literature', *American Journal of Medical Genetics* 41: 105–11. Much more ethnographic work in this area is required.

38 See *infra* text accompanying nn. 48–51 for a reconstruction of the notion of reassurance.

39 See *supra* nn. 31–2 and accompanying text.

40 This issue is discussed in A. Lippman (1991) 'Led astray by genetic

maps' (speech given Ottawa, Canada). Treatment, often said to be a goal of early identification of affected fetuses, becomes even less likely with CVS. Pharmaceutical companies will not be motivated to invest in developing treatments for conditions that 'need not occur'. Rarely will they base business decisions on their social worth rather than on their financial value.

This situation contains elements of an unusual conflict. Increasingly, geneticists are promising to have treatments available for a wide range of disorders and, for some conditions, therapeutic developments have occurred which make them far more benign than previously. The promises, and the available examples, are likely to be sufficiently persuasive that women 'at risk' may either make use of prenatal diagnosis less frequently or see less reason to abort an affected fetus than today. Yet, at the same time, the very availability of prenatal diagnosis and abortion may be seen as justifications for *not* investing in the further development of these therapies that parents will have been led to expect. Cf. Varekamp, Suurmeijer, Bröcker-Vriends *et al.* (1990) 'Carrier testing and prenatal diagnosis for hemophilia: experiences and attitudes of 549 potential and obligate carriers', *American Journal of Medical Genetics* 37: 147, 153 (noting decrease in haemophilia screening as treatment capabilities increased).

41 See Bell (1990) 'Prenatal diagnosis: current status and future trends', in *Human Genetic Information: Science, Law and Ethics*, 18–36 (Ciba Foundation Series). See also Kolker, above, n. 29, 612 (prevention is 'clearly cheaper than providing services for those with genetic disorders'); Modell (1990) 'Cystic fibrosis screening and community genetics', *Journal of Medical Genetics* 27: 475, 476 ('undesirable (diseases) may be all but eradicated'); Dalgaard and Norby 'Autosomal dominant polycystic kidney disease', 323–4 ('access to selective reproductive prevention' is important).

42 S. Wymelenberg (1990) *Science and Babies: Private Decisions, Public Dilemmas*, 130.

43 In fact, some consider the combined procedures of *in vitro* fertilization and embryo diagnosis to be 'ethically better' than prenatal diagnosis for detecting problems because it 'avoids' abortion. See Michael and Buckle (1990) 'Screening for genetic disorders: therapeutic abortion and IVF', *Journal of Medical Ethics* 16: 43. But see J. Testart (1990) *Le Monde diplomatique*, 24 (suggesting that it is the very need to consider abortion ('de terribles responsabilités') that is perhaps the best safeguard against ordinary eugenics ('l'eugenisme ordinaire')).

44 Brambati, Formigli, Tului and Simoni (1990) 'Selective reduction of quadruplet pregnancy at risk of β-thalassaemia', *Lancet* 336: 1325, 1326.

45 If nothing else, it is certainly preferable for their public image if geneticists are seen as reassuring women, rather than selecting their offspring.

46 Much of importance has been written about the link between prenatal diagnosis and eugenics; this dialogue, despite its importance, will not be repeated here. See generally T. Duster, *Backdoor to Eugenics*; Hubbard,

The Politics of Women's Biology; Degener (1990) 'Female self-determination between feminist claims and "voluntary" eugenics, between "rights" and ethics', in *Issues in Reproductive and Genetic Engineering* 3: 87; Hubbard (1987) 'Eugenics: new tools, old ideas', *Women and Health* 13: 225.

47 This point is not merely an argument of critics of prenatal diagnosis. Shaw, a geneticist-lawyer who strongly defends the principle of fetal protection, has written that 'any counselor who explains reproductive alternatives and offers a prenatal test to a counselee is a practicing eugenicist and any couple who chooses to avoid having babies with chromosome abnormalities or deleterious mutant genes is also practicing eugenics'. Shaw (1987) Letter to the Editor: 'Response to Hayden: presymptomatic and prenatal testing', *American Journal of Medical Genetics* 28: 765–6.

48 Rothschild (1989) 'Engineering birth: toward the perfectibility of man?' in S. Goldman (ed.) *Science, Technology and Social Progress* 2: 93.

49 See Anon (Dec. 1990) 'WIC program shows major benefits', *Nation's Health*, 3.

50 See Farrant (1985) 'Who's for amniocentesis? The politics of prenatal screening', in H. Homans (ed.) *The Sexual Politics of Reproduction*, 96, 120.

51 See Yankauer (1990) 'What infant mortality tells us', *American Journal of Public Health* 80: 653.

52 While those in need are identified explicitly as (certain) pregnant women, it is worth noting that clinical geneticists themselves have a need for this technology, too. For instance, when a child is born with a malformation, geneticists probably feel most 'helpful' when prenatal diagnosis, a technological palliative for the pains of etiologic ignorance, can be offered. Saying that the malformation is not likely to happen again, given the usually low empiric recurrence risks associated with most of these problems, is not nearly as comforting for genetic counsellors as is offering *in utero* detection. Counsellors 'need' this technique for the satisfactory performance of their jobs no less than they believe a family 'needs' prenatal diagnosis to prevent the birth of a second affected child.

53 See A. Lippman (1989) 'Prenatal diagnosis: reproductive choice? Reproductive control?' in C. Overall (ed.) *The Future of Human Reproduction*, 182, 187 (consideration of prenatal diagnosis as a professional resource).

54 See Nsiah-Jefferson (1988) 'Reproductive laws, women of color and low income women', in S. Cohen and N. Taub (eds) *Reproductive Laws for the 1990s*, 17–58 (discussing potential areas of cultural conflict in genetic counselling).

55 There is an extensive literature on 'medicalization' in general and on the medicalization of pregnancy and childbirth *per se* in which this discussion is rooted and from which it derives guidance. See, e.g., Oakley, *The Captured Womb*, 275. ('The medicalization of everyday life is a phenomenon described in many radical and liberal critiques of medicine.'); ibid., 276 ('For both birth and death normal signs have become neon lights flagging risks which demand and validate medical

intervention.'); Raymond (1984) 'Feminist ethics, ecology, and vision', in R. Arditti, R. Klein and S. Minden (eds) *Test-Tube Women*, 427–37; I. Zola (1977) 'Healthism and disabling medicalization', in I. Illich, I. Zola, J. McKnight *et al.* (1977) *Disabling Professions*, 41; Zola (1975). 'In the name of health and illness: on some socio-political consequences of medical influence', *Social Science and Medicine* 9: 83, 85–7 (noting that control by medical value is not achieved through political means but by 'medicalization'); Zola (1972) 'Medicine as an institution of social control', *Sociology Review* 20: 487; see also Lewin (1985) 'By design: reproductive strategies and the meaning of motherhood', in *Sexual Politics of Reproduction*, 123 (women 'must adapt' to 'motherhood' but can also approach it as 'active strategists').

56 See A. Oakley (1989) 'Smoking in pregnancy: smokescreen or risk factor? Towards a materialist analysis', *Sociology Health and Illness* 11: 311.

57 See Farrant, 'Who's for amniocentesis?', 96; Oakley, 'Smoking in pregnancy', 311.

58 See R. Hatcher and H. Thompson (1987) *Satisfaction with Obstetrical Care Among Canadian Women*, Kingston, Ontario: Health Services Research Unit, Department of Community Health, Queen's University (results of a survey showing pregnant women's reluctance to question medical authority).

59 See Lippman, 'Reproductive choice', 182. Physicians may pressurize women into being tested, even using false information to do so. Marteau, Kidd, Cook *et al.* (1989) 'Perceived risk not actual risk predicts uptake of amniocentesis', *British Journal of Obstetrics and Gynaecology* 96: 739.

60 See R. Hubbard and Henifin (1985) 'Genetic screening of prospective parents and of workers: some scientific and social issues', *International Journal of Health Services* 15: 231; B. Rothman 'The meaning of choice in reproductive technology', in *Test-Tube Women*, 23. I have previously discussed the 'burden' of decision-making in the context of genetic counselling and a similar 'burden' would seem to exist here. See Lippman-Hand and Fraser (1979) 'Genetic counseling I: parents' perceptions of uncertainty', *American Journal of Medical Genetics* 4: 51–71, 58–63; Lippman-Hand and Fraser (1979) 'Genetic counseling II: making reproductive choices', *American Journal of Medical Genetics* 4: 73–87. This theme is present in contemporary literature as demonstrated by Goldstein's reference to the 'momentous decision' that childbearing now involves. R. Goldstein (1983) *The Mind–Body Problem*, 200.

Hubbard and Henifin, in fact, identify a 'new Catch-22' wherein participating in a genetic screening programme may lead to a person's being identified as a 'genetic deviant', but failure to participate (or to abort a fetus diagnosed with a disorder *in utero*) may lead to her being labelled as a 'social deviant'. Hubbard and Henifin, 231–48.

61 The degree of this burden is demonstrated by the frequency with which women questioned about their reasons for having prenatal diagnosis say that they 'had no choice'. Sjögren and Uddenberg (1988) 'Decision making during the prenatal diagnostic procedure', *Prenatal Diagnosis*

8: 263. See Kirejczyk (1990) 'A question of meaning? Controversies about the NRT's in the Netherlands', *Issues in Reproductive and Genetic Engineering* 3: 23 (individuals often accept a medical technique because of fear that they might later regret not having done so); see also A. Finger (1990) *Past Due: A Story of Disability, Pregnancy and Birth*; Beck-Gernsheim (1988) 'From the pill to test-tube babies: new options, new pressures in reproductive behavior', in *Healing Technology: Feminist Perspectives* 23; Rapp (1987) 'Moral pioneers: women, men and fetuses in a frontier of reproductive technology', *Women and Health* 13: 101.

62 B. Rothman, *Recreating Motherhood*, 92–7. Women are expected to behave in accordance with norms set up by those in power. See Rodgers, 'Pregnancy as justifications for loss of judicial autonomy', in *The Future of Human Reproduction*, 174.

63 See, e.g., Fleischer (1990) 'Ready for any sacrifice? Women in IVF programmes', *Issues in Reproductive and Genetic Engineering* 3: 1 (referring to a 'code of good conduct' pregnant women ought to follow); see also M. De Koninck and F. Saillant (1981) *Essai sur la santé des femmes* Conseil du statut de la femme; A. Quéniart (1988) *Le Corps paradoxal: regards de femmes sur la maternité*; Simkin (1989) 'Childbearing in social context', *Women and Health* 15: 5 (all discussing the ideology of risk and behavioural expectations in pregnancy).

64 See B. Rothman, *Recreating Motherhood*, 92; Leuzinger and Rambert (1988) '"I can feel it – my baby is healthy": women's experiences with prenatal diagnosis in Switzerland', *Issues in Reproductive and Genetic Engineering* 1: 1153.

65 Cf. Levran, Dor, Rudak *et al.* (1990) 'Pregnancy potential of human oocytes – the effect of cryopreservation', *New England Journal of Medicine* 323: 1153, 1154 (hereinafter Levran); Sauer, Paulson and Lobo (1990) 'A preliminary report on oocyte donation extending reproductive potential to women over 40', *New England Journal of Medicine* 323: 1157, 1159.

66 See generally R. Blatt, *Prenatal Tests*; A. Lippman, 'Led astray by genetic maps'.

67 See Fuhrmann (1988) 'Impact, logistics and prospects of traditional prenatal diagnosis', *Clinical Genetics* 36: 378, 380. This categorization is more a cultural than biological creation. See Bourret (1988) 'Le temps, l'espace en génétique: intervention médicale et géographique sociale du gène', *Sciences Sociales et Santé* 6: 171; A. Lippman (1991) 'The geneticization of health and illness: implications for social practice' (manuscript in preparation based on presentation at National Association for Science, Technology and Society, Washington, D.C., 2 Feb. 1991). It reflects prevailing ideas about the kinds of children women should have and when the probability for them is or is not diminished. See Finkelstein (1990) 'Biomedicine and technocratic power', *Hastings Center Reports* 13, 14–16; see also *infra* n. 86 for a discussion of the role of genetics in creating these ideas.

Age has thus become more than an event, a birthday; it has been redefined as a marker, a risk, although nothing inherent in it makes it so. See Furhmann, *supra*, 380 (35 is the crucial age in North America);

J. Moatti, J. Lanoë, C. LeGalés *et al.* (1989) 'Economic assessment of prenatal diagnosis in France' (unpublished manuscript presented at Joint Meeting of European Health Economic Societies, Barcelona, Spain, 21–3 September) (age 38 in France); Sjögren and Uddenberg, 'Decision making', 263 (age 37 in Sweden). This age marker may even serve to stigmatize the 'older' woman. See Hubbard and Henifin, 'Genetic screening', 238. Further discussion of the arbitrariness of age 35 as a criterion for access to prenatal diagnosis can be found in 'Who decides?', 434; Vekemans and Lippman (1986) Letter to the Editor: 'Eligibility criteria for amniocentesis', *American Journal of Medical Genetics* 17: 531.

68   The many ways in which the concept of 'risk' is itself a cultural creation, unfortunately, cannot be given the attention they deserve here. However, it is useful to recall that the data used to assign people to risk categories reflects the information we choose to collect, and the problems that interest the collector. Alexander and M. Keirse (1989) 'Formal risk scoring', in I. Chalmers and M. Keirse (eds) *Effective Care in Pregnancy and Childbirth* I, 345, 346–7. It is also important to note that changes in the nature and number of things counted as risks are more prevalent than changes in the actual number of people 'at risk'; and that even using the term 'risk' to describe an event or experience is politically and socially dependent. Cf. L. Winner (1986) *The Whale and the Reactor: A Search for Limits in an Age of High Technology*, 142 (discussing risk versus hazards).

69   See Botkin (1990) 'Prenatal screening: professional standards and the limits of parental choice', *Obstetrics and Gynecology* 75: 875; Shiloh and Sagi (1989) 'Effect of framing on the perception of genetic recurrence risks', *American Journal of Medical Genetics* 33: 130.

70   A. Lippman, 'Led astray by genetic maps'. Human genome projects comprise the organized and directed international and national programmes to map and sequence all human genes. Some of these genes will be associated with recognizable disorders; others will be associated with biological variations of varying and mostly unknown consequence. See generally McKusick (1989) 'Mapping and sequencing the human genome', *New England Journal of Medicine* 320: 910; Watson, 'The Human Genome Project', 44. Differences between people will be identified, and while knowing the location and composition of human genes will add to our information about the latter, it will not reveal how the person with these genes will 'turn out'. See *supra* nn. 13–14 and accompanying text for a critical discussion of the limits of the genetic model.

71   Cf. Vallgarda (1989) 'Increased obstetric activity: a new meaning to "induced labor"?', *Journal of Epidemiology and Community Health* 43: 48, 51 (hypothesizing that, among other factors, the availability of new technologies such as electronic fetal monitoring leads to an increased number of interventions by practitioners).

72   This may be an example of what Tversky and Kahnemann have called the 'availability' heuristic. Tversky and Kahneman (1973) 'Availability: a heuristic for judging frequency and probability', *Cognitive Psychology*

5: 207. That is, having become familiar through constant reference to it and to prenatal diagnosis, Down syndrome may be perceived by the general population as 'worse' and as more frequent than it is statistically.

73 Until recently, the frequency of births of children with Down syndrome to women of different ages was the sole basis for estimating individual risks. Within the past few years, investigators have identified certain substances in blood samples from pregnant women that show a statistical association with the chromosomal status of the fetus. This additional information is now beginning to be used in conjunction with maternal age to estimate risks for Down syndrome. In some cases these data will increase a woman's putative risk above that associated with her age alone; in others, it will decrease it. When the numerical value of this risk equals or surpasses that associated with maternal age 35 alone ('35-equivalent'), prenatal diagnosis is generally offered. See Wald and Cuckle (1988) 'APF and age screening for Down syndrome', *American Journal of Medical Genetics* 31: 197.

74 J. Green (1990) *Calming or Harming? A Critical Review of Psychological Effects of Fetal Diagnosis on Pregnant Women*, Galton Institute 2nd series. In this context, the notion of 'iatrogenic anxiety' would seem pertinent. This anxiety may develop when laboratory analyses reveal chromosomal variations never before reported whose significance is unknown. The prevalence of iatrogenic anxiety among women being tested may be substantial, but its extent is currently unknown.

75 See Lippman, 'Research studies in applied human genetics'.

76 See, e.g., Modell (1990) 'Cystic fibrosis screening and community genetics', *Journal of Medical Genetics* 27: 475 ('Cystic fibrosis . . . is fast becoming preventable . . . [because] [t]he gene in which mutation can lead to CF . . . has recently been identified. . . . [This creates] an imminent need to set up population screening for CF carriers').

77 See, e.g., N. Zill and C. Schoenborn (1990) *Developmental, Learning, and Emotional Problems: Health of our Nation's Children*, National Center for Health Statistics, November 1990.

78 See H. Longino (1990) *Science as Social Knowledge: Values and Objectivity in Scientific Inquiry*, 38–48.

79 See Armstrong (1986) 'The invention of infant morality', *Sociology Health and Illness* 8: 211 (the idea of infant mortality was created by new measuring tools in statistics); Armstrong (1990) 'Use of the genealogical method in the exploration of chronic illness: a research note', *Social Science and Medicine* 30: 1225 (how increases in chronic disease are constructed).

80 Children with malformation and medical disorders will always be born, and avoiding their birth via prenatal diagnosis does not address the issue of preventing these problems or of ameliorating their effects on the child or the family. The former will require interventions that reduce environmental mutagens and teratogens, for example; the latter elicits interventions which have already been discussed. See *supra* text accompanying nn. 42–4.

81 See R. Hubbard, *The Politics of Women's Biology*, 198.

82 See Beck-Gernsheim, 'From the pill to test-tube babies', 28–9 ('It is

characteristic that new technologies, once available, produce new standards of what we ought to have.'); Lippman, 'Prenatal diagnosis', 182 (discussing professional establishment of criteria for testing and physicians' desires to comply with perceived medical standards).

83   These techniques are likely to be driven by financial considerations of the pharmaceutical companies developing them. See, e.g., D. Nelkin and L. Tancredi (1989) *Dangerous Diagnostics: The Social Power of Biological Information*, 33–6; A. Lippman, 'Led astray by genetic maps'; cf. Note (1991) 'Patents for critical pharmaceuticals: the AZT case', *American Journal of Law and Medicine* 17: 145 (analysing the validity of pharmaceutical companies' claims that without a federally granted monopoly, they would not have the incentive to research and develop orphan drugs).

84   See Shiloh, Waisbren and Levy (1989) 'A psychosocial model of a medical problem: maternal PKU', *Journal of Primary Prevention* 10: 51.

85   For thorough analyses of the question of women's control, see generally R. Rapp (1988) 'Chromosomes and communication: the discourse of genetic counseling', *Medical Anthropology Quarterly* 2: 143.

86   In fact, the avilability of amniocentesis 'influenced legislation so that the upper limit of gestational age for legally tolerated termination of pregnancy was adjusted to the requirements of second-trimester prenatal diagnosis in several countries'. Fuhrmann, 'Impact, logistics and prospects', 378. Evidently, geneticists can accomplish what women's groups cannot: a revisioning of abortion.

87   The term 'social control' is used in accord with its original use to embrace 'the widest range of influence and regulation imposed by society upon the individual'. D. Gordon (1988) 'Clinical science and clinical expertise: changing boundaries between art and science in medicine', in *Biomedicine Examined*, 257.

88   Lippman, 'Reproductive choice?', 187–92.

89   Finkelstein, 'Biomedicine and technocratic power', 14–16.

90   Fetal abnormality as grounds for abortion is of fairly recent vintage, having first become 'legal' in the United States in 1967 in response to a rubella epidemic. The Canadian Medical Association gave its approval the same year. Beck (1990) 'Eugenic abortion: an ethical critique', *Canadian Medical Association Journal* 143: 181–4. Today, members of the general population as well as physicians regularly and strongly agree that fetal abnormality is a justification for abortion. See Annas (1989) 'The Supreme Court, privacy and abortion', *New England Journal of Medicine* 321: 1200; Breslau (1987) 'Abortion of defective fetuses: attitudes of mothers of congenitally impaired children', *Journal of Marriage and Family* 49: 839; Varekamp *et al.*, 'Carrier testing and prenatal diagnosis', 147.

91   See Fuhrmann, 'Impact, logistics and prospects', 383–4. A recent example of the use of genetics to set social policy in this area is the position taken by the American Society of Human Genetics with respect to possible restrictions on abortion under consideration in various parts of the United States. This professional group has proposed as model legislation

that any pregnant female whose pregnancy has not reached the point of viability and who has been informed by a licensed or certified health care professional that her fetus (or fetuses) is/are likely to have a serious genetic or congenital disorder shall have the right, among other options, to choose to terminate her pregnancy. This right shall extend to situations where the female is at significantly increased risk of bearing a child with a serious disorder for which precise prenatal diagnosis is not available.

Letter from Phillip J. Riley to the author. The merits for/against this position aside, it certainly demonstrates how geneticists seek to influence the resolution of fundamentally political, legal (and ethical) problems.

92 Nsiah-Jefferson, 'Reproductive laws', 31–7, 39–41.
93 Billings (1990) 'Genetic discrimination: an ongoing survey', *Genewatch*, May 1990, 7–15.
94 See Billings, Kohn, de Cuevas and Beckwith (1991) 'Genetic discrimination as a consequence of genetic screening', *American Journal of Human Genetics*; see also Gostin (1991) 'Genetic discrimination: the use of genetically based diagnostic and prognostic tests by employers and insurers', *American Journal of Law and Medicine* 17: 109.
95 Brody (1990) 'A search to ban retardation in a new generation', *New York Times*, 7 June 1990, B9, col. 1 (citing Carol Kaufman) (the four states are Massachusetts, Montana, Texas and Washington). PKU reflects an inability to metabolize phenylalanine properly. It can be controlled by dietary restrictions.
96 Drugen, Greb, Johnson and Krivchenia (1990) 'Determinants of parental decisions to abort for chromosomal abnormalities', *Prenatal Diagnosis* 10: 483.
97 See Lippman-Hand and Fraser, 'Genetic counseling I', 51; 'Genetic counseling II', 73; Harper and Harris (1986) Editorial: 'Medical genetics in China: a western view', *Journal of Medical Genetics* 23: 385, 386–8 (noting role of 'genetic counselor as arbiter for permission to have additional children in China' or to abort child); Rapp, 'Chromosomes and communication', 143 (analysing messages conveyed in genetic counselling discourse); see also Puck (1981) 'Some considerations bearing on the doctrine of self-fulfilling prophecy in sex chromosome aneuploidy', *American Journal of Medical Genetics* 9: 129 (noting use of term 'syndrome' in prenatal diagnosis).
98 Homes-Seidle, Ryynanen and Lindenbaum (1987) 'Parental decisions regarding termination of pregnancy following prenatal detection of sex chromosome abnormality', *Prenatal Diagnosis* 7: 239, 241–3. See also Robinson, Bender and Linden (1989) 'Decisions following the intra-uterine diagnosis of sex chromosome aneuploidy', *American Journal of Medical Genetics* 34: 552. This raises an interesting question for the future as screening is further routinized and moves increasingly from geneticists to obstetricians.
99 Lorenz, Botti, Schmidt and Ladda (1985) 'Encouraging patients to undergo prenatal genetic testing before the day of amniocentesis', *Journal of Reproductive Medicine* 30: 933.

100 As possibilities for screening and testing expand, so, too, will the need to provide genetic counselling services to participants. The size of the resources required to do this appropriately may be enormous, if existing models for genetic counselling are to be followed. See Fraser (1974) 'Genetic counseling', *American Journal of Human Genetics* 26: 636. The consequences may also be enormous – however the programmes are designed.

101 Kranzberg (1990) 'The uses of history in studies of science, technology and society', *Bulletin of Science Technology and Society* 10: 6. These technologies are not neutral objects waiting for us to make good or evil use of them. Rather, the 'politics embodied in material things' from the very start (Winner 'Is there any light?', 12) give them 'valence' and make it essential to understand the social context in which a new device or practice is offered. Bush (1983) 'Women and the assessment of technology: to think, to be; to unthink, to free', in J. Rothschild (ed.) *Machina Ex Dea: Feminist Perspectives on Technology*, 154–6. The context, itself, not only influences the technologies we choose to develop but also presupposes certain approaches to their use. In turn, the use of any given technology will change the context, will change us. Technology is like a 'new organism insinuating itself and altering us irrevocably'. Boone (1988) 'Bad axioms in genetic engineering', *Hastings Center Reports*, Aug.–Sept. 1988, 9.

102 This issue is presented in fairly general terms here without the in-depth consideration that is being (and will be) developed elsewhere in the context of my larger project.

103 Waxler 'The social labeling perspective on illness and medical practices', in L. Eisenberg and A. Kleinman (eds) *The Relevance of Social Science to Medicine*, 283; Young, 'The anthropologies of illness and sickness', 257; Young, 'Rational men and the explanatory model approach', 57.

104 A recent example is the differential in rates of substance abuse reporting during pregnancy to public health authorities in Florida, with poor women being reported more often than others. Chasnoff, Landress and Barrett (1990) 'The prevalence of illicit drug or alcohol use during pregnancy and discrepancies in mandatory reporting in Pinellas County, Florida', *New England Journal of Medicine* 322: 1202. See also L. Whiteford and M. Poland (1989) 'Introduction', in L. Whiteford and M. Poland (eds) *New Approaches to Human Reproduction*, 1.

105 See Townsend (1990) 'Individual or social responsibility for premature death? Current controversies in the British debate about health', *International Journal of Health Services* 20: 373, 382–4 (noting that lifestyle is not just a matter of choice, and presenting an analysis of the many forces that shape what we too easily call choice); cf. Rosén, Hanning and Wall (1990) 'Changing smoking habits in Sweden: towards better health, but not for all', *International Journal of Epidemiology* 19: 316 (providing an example of where education contributes to increased inequities in health).

106 Young, 'Rational men and the explanatory model approach', 57.

107 See Kickbusch (1989) 'Self-care in health promotion', *Social Science and Medicine* 29: 125.

108 Other stratifications of consequence here based on ability, race, etc. are considered elsewhere. See generally A. Lippman, 'Led astray by genetic maps'; T. Duster, *Backdoor to Eugenics* (emphasizing racial and ethnic strata). In addition, inequities attached to genetic screening and testing relating to employment discrimination, insurance refusals and racial prejudice, for example, have been considered in detail elsewhere and these situations will not be reviewed specifically here. See, e.g., T. Duster, *Backdoor to Eugenics*; N. Holtzman (1989) *Proceed with Caution: Predicting Genetic Risks in the Recombinant DNA Era*; Billings, 'Genetic discrimination', 7, 15; Council for Responsible Genetics, 'Position paper on genetic discrimination', 287.

109 Some even suggest that they have been developed and used specifically to maintain gendered distinctions and increase patriarchal power. See, e.g., Morgan (1989) 'Of woman born? How old fashioned! – new reproductive technologies and women's oppression', in *The Future of Human Reproduction*, 60; Rowland (1984) 'Reproductive technologies: the Final Solution to the woman question?', in *Test-Tube Women*, 356.

110 See L. Whiteford and M. Poland (1989) *New Approaches to Human Reproduction* 1: 8–9; Raymond (1990) 'Reproductive gifts and gift giving: the altruistic woman', *Hastings Center Reports*, Nov.–Dec. 1990, 7; see also *supra* n. 61.

111 See, e.g., M. Warren (1985) *Gendercide: The Implications of Sex Selection*; B. Hoskins and H. Holmes (1984) 'Technology and prenatal femicide', in *Test-Tube Women*, 237; Rothschild, 'Engineering birth', 107.

112 E.g., Fletcher (1983) 'Is sex selection ethical?' in K. Berg and K. Tranoy (eds) *Research Ethics*, 333; Wertz and Fletcher (eds) (1988) 'Ethics and medical genetics in the United States: a national survey', *American Journal of Medical Genetics* 29: 815, 821 (Table V).

113 'Who decides?', 434; 'Reproductive choice?', 182.

114 Raymond (1981) 'Introduction', in H. Holmes, B. Hoskins and M. Gross (eds) *The Custom-Made Child? Women Centered Perspectives*, 177 (defining previctimization as 'the spectre of women being destroyed and sacrificed before even being born').

115 See generally G. Corea, R. Klein, J. Hanmer *et al.* (1987) *Man-Made Women: How New Reproductive Technologies Affect Women*; J. Hanmer (1983) 'Reproductive technology: the future for women?', in *Machina Ex Dea*, 183, 191 ('The questions of social scientists imply that sex predetermination is an accepted and acceptable idea. It is just a matter of finding out which method is preferred and when and how many children are desired.'); R. Rowland (1987) 'Technology and motherhood: reproductive choice reconsidered', *Signs* 12: 512.

116 Cf. E. Martin (1987) *The Woman in the Body: A Cultural Analysis of Reproduction*.

117 D. Nelkin and L. Tancredi, *Dangerous Diagnostics*, 17 (testing creates social categories 'in order to preserve existing social arrangements and to enhance the control of certain groups over others').

118 See *supra* nn. 67–71 and accompanying text.

119 These circumventions pale in comparison to the variety of pharmaceutical and surgical methods that can be applied to remove all age limits on the possibility of pregnancy for a woman. See, e.g., Levran *et al*. 'Pregnancy potential', 1153; Sauer, Paulson and Lobo 'A preliminary report on oocyte donation', 1157.

120 Hook, Cross and Schreinemachers (1983) 'Chromosomal abnormality rates at amniocentesis and in live-born infants', *Journal of the American Medical Association* 249: 2034.

121 Hubbard and Henifin, 'Genetic screening', 238.

122 Hubbard, *The Politics of Women's Biology*; Hubbard (1984) 'Personal courage is not enough: some hazards of childbearing in the 1980s', in *Test-Tube Women*, 331, 339.
      When amniocentesis was first introduced, 40 years was the age cut-off. This has dropped to 35 in North America, and recommendations that it be lowered further have been made. President's Commission, 81; Crandell, Lebherz and Tabsh (1986) 'Maternal age and amniocentesis: should this be lowered to 30 years?' *Prenatal Diagnosis* 6: 237, 241.

123 See *supra* n. 73.

124 See L. Rindfuss and Bumpass (1978) 'Age and the sociology of fertility: how old is too old?' in K. Taueber, L. Bumpass and J. Severt (eds) *Social Demography*, 43 (providing an overview of social definitions of childbearing age).

125 Its impact on their experience of pregnancy is enormous but will not be considered here. See Beeson (1984) 'Technological rhythms in pregnancy', in T. Duster and K. Garrett (eds) *Cultural Perspectives on Biological Knowledge*, 145; A. Lippman 'Led astray by genetic maps'; see also B. Rothman (1986) *The Tentative Pregnancy: Prenatal Diagnosis and the Future of Motherhood*.

126 See generally K. Michaelson (1988) 'Childbirth in America: a brief history and contemporary issues', in *Childbirth in America*, 1; A. Oakley, *The Captured Womb*; Fraser (1983) 'Selected perinatal procedures: scientific bases for use and psycho-social effects. A literature review', *Acta Obstetrica et Gynecologica Scandanavia* 117: 6 (Supp.); O'Reilly (1989) 'Small "p" politics: the midwifery example', in *The Future of Human Reproduction*, 159.

127 Board of Trustees, American Medical Association (1990) 'Legal interventions during pregnancy. Court-ordered medical treatments and legal penalties for potentially harmful behavior by pregnant women', *Journal of the American Medical Association* 264: 2663; Landwirth (1987) 'Fetal abuse and neglect: an emerging controversy', *Pediatrics* 79: 508 (discussing tension between fetal interests and maternal rights to privacy and self-determination).

128 Petchesky (1987) 'Fetal images: the power of visual culture in the politics of abortion', in M. Stanworth (ed.) *Reproductive Technologies: Gender, Motherhood and Medicine*, 57.

129 Morgan, 'Of woman born?', 65. For recent use of this term in the context of scientific studies, see *supra* n. 65 and accompanying text.

130 See Robertson (1983) 'Procreative liberty and the control of conception, pregnancy and childbirth', *Virginia Law Review* 69: 405, 438–43; Shaw

(1980) 'The potential plaintiff: preconceptional and prenatal torts', in A. Milunsky and G. Annas (eds) *Genetics and the Law* 2: 225.

131 E.g., Lazarus (1988) 'Poor women, poor outcomes: social class and reproductive health', in *Childbirth in America*, 39; Silins, Semenciw, Morrison *et al.* (1985) 'Risk factors for perinatal mortality in Canada', *Canadian Medical Association Journal* 133: 1214 (listing social class as a risk factor in stillbirths and infant deaths up to 7 years of age); Yankauer (1990) Editorial 'What infant mortality tells us', *American Journal of Public Health* 80: 653.

132 See *supra* text accompanying nn. 104–7.

133 Beeson 'Technological rhythms', 145; Roghmann, Doherty, Robinson *et al.* (1983) 'The selective utilization of prenatal genetic diagnosis: experiences of a regional program in upstate New York during the 1970s', *Medical Care* 21: 1111, 1122 (concluding that in use of prenatal genetic testing, '[t]he primary factor appears to be emotional acceptance by the patient . . . [but] [l]ack of knowledge, financial barriers, earlier prenatal care, and cooperation from the primary care sector are important'); Sokal, Byrd, Chen *et al.* (1980) 'Prenatal chromosomal diagnosis: racial and geographic variation for older women in Georgia', *Journal of the American Medical Association* 244: 1355 (study showing that 15 per cent of Georgia women 40 years and older underwent prenatal chromosomal diagnosis; use ranged from 60 per cent among whites in two large urban counties to 0.5 per cent among blacks outside Augusta and Atlanta health districts).

134 Lippman-Hand and Piper (1981) 'Prenatal diagnosis for the detection of Down syndrome: why are so few eligible women tested?', *Prenatal Diagnosis* 1: 249, 250.

135 Professional underreferral seems to be a factor in underutilization of prenatal diagnosis. Ibid., 255.

136 I do not suggest that all women *should* have an ultrasound exam early in a 'normal' pregnancy but merely point out what one of the effects of such a policy might be.

137 Bowman (1989) 'Legal and ethical issues in newborn screening', *Pediatrics* 83: 894, 895 (Supp.) ('If we ask poor mothers to participate in newborn screening programs and do not fight for universal prenatal care, equitable health care delivery, education, and adequate housing and food, then we are coconspirators in health deception.'); Lippman, Messing and Mayer, 'Is genome mapping the way to improve Canadians' health?', 398; Lippman, 'Genetics and public health'; Lippman, 'The geneticization of health'.

138 Acheson (1990) 'Public health – Edwin Chadwick and the world we live in', *Lancet* 336: 1482, 1483 (United Kingdom study suggesting that inequalities in health are present everywhere).

139 Cf. Stewart (1990) 'Access to health care for economically disadvantaged Canadians: a model', *Canadian Journal of Public Health* 81: 450, 452–3 (advocating education as one of four strategies to increase health care access for the poor). Omitted from discussion here, since it is being treated in detail elsewhere, is the marketing of susceptibility screening as a form of preventive medicine and its failure to acknowledge the

historical, political and economic determinants of health (by its focus on individuals) or the constraints on behavioural choice created by class (and other) stratifications. Lippman, 'The geneticization of health'.

140 See Andrews and Jaeger (1991) 'Confidentiality of genetic information in the workplace', *American Journal of Law and Medicine* 17: 75.

141 Dunstan (1988) 'Screening for fetal and genetic abnormality: social and ethical issues', *Journal of Medical Genetics* 25: 290.

142 Dunstan thus sees genetic screening and 'selective abortion' as a 'rationalized adjunct to natural processes' in which 'defective products' (babies) are 'discard[ed] spontaneously'. Ibid., 292.

143 For a full development of these ideas, see Asch (1988) 'Reproductive technology and disability', in *Reproductive Laws for the 1990s*, 69; A. Asch and M. Fine (1988) 'Shared dreams: a left perspective on disability rights and reproductive rights', in M. Fine and A. Asch (eds) *Women with Disabilities*, 297.

144 There would seem to be similar assumptions beneath the transformation of problems with dirty workplaces into problems with women workers who may become pregnant. See, e.g., Bertin (1988) 'Women's health and women's rights: reproductive health hazards in the workplace', in *Healing Technology* 289, 297 (advocating legislation requiring safe workplaces and prohibiting sterility requirements); Woolhandler and Himmelstein, 'Ideology in medical science', 1205.

145 Levin (1990) 'International perspectives on treatment choice in neonatal intensive care units', *Social Science and Medicine* 30: 901, 903 (citation omitted).

146 For a further discussion on this, see McDonough, 'Congenital disability', 149.

147 Powell-Griner and Woolbright (1990) 'Trends in infant deaths from congenital anomalies: results from England and Wales, Scotland, Sweden and the United States', *International Journal of Epidemiology* 19: 391, 397 (probable that level of infant mortality will be influenced by prenatal screening and selective abortion); Saari-Kemppainen, Karjalainen, Ylostalo *et al.* (1990) 'Ultrasound screening and perinatal mortality: controlled trial of systematic one-stage screening in pregnancy', *Lancet* 336: 387, 391 (Researchers of ultrasound screening in Helsinki, Finland, concluded that '[t]he decrease in perinatal mortality of about half in this trial can be explained mainly by the detection of major fetal anomalies by ultrasound screening and the subsequent termination of these pregnancies').

148 Lippman, 'Genetics and public health'. See Finger, *Past Due*; P. Kaufert (1990) 'The production of medical knowledge: genes, embryos and public policy' (paper presented at Gender, Science and Medicine II conference, Toronto, Ontario, 2 Nov. 1990). Moreover, illness and disability are *hard* (i.e., difficult) issues partly because society defines them as such, in its decisions about how (not) to allocate resources to deal with them. Unfortunately, since resources are always 'scarce', the programmes that do (not) get supported will merely be those which policymakers choose (not) to fund. No specific choice is inherent in the limited budgets available, although the requirements that choices be

made is. In choosing how to deal with health problems, budget limitations may sometimes be secondary to limitations in our visions about what to do. And, in choosing how to approach (even) 'hard' issues, genetic prevention is only one possibility.

149 Asch, 'Reproductive technology and disability', 70.

150 Cf. Winner, *The Whale and the Ractor.*

151 See Friedmann (1990) 'Opinion: the human genome project – some implications of extensive "reverse genetic" medicine', *American Journal of Human Genetics* 46: 407, 412.

152 Ibid., 411.

153 Lippman, Messing and Mayer, 'Is genome mapping the way to improve Canadians' health?', 397.

154 McDonough, 'Congenital disability', 149.

155 See, e.g., Cunningham and Kizer (1990) 'maternal serum alpha-fetoprotein screening: activities of state health agencies: a survey', *American Journal of Human Genetics* 47: 899 (arguing that state health agencies must accept that genetic services constitute a public health responsibility).

156 Lippman, 'Genetics and public health'. Cf. Shannon (1990) 'Public health's promise for the future: 1989 Presidential address', *American Journal of Public Health* 80: 909 (need for public health programmes to promote social justice).

157 Ryan, (1990) 'The argument for unlimited procreative liberty: a feminist critique', *Hastings Center Reports*, July–Aug., 6 (cautioning that human relationships must not be overlooked in the argument for an unlimited right to procreate).

158 See R. Chadwick (1987) 'Having children', in R. Chadwick (ed.) *Ethics, Reproduction and Genetic Control*, vol. 3 (prenatal diagnosis is not only a private matter); see also Edwards (1988) 'The importance of genetic disease and the need for prevention', *Philosophical Transactions of the Royal Society of London* 319: 211. Edwards identifies the 'conveyance of our genetic material from one generation to the next with the minimum of damage' as the 'biggest public health problem facing our species'. Ibid., 112. I adapt his comments as a further reminder of the essential interconnections between genes and culture: mutations cause genetic damage and we do make social and political choices that influence the rate of mutation.

159 I thank Margrit Eichler for suggesting this term and apologize if my use distorts her concept inappropriately.

160 Cf. Danis and Churchill (1991) 'Autonomy and the commonweal', *Hastings Center Reports*, Jan.–Feb. 1991, 25 (suggesting we can no longer avoid the conflict between individual wishes and societal needs and proposing, though with respect to other technologies, that we consider the concept of 'citizenship' in attempting to accommodate both levels); see also Fox (1990) 'The organization, outlook and evolution of American bioethics: a sociological perspective', in G. Weisz (ed.) *Social Science Perspectives on Medical Ethics*, 201.

161 Given that even viewing private and public as alternatives reflects our prior western beliefs that these are necessarily distinct spheres, it is of

interest that the notion of disjuncture seems to echo the lingering historical debate between 'healers' and 'hygienists' about the best way to deal with health problems. Generally, heroism in healing has had more appeal than the supposedly less glamorous work of the hygienist. See Loomis and Wing (1990) 'Is molecular epidemiology a germ theory for the end of the twentieth century?', *International Journal of Epidemiology* 19: 1.

162   Important to understanding this idea is the distinction between 'fetalists' and 'feminists'. J. Raymond (1987) 'Fetalists and feminists: they are not the same', in P. Spallone and D. Steinberg (eds) *Made to Order: The Myth of Reproductive and Genetic Progress*, 58. 'Feminist positions on the NRTs [new reproductive technologies] highlight the explicit subordination and manipulation of women and their bodies that are involved in these reproductive procedures . . . [while f]etalists are concerned with what they express as the "violence" done to the conceptus, embryo, or fetus in procedures such as IVF.' Ibid., 60–1.

163   In fact, we must be careful not to assume that all the social implications are ethical ones and to acknowledge that even deciding *what* the moral/ ethical questions are is not 'value free'. This is especially important because bioethical analyses tend to emphasize individual rights rather than the 'mutual obligations and interdependence' that may be critical determinants. G. Weisz (1990) 'Introduction', in *Social Science Perspectives*, 1, 3.

164   Fletcher (1989) 'Where in the world are we going with the new genetics?', *Journal of Contemporary Health Law Policy* 5: 33.

Chapter 8

Medical genetics and mental handicap

Lydia Sinclair and Matthew Griffiths

MENTAL HANDICAP

People with a mental handicap have difficulties both in understanding the world and how it works, and in operating successfully and effectively within it.

They have these difficulties because of an impairment. This impairment has been described as 'arrested or incomplete development of mind which includes impairment of intelligence and social functioning' (Mental Health Act 1983). These are difficulties of understanding (impairment of intelligence) and of operation (of social functioning).

The terminology used to describe these difficulties is subject to much debate. This chapter uses the term 'mental handicap' throughout to cover the Mental Health Act definitions of both 'mental impairment' and 'severe mental impairment' (*Re J* 1990). Mental handicap was chosen as being the most widely understood description of the difficulties people face in every aspect of their everyday lives. Other current terms include:

learning difficulties (education and educational legislation);
learning disabilities (Department of Health);
intellectual impairment;
intellectual disability;
mental disability;
intellectually challenged.

Whatever terminology is used to describe this impairment, we consider that it must be valid in a particular, specific or general context. For example, a child may quite correctly be described as having 'severe learning difficulties' by his teacher and an 'intellectual impairment' by a psychologist. If he is displaying bizarre behaviour, however, his mother is more likely to say, 'Please help me to hold on to my son – he has a mental handicap'. Mental handicap, in our view, includes a wide range of difficulties, which range from problems with abstract thought on the one hand, to an apparent unawareness of the world on the other.

Adults with a mild degree of mental handicap may never have the term applied to them at all. The difficulty they experience may not be generally apparent in their everyday lives. They may be in regular, unskilled or routine employment, be married, have children, and take part in the usual activities of their community. Their difficulties with abstractions, generalizations and sophisticated symbolic representation may never affect their social functioning, although they may be regarded as 'not very bright'.

People with a moderate mental handicap will be identified as having a disability. They will need support and some specialized services to enable them to operate in everyday life. They may benefit from the services provided for people with mental handicap, but they may also be stigmatized through being defined as individuals with a mental handicap. Benefits could be, for example, specialized services, additional social security entitlements, or exclusion from payment of Council Tax. However, the social stigma of disability and the label of mental handicap may well outweigh these material advantages.

People with a moderate mental handicap may also lack the capacity to make complex decisions, and many decisions will often be made by others on their behalf. Many decisions may be made without full consultation with the persons concerned even though they could, in fact, be involved.

People with a severe mental handicap will need considerable support in all or most aspects of day-to-day living. Although they may lack the capacity to make major decisions in their lives, they will be able to make choices with support and help if the information and decisions to be made are correctly presented.

People with profound mental handicap will often have additional physical or sensory disabilities, and will need to have all their needs met by others. They will need to be dressed, kept clean and safe. They will be able to respond and co-operate and participate.

The degree of impairment which a person is judged to have will influence:

his or her status in law;

his or her entitlement to financial support;
how life decisions are made on behalf of the person;
society's perception of the person's usefulness and worth.

MEDICAL DEFINITIONS OF MENTAL HANDICAP

Medical and legal intervention have resulted in mental handicap
being perceived in medico-legal terms. This is an inappropriate
model for difficulties which are actually cognitive and social and not
medical. Both doctors and lawyers make decisions which affect
many aspects of the life of a person with a mental handicap. These
include:

management;
care;
education;
(re)habilitation;
employment;
life decisions.

For example the diagnosis of Down syndrome is medical, and is
based on the presence of a specific extra chromosome. An individual
who has Down syndrome may be classed as severely mentally
impaired in law simply because he/she has that particular medical
condition. However, in reality, the diagnosis cannot predict anything
very specific about an individual's cognitive or social functioning.
He or she may have a mild, moderate, severe or profound mental
handicap. A few people with Down syndrome function within the
normal range. Medical and legal labelling processes may not recognize that two people with the same diagnosed condition, of the same
age, can be totally different in terms of both cognitive functioning
and social ability.

A mental impairment, defined in legal terms and based on a
medical diagnosis, may result in a range of decisions being taken
which are not taken by, or on behalf of, the rest of the population.
These decisions start before birth and may continue to be taken
throughout the individual's life.

Pre-birth

If a fetus is identified as having the potential or possibility of
developing into a baby who may have severe mental handicap, a

decision will be taken as to whether the pregnancy should be terminated or not (Abortion Act 1967; Human Fertilization and Embryology Act 1990). Severe disability is specifically singled out as grounds for termination.

This chapter will explore the ethical aspects of prenatal diagnosis and screening for genetic conditions, and the decisions which will be necessary if prenatal diagnosis or screening takes place.

At birth

If a child is born with the likelihood of a severe mental impairment together with a life-threatening condition, a decision may be taken about possible therapeutic interventions. Interventions which would be routine for non-intellectually impaired babies may be given only after a specific decision if the child has an impairment. The case of baby J illustrates this (*Re J* 1990). Baby J was born prematurely weighing 2 lbs and was kept alive on a ventilator after birth. He was considered to be severely brain-damaged with the likelihood of paralysis in all four limbs. He was made a ward of court. The High Court order that reventilation of J would not be in his best interests was approved by the Court of Appeal. This was on the grounds that it would not be in J's best interests for him to be given treatment (in this case reventilation if he should stop breathing) because it would cause increased suffering to J with no real benefit. The court came to the view that reventilation of J was distressing for him and hazardous to his life. Lord Justice Taylor reaffirmed the principle that a court could never sanction steps to terminate life and was only concerned with steps which should be taken to prolong life. The Court held that a court should judge the qualify of life which the child would have if the treatment were to be given and decide, on behalf of the child, whether such a life would be intolerable. Factors to consider would be the degree of disability, and any additional suffering or exacerbation of the disability that the treatment would cause.

In this case the court accepts its right to make judgements about the future quality of life of the child and to make assumptions about the child's own views, i.e. substituted judgements. The test was stated to be 'whether the child, if capable of exercising sound judgment, would consider the life tolerable'.

In childhood

Education

If a child has 'learning difficulties' within the meaning of the 1981 Education Act, a decision will have to be made about whether he or she is educated in an ordinary or a special school. This will be coupled with decisions about the curriculum he or she receives.

Medical treatment

Decisions may be made to carry out or withhold medical treatment which for other 'normal' children would be routine. For example:

removal of birthmarks;
pinning back protruding ears;
correcting squint;
cosmetic or corrective dentistry;
orthopaedic corrections.

In adolescence

During adolescence, decisions continue to be made about the education, social opportunities and medical care of young people with a mental handicap.

As young people get older, bigger and stronger, those who have difficult behaviour may be subject to decisions about restraint, either physical or through medication.

Young people with a mental handicap may also be the subjects of decisions about sterilization, the inhibition of menstruation or the chemical suppression of sexuality.

In adulthood

Any or all of the decisions which affect children in adolescence may be made or continued. Adults with a mental handicap are also subject to various decisions about their capacity to undertake a range of adult activities. These include:

consent to sexual activity;
consent to medical treatment;
capacity to vote;

competency to make a will;

competency to sign a contract, including a contract of marriage, a tenancy agreement, or the purchase or sale of a house etc.

Decisions may also be made about their competence to enter employment, become parents or manage any or all of their own affairs.

The authors believe that the ethical issues raised by these decisions are ignored in favour of 'practical' or pragmatic solutions.

The current state of legislation is not helpful to people making ethical judgements because there is an anomaly at the heart of all the legislation which seeks to give extra protection or extra entitlement to people with a mental handicap.

HUMAN AND CITIZENS' RIGHTS FOR THOSE WITH MENTAL HANDICAP

Problem: Lack of full educational, social, employment and other citizens' rights.

Attempted solution: Compensatory legislation for those with additional needs:

Education Act, 1981;
Children Act, 1989;
Disabled Persons Act, 1986;
Chronically Sick and Disabled Persons Act, 1970.

In the core areas, individuals are denied common citizens' rights. They are then given a range of extra exemptions and additional supports which should, in theory, compensate for the deficits in the core areas. Supportive, facilitating or protective legislation cannot, however, fully correct the effects of the fundamental non-observance of human and citizens' rights. For example, a person who is deprived of his citizen's rights to use public buildings and public transport is given a mobility allowance to compensate for this – but this attempt at compensation is of only limited value. This limitation arises both because of the inherent facts of disability, and because we live in a society which gives only patchy provision and support for the difficulties that accompany the disability, both for the affected individual and for his/her family.

How do prenatal genetic diagnosis and screening relate to this?

Genetic screening before birth is used (rarely) to allow the amelioration of some conditions, but is much more commonly used to select those pregnancies in which a termination may be the only medical intervention available. Testing seeks to identify disability or impairment in a fetus. Subsequent decisions will be based on the premise that an individual's likely disability is of such central importance in determining the worth of his/her life that those invididuals who may be disabled will be subject to different rules in deciding about termination during pregnancy (Abortion Act 1967; Human Fertilization and Embryology Act 1990). If tests are carried out, and the fetus is found to be at risk of disability, the question will be put: Should this impaired fetus be allowed to develop, or should the pregnancy be terminated?

MEDICAL/SCIENTIFIC TECHNOLOGY AND PERSONAL DECISIONS

The context of prenatal testing

There are, broadly, two groups of women who will undergo prenatal testing of the fetus during pregnancy, and who may be confronted by the question of whether to abort the pregnancy or to continue it and to plan for the future.

The first group comprises women who are identified as being in a 'high risk' category. These will include: women who are aware of genetic abnormality in their own or their partner's family; women who have already given birth to a child with a disability; and women who are concerned about health or environmental hazards during pregnancy. Many of these women will have been referred for diagnostic testing and, ideally, pre- and post-test counselling. Families tested will include those who know about or have thought about the practical, personal and ethical issues of giving birth to and bringing up a child with a disability. Each family will have unique personal and practical experiences to bring to this decision-making.

The second group comprises women who have not previously been identified as being at 'high risk', and for whom identification of disability in their fetus was made during routine prenatal screening. These women and their families may have no practical or personal experience of disability, and they will be faced with difficult practical and ethical decisions for which they have not been prepared. Counselling for these families is also essential and may not be so readily available because their needs have often not been properly recognized within NHS planning. In contrast to the first group, these women will be very largely dependent upon health-care professionals for information concerning the condition that has been identified in the fetus.

For both groups of women and their families the knowledge of a fetal disability is devastating, and the consequential decisions will be painful and difficult. A further concern is that the medical technology available to detect fetal abnormality has raced ahead of professional thinking about the effects of screening and the ethical issues which are raised. These difficulties are graphically illustrated in cases where the screening produces inaccurate information, or information of uncertain significance; no test is 100 per cent reliable, but fetal ultrasonography regularly reveals unusual features of uncertain prognostic importance. A further problem is that parents may have no knowledge of the technology and may find the information and scientific explanation difficult to understand. Patient and sympathetic professionals must explain and counsel families before and after testing. Treatment for detected abnormalities is far behind the advances in screening technology. Much medical information will therefore be given to families without any accompanying 'treatment programme'. Patients and their families usually expect a treatment plan from their doctor, and in this situation their expectations will be disappointed.

The fetal screening and diagnostic tests currently available to pregnant women include: (1) fetal ultrasonography, (2) amniocentesis, (3) chorionic villus sampling (CVS), and (4) maternal serum screening. Techniques for prenatal diagnosis carried out on test-tube conceptions before implantation in the womb are being developed. Of possibly wider future application may be the isolation and testing of fetal cells from blood samples taken from women in early pregnancy; this may become a practical proposition as a screening test to be offered to all pregnant women.

Amniocentesis, ultrasonography and CVS

A woman in a 'high risk' category will seek out or be advised to undergo chorionic villus sampling or amniocentesis, usually in conjunction with fetal ultrasonography. These tests will identify the baby's sex and be able to detect the specific chromosome abnormality, enzyme deficiency, or metabolic defect for which testing has been carried out. DNA analysis will identify genetic markers for certain inherited conditions including Huntington's disease, some muscular dystrophies and cystic fibrosis.

Women at standard risk of fetal abnormality will be offered the 'routine' tests. Ultrasonographic imaging of the fetus will identify disturbances of growth and malformations such as neural tube and skeletal defects and congenital heart disease. Amniocentesis (sampling the fluid from around the fetus) has been available for some years, and has become part of the 'routine' care offered to pregnant women of 35 years or older; in this context, it is performed primarily to detect fetuses with Down syndrome. It is also used to perform specific tests if a woman is at increased risk of carrying a fetus with certain other genetic conditions, or with a congenital malformation such as a neural tube defect. Chorionic villus sampling entails sampling the tissues that are derived from and that surround the fetus, and can be used instead of amniocentesis to examine the fetal chromosomes; it can also be used to detect metabolic abnormalities or to examine the fetal DNA when the fetus is already known to be at increased risk of certain specific inherited conditions. Although CVS can be used to obtain results at 10–12 weeks in a pregnancy instead of 4–8 weeks later, as with amniocentesis, CVS has the disadvantage of being associated with a higher risk of miscarriage. Maternal serum screening for alpha-fetoprotein and other substances can be used to identify pregnancies at increased risk of open neural tube defect (spina bifida or anencephaly) or of Down syndrome; it is not itself a diagnostic test, and so an obstetrician would usually suggest some other investigation (ultrasound or amniocentesis) if the serum screening indicated a risk that caused concern.

The information obtained from these commonly offered, 'routine' tests is not 100 per cent reliable, and for many of the conditions detected by the tests there is no effective treatment or cure. For these and other reasons the rationale for comprehensive screening has been questioned.

Advantages of testing

There are very few treatments for conditions identified by the routine ultrasound or amniocentesis screening tests. Treatment for some identified abnormalities may be available *in utero*. This applies, for example, in the case of the rhesus-positive fetus of a rhesus-negative mother who is producing antibodies that damage the fetal red blood cells, and where the fetus can benefit enormously from blood transfusions given over a period of weeks or months before the birth. However, this is not usually detected by fetal ultrasound or amniocentesis, and it is very uncommon for these routine genetic screening tests to detect conditions where such treatment *in utero* is beneficial to the fetus.

Some treatments immediately after birth may be important, and the knowledge of the abnormality during pregnancy will allow families to be informed, to seek professional advice and to make appropriate plans. Examples here include surgery for heart defects, blood transfusions for babies with anaemia, correction of sex hormone abnormalities, and corrective surgery and medication for some other conditions. However, in most circumstances the fact of diagnosing the condition before birth will make little difference to the outcome for the infant.

Difficulties of prenatal testing

For many fetal abnormalities there is no treatment and no cure. These are harsh and unremitting facts for women and their families to absorb. They will be presented with painful and difficult choices.

Although each family is in a unique position, the choices will be difficult both for those already identified as 'high risk' and for those who have just been made aware of their position. The prevailing social policy in England and Wales is reflected by the law providing for abortion. Under the Human Fertilization and Embryology Act (1990) and the Abortion Act (1967), abortion is generally available on medical and social grounds with the recommendations of two doctors, up to 24 weeks of gestation.

An exception to this is in cases where medical evidence indicates that 'there is substantial risk that if the child were born it would suffer from such physical or mental abnormalities as to be seriously handicapped' (Human Fertilization and Embryology Act 1990 S37 1(d)). In these cases an abortion is legal after 24 weeks of gestation. This law emphasizes the social policy of giving choice to women to decide about their own bodies and their future lives. The law also reflects another set of social attitudes which is that a 'damaged' or 'defective' fetus warrants special legal treatment becaue it is of less value than an 'undamaged fetus'. The mother's choice here is not simply to abort a baby for reasons connected with her own personal, medical or social circumstances but for reasons to do with the value of the fetus and its future as a person.

The laws in this country do not yet generally recognize the rights of a fetus as an independent person, a distinct individual. The debate about the rights of the fetus and personhood is important but will not be addressed in this article. The English legal system does recognize that a fetus damaged *in utero* by negligence can bring an action for damages (Re Congenital Disabilities (Civil Liability) Act 1976). There is, however, no right, in England, for the fetus to sue his or her mother.

It has been argued that the Human Fertilization and Embryology Act (1990) also reflects a social policy which wishes to restrict the birth of profoundly handicapped people. A disabled child will make enormous demands – practical, emotional and financial – on his or her immediate family, and also on social and medical provision by society. Parents of children with a mental handicap and workers in the field of mental handicap are very aware of the social, emotional and physical realities of caring for such a child. There is not enough social support, housing, education, jobs, day services and social security money to provide a dignified and caring environment for all babies with a mental handicap who will grow into adults.

PRENATAL TESTING AS DISCRIMINATION

These realities in themselves, however, should not influence decisions about the termination of pregnancies. To allow these reasons to be considered would be a dangerous step on a slippery slope to population selection on economic grounds. Society cannot, tacitly or actively, encourage measures to select for non-dependent members on the grounds that this is cost-effective.

'High-risk' mothers have other choices than termination of pregnancy. These include sterilization, adoption, artificial insemination by donor (AID), surrogacy or medical intervention where appropriate (e.g. diet). These choices all involve an assessment of future risk and preventative planning. All should be clearly explained.

Many decisions are made on the assumption that disability is itself a bad thing and should be avoided. That a child who is whole, healthy and 'undamaged' will have a 'better life', and that the mother and father and the rest of the family will have a better life is a powerful principle. Concerns to plan families, limit numbers of children and have healthy children are legitimate concerns for mothers and families. Decisions about 'quality of life' to do with size of family, economic stability, emotional strength also affect decisions to terminate a 'normal' fetus, e.g. 'three children would be too many'.

The difference in deciding not to give birth to a 'damaged' or 'disabled' child is that this decision selects the quality of the fetus as the major, or a major, reason for termination. The law allows this, and creates a special case for such 'late abortions' on the grounds of preventing future handicap. Other factors will influence a decision, but the crucial question here is the quality of the future child, currently *in utero*.

We argue that this social attitude of discrimination extends to post-birth situations and underlies social policy in planning for disability. Discrimination against people with disability is commonplace in this country. People with mental handicap are no exception. There is, as yet, no public or legal acknowledgement of this, and there are no plans to outlaw discrimination by statute. The provision of services for people with a mental handicap is a very low priority in most social and medical programmes.

We further argue that an assessment of the quality of a child, of a person, is an impossible task and should not be encouraged by statute or by social planning. There is no recipe for a 'healthy, happy, successful life' for either individuals or families. This will not depend on IQ, physical prowess, beauty, competence or any concept of 'wholeness' or 'damage'. It does depend, however, on life decisions.

The next section will look at some of these life decisions made by or for people with a mental handicap and the choices they face.

LEGAL DEFINITIONS

Legal definitions can change lives.

The Mental Health Act (1983) defines mental impairment as 'a state of arrested or incomplete development of mind which includes (severe or significant) impairment of social functioning and is associated with abnormally aggressive or seriously irresponsible conduct on the part of the person concerned' (Section 1(2) of the Mental Health Act (1983)). The definition used in the Mental Health Act (1959) was 'subnormality', and terminology used in the Mental Deficiency Act (1913) included 'idiot', 'imbecile' and 'feeble-minded'.

Mental health legislation in England and Wales and in Scotland is concerned mainly with compulsory admission and treatment of patients in hospital. This includes people with a mental handicap (impairment, disability) but the 1983 Act, by using the above definition, excludes from long-term compulsory admission all those who do not have a behavioural difficulty. The Act also uses a generic term of 'mental disorder' to allow short-term compulsory admission to hospital and this definition is broad enough to include people with a mental handicap who do not have 'difficult' behaviour. Mental disorder means 'mental illness, arrested or incomplete development of mind, psychopathic disorder and any other disorder or disability of mind' (S1 (2) Mental Health Act (1983)). In this Act the use of terminology has specific implications for admission to hospital, reception into guardianship, and the use of compulsion and imposition of hospital orders. The Act also provides for the management by the courts and the administration of the property and affairs of those who are 'incapable by reason of mental disorder' from doing those things for themselves (Section 93 (2), Mental Health Act (1983)).

Definitions of mental handicap, impairment and disability are used in other legislation, including the Sexual Offences Acts of 1956 and 1967. Under the provisions it will be an offence to have sexual intercourse with a person who has a 'severe mental handicap' and who cannot consent to sexual intercourse (Sexual Offences Acts (1956) Section 7, and (1967) Section 1(3) GA).

The clarification of severe mental impairment is important in assessing a person's capacity to consent to marriage, to make contracts, to make a will, to sign a tenancy agreement and to qualify for Council Tax exemption.

To qualify for services under the National Assistance Act 1948, the Chronically Sick and Disabled Persons Act 1970, the Education Act 1981, the Children Act 1989 and the NHS and Community Care Act 1990, a person must be assessed as 'disabled', 'a child in need', or 'a child with special educational needs'.

The National Assistance Act 1929 defines disability as follows:

persons who are blind, deaf or dumb or who suffer from mental disorder of any description and other persons who are substantially and permanently handicapped by illness, injury or congenital deformity or such other disability as may be prescribed by the Secretary of State.

The definition/labelling process is now essential to secure services or an assessment of needs. There is increasing pressure to establish registers of disabled adults and children for purposes of community planning. This process can be stigmatizing and is often viewed by carers and individuals with a disability as unproductive – a negative process with no positive benefits. Discrimination on grounds of disability remains a serious issue in this country. Disabled people continue to experience severe economic deprivation and social disadvantage (Bynoe *et al.* 1991).

People with a disability including mental handicap are subject to separate social and educational provision. This is despite the integrationist philosophy of the 1981 Education Act and the move towards 'normalization' and community living. Most people with a mental handicap, adults and children, live at home with their families or in community houses and a minority continue to live in long-stay institutions. They are subject to a whole range of decisions made on their behalf by parents/carers/professionals and others. This remains true despite the increase in self-representation by people with a mental handicap and despite the advocacy by others on their behalf.

Decisions are made by others usually on the grounds that this is in the person's 'best interests'. For all children who are under the age of 18, decisions are routinely made by parents or guardians – and for most personal matters the parents and guardians have the legal authority to do this.

All adults who are over the age of 18 have the right to make their own decisions, but for adults with a mental handicap many decisions continue to be made in their 'best interests' by others. These can be difficult personal decisions which involve important ethical questions and they may have serious practical consequences, especially in the area of relationships.

SEXUALITY, PERSONAL RELATIONSHIPS, MARRIAGE, REPRODUCTION

The following cases illustrate some ethical dilemmas.

(1) Jane is 20 years old. She has Down syndrome and is described as 'moderately mentally handicapped'. Jane has always lived at home. Since her parents' divorce, when she was 15 years old, she has lived with her mother. For two years, Jane's mother has discouraged her from attending a day activity centre because she is worried about her safety. Jane can read, play the piano and swim. Her father is concerned that she has little contact with friends of her own age and

no opportunities to develop her skills. Jane is competent to make her own decisions but has limited opportunity to obtain information for herself and to make decisions about her future.

When Jane was 14 years old she underwent surgery for removal of her appendix. At the request of her parents she was also sterilized. This was not discussed with Jane prior to her operation.

Jane's life has been 'protected' and 'guided' by her parents. She lives in a caring but limited environment with restricted choice of friends, relationships, education, jobs, housing. She is loved and well cared for but does not have control over her life. Decisions are made for her on the basis that she should not have a family life, marriage, children, a job or independent housing.

(2) Ann is 29 years old. She is described as 'severely mentally handicapped' and lives in a house provided by a voluntary organization with three other residents who are mentally handicapped. Ann had previously lived with her parents and moved to the house three years ago when her father had a heart attack. Ann goes to a day activity centre four days a week and takes part in most of the house activities. She needs help with washing, dressing and eating, but is slowly becoming more independent. She has made friends with a male resident, John, and enjoys parties and outings. She says she loves John.

Ann's parents have requested that she should not be alone with John and should not be given sex education or advice about contraception. They do not approve of her friendship with John and do not want her to have a sexual relationship. They are worried she might become pregnant and have asked Ann's doctor to recommend that she be sterilized.

Ann is an adult. She is unable to make a relationship with John without advice and help; she has no independent advocate to speak for her.

(3) Mary (29) and Jim (27) are a married couple, both of whom are described as 'moderately mentally handicapped'. They live together in a flat in a local authority housing project supported by a social worker and an advocate. Mary is pregnant. She has been told that social services will apply to the court for an order to remove the baby from her care after birth and that this will be with a view to long-term fostering and adoption. Mary's lawyer is now seeking expert medical and social evidence to prove that she and Jim are capable of being adequate parents and to identify the support they will need to do this.

Mary and Jim live in a social and legal system which establishes standards for acceptable child-rearing and family life. Their 'disability' may disqualify them from being parents unless they can prove otherwise.

All these cases illustrate how decisions are made on behalf of and about people with a mental handicap. Decisions are often made without consultation, and are based on judgements about what is socially acceptable and convenient.

This current situation is unacceptable; it fails to recognize the rights of people with mental handicap. Lawyers and others are currently debating the matter of who makes decisions for those who are not able to do so for themselves. The Law Commissions in England and Scotland have produced discussion documents about this, and have considered proposals for change (Scottish Law Commission, Discussion Paper 94; Law Commission, Consultation Papers 119 and 128, 129, 130).

The courts have, in recent years, addressed the question of medical treatment for people with mental handicap who are unable to make decisions about medical care.

The House of Lords' decision in the case of Re: F has endorsed the practice of sterilization for women (adults and minors) who lack capacity and for whom the operation is medically and/or socially recommended (Re F. H. L. 1989). The courts have declared that such operations are not unlawful if they are shown to be in the 'best interests' of the individual; 'best interests' are decided by the person's doctor.

Jane and Ann, described above, have been denied the right to make their own decisions about sexuality and parenthood. The courts have endorsed the practice of sterilization on medical and non-medical grounds. Social attitudes to sexuality, relationships and marriage for people with mental handicap reflect the view that decisions about these matters can be made by others in the person's 'best interests'.

Decisions about these matters are complex and difficult ones for everyone. For people who are mentally handicapped there may be additional practical, emotional and medical problems. There is real concern about exploitation and a need to protect vulnerable people from harm and abuse. This must be balanced with a respect of autonomy, a wish for personal development, and a real need to establish and enable advocacy by and on behalf of people with a mental handicap.

Sterilization of women who are mentally handicapped is usually proposed for a mixture of medical and social reasons. Different reasons are given to justify this drastic and often irreversible procedure. Problems with periods, risks of pregnancy, inability to be a mother are often cited reasons. Since the House of Lords' decision in Re: F, the courts continue to endorse sterilization on the grounds that this is in the person's 'best interests'. Court approval is not required if the operation is purported to be for strictly medical reasons. There has been very little publicly expressed concern about this, despite the serious nature of this procedure and the enormous ethical questions it raises.

RESOURCES: MEDICAL AND SOCIAL SUPPORT

It is the case that persons with disabilities will require support from their families and from society if they are to live a full life. This principle is recognized in government circulars, guidance and in legislation. The National Assistance Act 1948, the Disabled Persons (Consultation, Representation and Services) Act 1986, the Education Act 1981, the Children Act 1989 and the NHS and Community Care Act 1991 all reflect this commitment to social responsibility, to provision of service and support by the state. The reality is often disappointing, with inadequate or inappropriate day services, and insufficient residential care, housing, support and education.

The following case illustrates this failure:

(4) Lucy and Janet are in their twenties. They are described as 'moderately mentally handicapped' and were housed by social services in a council flat after many years of living in a long-stay hospital. They were assessed for independent living and supported in their move to this flat. After one month the social service file was closed and Lucy and Janet gradually became unable to manage. They lost their jobs, failed to pay their rent and other bills, removed all their furniture, and failed to eat properly or to clean the house. After two years they were discovered living in a dirty flat, with £3,000 rent arrears. This independent living arrangement failed because of inadequate practical and social support.

Although such problems can arise, those with mental handicap can be cared for successfully in the community.

(5) The final story is about Richard, a young man now aged 15 who

has a severe mental handicap caused by a genetic disorder and who has lived happily at home in the community with help and support. Richard might well have been aborted, but for a series of circumstances which meant that he was never identified as being likely to have a severe disability. His condition, Lesch-Nyhan syndrome, has been detectable *in utero* since the late 1960s because of a deficiency of a specific enzyme (HGPRT) in the brain, red blood cells and amniotic cells. Lesch-Nyhan syndrome is a sex-linked recessive condition that usually causes very severe and complex intellectual and physical disabilities.

Although Richard was his mother's sixth child, and all five of his older half-siblings were affected by the syndrome, she did not receive any counselling or advice, because the children were dispersed, either into local authority care or to live with other family members from the early months of their lives. This meant that the children were never seen together as a family, and so the fact that all three of the boys had severe disabilities and all three girls had mild disabilities did not have the impact it would otherwise have done. His mother was therefore not identified as being at high risk of a further handicapped child, and no specific tests were offered during her pregnancies.

Tests on all the half-siblings were carried out when Richard was 11, when one of the girls gave birth to a severely disabled baby. The family members were then traced, and tests were carried out on the five remaining children. The eldest boy was dead, the three girls are carriers and have mild mental handicaps and the two younger boys are severely affected by the syndrome.

Richard was born with severe disabilities. In addition to the Lesch-Nyhan syndrome he had Hirschprung's disease. A section of his colon had to be removed, and for a time he required a colostomy.

He was taken into care at three months and spent most of his early life in hospitals. At that time it was believed that he was too severely disabled ever to be placed in a family. His ethnic origins added to the problems of placing him (his 'un-place-ability'). Attitudes have changed since the early 1980s, but at that time only the belief and commitment of a senior social worker pioneered his move into a foster family as a first step towards finding a permanent family for him.

The search was successful. Richard has grown up in a family, attends a day school for children with severe learning difficulties, and is a member of an integrated youth club which he attends on Saturdays and during school holidays. He has very severe and complex disabilities, including the characteristic self-mutilation of Lesch-Nyhan syndrome; he bites his fingers severely from time to time and also bites the inside of his mouth and his upper arms. He cannot sit unsupported, has many athetoid movements, is doubly incontinent, has chewing and swallowing difficulties and his language development and speech are both very much affected. He requires total care in every aspect of his life. He is, however, alert, friendly and communicative. He enjoys many of the activities of other boys his age, including going to parties, ten-pin bowling, watching videos, swimming, and outings with family and friends. He is healthy, happy and enjoys life. His future is, however, less certain. He will always need a very high level of care and stimulating activity. Services for adults do not currently provide the range and intensity of support to meet his needs.

CONCLUSION

Despite advances in genetic screening and the availability of terminations of pregnancy, there will always be children born with mental handicap who will grow up to be adults. These will include children whose disability was:

non detected by prenatal diagnosis or screening;
undetectable by prenatal diagnosis or screening;
caused by factors occurring post-screening, or at birth;
caused during infancy or early childhood.

Among these will be children with profound, severe, moderate or mild handicap. They will all be subject to definitions for the purposes of entitlement to services and benefits. They will also be subject to discrimination and exclusion from society to a greater or lesser degree.

If advances in genetic screening and an acceptance of selective conception and abortion reflect and endorse the view that disability is undesirable, then these individuals will be excluded from society still further. Genetic screening programmes constitute an important means of 'legitimizing' discrimination and the exclusion of those with mental handicap from society.

Abby Lippman, in Chapter 7, 'Prenatal genetic testing and screening: Constructing needs and reinforcing inequities' (see pp. 142–86), forcefully argues for an honest analysis of scientific advances in genetic screening. She uses the term 'geneticization' to describe the process whereby individuals are reduced to identification by the DNA codes. She further identifies the contradictory principles inherent in prenatal diagnosis. These are that the testing is designed as a form of quality control for fetuses, but it is also a way to give women control over their pregnancies and their right to choose which children they will bear. The testing is also a means of reassurance to those women whose babies are found to have no detectable disorders.

The choice of termination is not always a real choice for families where the birth of a disabled child causes real hardship because there is inadequate social support. The decision will be forced by circumstances, and hence will inevitably be heavily influenced by social policy.

Clarke (1991), in addressing the work of clinical geneticists, argues that prenatal diagnosis and the 'offer' of pregnancy termination have secondary effects both on the mother's social and psychological welfare, and on people with a mental handicap who are living in society. He identifies the possible effect of this on the status of people with a mental handicap and on the provision of future service. These concerns are well founded. The conflicting reasons for genetic counselling, however, are not necessarily incompatible. Autonomy and choice for women must be based on full information about the medical/genetic facts of inheritance and about possible problems. This need for information will not necessarily conflict with a real commitment to valuing people with disability equally with all other members of society. To achieve this, a real dedication of educational, social and medical resources is necessary. Anti-discrimination legislation is needed to challenge unjustified discrimination and as a public statement of intent. A legal structure which addresses the human rights of all citizens is equally vital; the rights of those designated as belonging to supposedly 'less fortunate groups' should not be protected less securely than others'. The abortion law in England and Wales does exactly this – it selects a particular fetus for special treatment.

Whatever the future developments in the field of genetic screening, social attitudes of discrimination and exclusion must not be created or reinforced by social policy, or be reflected in present or future legislation. Ethical questions must be addressed alongside scientific ones. The power to do something does not necessarily justify it or make it the right thing to do.

REFERENCES

Bynoe, I., Oliver, M. and Barnes, C. (1991) 'Equal rights for disabled people. The case for a new law', Institute for Public Policy Research.

Clarke, A. (1991) 'Is non-directive genetic counselling possible?', *Lancet* 338: 998–1001.

Re Congenital Disabilities (Civil Liability) Act 1976, and *B.V. Islington Health Authority* v *Merton and Sutton Health Authority*, Court of Appeal 18 March 1992.

Re F. H. L, 4 May 1989.

Re J: A Minor (Wardship Medical Treatment) (1990) *The Times* Law Report 23 October 1990.

The Law Commission, Consultation Paper 119. 'Mentally incapacitated adults and decision making: an overview', and Consultation Papers 128, 129, 130, HMSO.

Scottish Law Commission, Discussion Paper 94. 'Mentally disabled adults: legal arrangements for managing their welfare and finances'.

Chapter 9

The rights and interests of children and those with a mental handicap

Jonathan Montgomery

Interests and rights are not identical concepts, although there is a link between them. In essence, my interests comprise those things that will bring me benefits. It is in my interests to remain healthy, receive good advice and be wealthy. But this does not mean that I have a right to all these things. We say that people have rights when their interests have been granted a special status. If a person has a right, then their interests justify imposing duties on others to respect or further those interests (Raz 1986: 165–92). Rights are therefore protected interests. Usually we are free to promote our own interests, even at the expense of others. However, when the rights of others are at stake, we are no longer free to pursue our own self-interest without regard for others. We must pay greater respect to the rights of others than we need pay to their general interests.

The way in which interests are upgraded into rights is also important. Rights can be merely moral rights, when the duties to respect them are no more than moral duties. They can also be legal rights, when a person's interests have led to other people being subject to legal obligations. Legal rights have more bite than moral ones because of the nature of the sanction that backs them up. There is also less controversy over whether legal rights exist than where moral rights alone are at issue, for legal rights can be identified in a more concrete way, through statutes and cases. Nevertheless, there is a wide range of methods that the law has used to enforce rights, and defining legal rights precisely is not always easy.

Rights therefore have greater force than ordinary interests because they enable the right-holder to claim respect from other people. Legal rights have a particular type of force: they are backed up by the threat of sanction. This chapter discusses the interests and legal rights of children and those with learning difficulties. This involves identifying the interests that are at stake, and whether they have been accorded priority over other people's freedom to do as they will, so that legal protection has been conferred. It also requires consideration of how the law prevents rights from being breached. Before this, however, it is necessary to ask what it is that distinguishes children and those with a mental handicap from other groups with whom genetic counsellors are concerned.

THE MENTALLY INCAPACITATED ADULT

In most cases, health professionals regard the agreement of their patients and clients as a precondition of any treatment they offer. To continue health care without consent would be both unethical and illegal. This basic rule is an expression of the right to determine what happens to one's own body. So far as the mentally incapacitated are concerned, the normal approach is impossible to operate. The defining characteristic of this group is precisely that they are unable to make the necessary choices. In these circumstances, any claim to a right to decide is meaningless. English law recognizes this and absolves health professionals of the obligation to obtain consent in relation to adults who lack the mental capacity to accept or refuse the care in question. Instead, the legal duty of the health professional is to act in the best interests of their patient or client. Should there be a dispute as to what is in their best interests, then care will be lawful provided that a responsible body of professionals in the relevant field accept that to provide it was within the margins of reasonable disagreement (*F* v *W. Berkshire HA* 1989). In effect, the law merely enforces the standards of the health professions.

It is therefore crucial to determine whether a client is competent to decide whether to accept the services of the genetic counsellor. If they are, then it is up to them what services to accept. If they are not, then the onus is on the professionals to do what they think is best for their clients. The views of the relatives of an adult who cannot consent have no legal status (other than as evidence as to what would be best for the client). The position in relation to children is more complex.

In England, the legal test for capacity has been developed primarily in the context of children, but it has general application. It is based on competence to understand the choices being made. Where a patient is able to understand the options they have the legal capacity to make the choice. Capacity must be assessed according to the particular decision in issue. The more serious the choice, the greater the understanding that is required. Life-and-death issues thus require a higher degree of comprehension of what is at stake than routine treatment for minor ailments (*Re T* 1992). It is unclear how much needs to be understood about the context in which the decisions are being taken. It has been argued by some judges that where contraception is concerned, children will have capacity to consent to treatment only when they can appreciate the moral and social implications of what they are doing. Others in the same case indicated that a narrower understanding of the issues would suffice (*Gillick* v *W. Norfolk & Wisbech HA* 1985).

Regrettably, this conflict has not been resolved and it remains unclear how much a client must be able to understand to consent to the investigation of their genetic status. However, it seems highly improbable that the courts would hold that genetic counsellors can only regard consent as valid when it is based on an understanding of eugenic issues. That would prevent many adults of average intelligence from being able to give a valid consent. It is likely that a lower degree of capacity will suffice. Clients are probably able to consent if they appreciate what they will have to do to provide a sample for a genetic test, what sort of information it is likely to provide, and (in outline) what will be done with that information. Where they have this degree of understanding, they should be treated as any other adult, whether or not they are defined as mentally handicappped for other purposes.

CHILDREN

The position in relation to children is more elaborate than that applying to mentally incapacitated adults. The difficulties can be divided into two categories. The first is concerned with determining when children should in fact be treated as adults, able to decide for themselves what happens to them. The second deals with the rights and responsibilities of parents.

Statute provides that children are able to consent to medical treatment as if they were adults once they reach the age of 16 (Family Law Reform Act 1969, section 8). However, this will not necessarily determine whether a child can consent to undergoing tests for their genetic status or receiving counselling. A young person who lacks the requisite understanding will be unable to consent even if they are 17. In addition, a younger child who can understand will be able to give a valid consent even though they have not reached the statutory age. The key is the degree of intellectual capacity, not age. The same problems arise as were outlined above in defining precisely what is required by way of understanding.

Where the position of children differs most from that of the mentally handicapped is in relation to what happens when they cannot validly consent. In relation to adults, responsibility for acting in the interests of the client passes to the health professional. Where children are concerned, it falls upon the parents to take decisions on their behalf. Geneticists must therefore turn to the parents for any consents that are needed. Parents are expected to exercise their rights to consent on behalf of their children in the interests of the children, but it is their responsibility to judge where those interests lie, not that of the health professionals. Although children will normally become competent to decide for themselves by at least the age of 16, the parental power to consent on their behalf continues until they are 18. The main implication of this is that where young people have learning difficulties and are incapable of choosing, their parents can consent on their behalf (see below for discussion of parental consent when a child can consent).

For legal purposes not all genetic parents will have the necessary status to give a legally valid consent. The crucial question is whether they have 'parental responsibility'. Mothers always will have, but a father will only automatically have it if he is married to the mother (either at the time of the birth or subsequently). A father who has never been married to the mother will only have parental responsibility if he is given it by court order, or if he has made a 'parental responsibility agreement' with the mother and registered it with the court. This agreement must be made on a prescribed form. If there are two people with parental responsibility, the consent of either of them will generally suffice. However, this rule will be displaced if a court order has been made specifically dealing with the matter.

An added complication has now been introduced to this area by two Court of Appeal decisions, led by Lord Donaldson, who has recently retired from the judiciary, that suggest that parents can consent even when their children refuse (*Re R* 1991; *Re J* 1992a). It used to be thought that once children were mature enough to be able to consent, their parents could no longer authorize treatment or tests. This meant that, once children were able to consent, they were in exactly the same position as adults. Counsellors would treat the competent child as their principal client in the same way as they would treat an adult. If the Court of Appeal is right to say that parents may consent even when a child refuses to do so, the position is much less clear. It would seem that parents may force their children to have genetic tests even against their wishes. Practical considerations indicate that this cannot really be the case in respect of counselling. Parents may force a child to attend a counsellor, but they cannot make them listen.

However, the effect of these two decisions on genetic counselling is likely to be limited. First, it is possible that the judgements will be overruled. The reasoning has been widely criticized as incompatible with general principles and in particular with the decision of the House of Lords in the Gillick decision (Montgomery 1992). Second, the mere fact that the parents consent does not mean that care must go ahead. The law ensures that decisions are taken jointly by parents and professionals. Parents have a veto because testing cannot be carried out without their consent, but by giving their consent they do no more than permit professionals to give care. To use the metaphor adopted by one judge, consent unlocks the door, but it is up to the health professions whether to go through it (*ReJ* 1990). It is now clear that the courts will not force health professionals to treat patients against their clinical judgement (*Re J* 1992b). Genetic counsellors are thus able to adopt the view that, even if it is legal to test for genetic status against the wishes of a child, it will rarely be ethical to do so.

In order to decide whether to make use of their power to obstruct parents who wish to force their children to be tested, counsellors will need to consider the rights and interests of the children concerned. The nature of these interests must therefore be examined.

THE RIGHTS AND INTERESTS AT STAKE

It has become orthodox to look for a framework for medical ethics to four cardinal principles: non-maleficence, beneficence, justice and autonomy (Beauchamp and Childress 1989; Gillon 1986). These principles are a means of expressing the moral (and often also legal) duties of health professionals to their patients and clients. They can also be described as defining those people's rights because the duties exist to protect their interests in being protected from harm, treated well, treated fairly and being free to determine the course of their own lives. In many respects, the interests and the rights of children and the mentally handicapped are the same as those of adults. The four basic principles apply.

However, the vulnerability of these groups, and the fact that they often play a dependent role within a family group, give rise to additional problems (Pullen 1990). It is therefore necessary to consider the need for extra protection to ensure that the interests that they have in common with adults are met as well as they would be with adults. There may be a need for health professionals to play an advocacy role to protect their clients that is unnecessary with articulate adults. Finally, it is worth considering whether there are additional rights, peculiar to the categories of people in question. These would reflect special interests that they have over and above those that the 'normal' adult population possesses.

Like everybody else, children and those with learning difficulties need to be protected from harm. This entails the existence of duties, both moral and legal, on others to refrain from causing such harm. In orthodox medical ethics this has become known as the principle of non-maleficence. Health professionals, parents and carers have a fundamental obligation to avoid harming those for whom they are responsible. If they do harm them, then they may be called to account in law, in extreme cases even by the criminal law.

In genetic counselling, the main concern will be for the potential that knowledge has for causing harm. Confronting a child with distressing and unsolicited information about their 'defective' genetic status can be defined as harmful. So too can revealing such information to others if it leads to embarrassment or ostracism, prejudices employment prospects, or reduces the availability of life or health insurance (or increases its cost). In one New Zealand case, a court found against a doctor who had informed a patient's husband that she was diagnosed as suffering from mental illness. The husband then confronted her with this information, causing her great distress. The court found that the doctor was obliged to compensate the patient for the harm caused by the negligent disclosure of his opinion of her (*Furniss* v *Fitchett* 1958).

A second cardinal principle of orthodox medical ethics is that of beneficence. Health professionals are not only bound to refrain from harming their patients/clients, they are also morally obliged to do them good. They should therefore practise in a way which actively promotes the well-being of their clients. Two major difficulties arise in respect of genetic counselling and those unable to take decisions for themselves. The first concerns the concept of benefit. There will be some cases where accurate identification of a genetic condition will lead to improved clinical management. Here it is clear that geneticists are able to promote patient health. However, genetic counselling is not usually aimed at 'curing' a client's condition. It is more often intended to enable them to make more informed choices about the way in which they live, and in particular about their reproductive plans. When clients cannot make these choices for themselves this type of benefit cannot be achieved (although it may be achievable in the future where children are concerned). Where this is the case, it is possible that the attempt to do good by counselling should be abandoned.

The second problem concerns the identity of the genetic counsellor's client. It is tempting to avoid the first problem by treating an adult carer as the person to be counselled. On this view the counsellor's duty to do good is satisfied by giving the carer the information needed to support their decisions. This makes sense where the decisions that carers will take will be intended to benefit the child or person with a mental handicap. However, genetic counsellors must be alert to the possibility that carers want information as much for their own benefit as for that of their charges. Where there is reason to believe that a carer will not act in the interests of the incapacitated person, then the principle of beneficence cannot justify counselling the carer, because it will be against the interests of the real client, the child or person with learning difficulties. Against this, counsellors will need to balance the possibility that carers will take decisions based on poor information if they are not counselled and that these may be even less in the interests of their charges. What is essential is that the interests of the child or handicapped person are distinguished from those of the carers and given precedence where they diverge.

Limited legal recognition is given to the principle of beneficence. All health professionals must live up to the standards of their calling. If they fail to practise in a way acceptable to a responsible body of their peers, they will be negligent (*Bolam* v *Friern HMC* 1957). Where a specialist area such as genetic counselling is concerned, then the standards will be set by practitioners in that speciality. Those who fail to reach the required standard can be made to pay compensation for any damage they cause by their negligence. As responsible genetic counsellors will seek to benefit their clients, the law of negligence requires that the principle of beneficence be respected. However, its scope is necessarily no wider than professional ethics dictates.

The third of the cardinal principles is that of justice. This can mean two main things in our context. The first is that those who cannot choose for themselves should not be denied access to appropriate services. This claim is poorly protected by law. The courts have refused to allow individuals to enforce the rights to services that are ostensibly set out in the National Health Service Acts. They have accepted that managerial decisions on resource allocation, and clinical judgements that services are not appropriate, cannot be overridden by judges (*R* v *Secretary of State for Social Services, W. Midlands RHA & Birmingham AHA, ex parte Hincks* 1980; *Re J* 1992b). The failure of courts to intervene means that access to genetic counselling services is dependent on health authorities voluntarily providing the necessary resources and on counsellors accepting clients. In this context, it may be in the interests of children and the mentally handicapped to have access to services, but those interests are not protected by the law and these groups cannot be said to have a legal right to services.

The second application of the principle of justice is that within a service that is offered, all clients should be treated fairly. It would be incompatible with this approach to regard the interests of the mentally incapacitated as less important than those of others, including carers. Here, the law provides some protection. Decisions that are made on the basis of irrelevant considerations may be struck down by the courts (*R* v *St Mary's Hospital, ex parte Harriott* 1988). However, whether the courts would consider the mental capacity of a client to be relevant or not to genetic counselling decisions is unclear. Treating people fairly does not always mean treating everyone the same. It may be quite proper to decline to offer genetic testing and counselling in respect of those who cannot choose for themselves what use to make of it. If the main purpose of counselling is to enhance autonomy and the clients will be unable to benefit, then it is rational to apply scarce resources on behalf of others.

The first sense of the principle of justice should be subordinated to the second. A denial of access to services will not be unjust if it is based on a fair consideration of a client's position. The crucial point is that decisions must be made about the positions of individual clients, and not on the basis of stereotypes. To fail to treat those who lack mental capacity as individuals with unique interests would be unjust. To decide that their interests do not indicate that genetic counselling services are appropriate, or point away from particular aspects of available services, can be perfectly just if it is based on unbiased consideration.

The final principle is the principle of autonomy. This demands that people should be free to shape the course of their own lives. Clearly, the application of autonomy to those with a mental handicap and to children is problematic. It is precisely their incapacity to make choices that marks them out from the 'normal' adult population. At this point, the two categories of people should be distinguished. The interests of children are very different from those of adults with learning difficulties. The former can be expected to become autonomous adults in the future, given the opportunity to do so. The latter may never attain the degree of mental capacity necessary to take control of their lives.

Where the client is a mentally handicapped adult the principle of autonomy requires little more than a sympathetic attitude. First, counsellors must presume that their clients are competent to take decisions. Only when they are fully satisfied that the clients are not competent should they disregard their claim to autonomy. Second, counsellors should explore different ways of explaining things to their clients. An apparent lack of mental capacity may be overcome by imaginative techniques of communication. In particular, the experience of the client should be examined to see whether it includes things that might provide meaningful analogies. Third, consideration should be given to the degree of technicality that is required when counselling is offered. It may be possible to provide sufficient information to broaden the choices available to a client, even when they cannot understand the full picture. These suggestions are all ways of seeking to provide autonomy. If no autonomy can be provided, then the principle can have no force.

These principles would also apply in the case of children, but there is more that can be said. The interest of children in autonomy is primarily that they should be able to exercise it in the future. Gerald Dworkin has explained this as follows:

> In the case of children . . . if it is expected that competence will be attained at some point, we ought to choose for them, not as they might want, but in terms of maximising those interests that will make it possible for them to develop life plans of their own. We ought to preserve their share of what John Rawls calls 'primary goods'; that is, such goods as liberty, health and opportunity, which any rational person would want to pursue whatever life plan he chooses.

> (Dworkin 1988: 96–7)

This insight highlights two crucial matters. The first is general, that children are entitled to the basic preconditions of life that will enable them to develop the skills of autonomy in the future. This can be expressed in terms of the principles of beneficence and non-maleficence. A proper understanding of beneficence would include working to help children to develop their ability to take choices. More fundamentally, the principle of non-maleficence includes maintaining a standard of health that will enable the child to act upon autonomous choices when they are older. Priority must be given to these tasks, for without them no other claims built on autonomy can bear fruit (Eekelaar 1986).

The second point that Dworkin's position identifies is particularly important for the genetic counsellors. It is that we should, where possible, seek to refrain from choosing on children's behalf. Instead, we should ensure that they can choose for themselves later. Some steps cannot be reversed once made. Generating genetic information is one of these. If the genetic status of children is identified, it precludes them from deciding (once able to do so) that it would be better if no one knew. The courts have recognized that if possible irreversible decisions should be left for children to make when they reach maturity (*Re D* 1976). This would suggest that where the principles of non-maleficence and beneficence do not provide a justification for immediate testing, it would be against the interests of children for their genetic status to be established. In such cases, the objective of counselling in respect of children should be to preserve their right to decide for themselves.

Before closing the catalogue of rights and interests, it is necessary to discuss the problems of control of information. In relation to adults, this can be linked to the principle of autonomy. There confidentiality exists to preserve the ability of clients to choose to keep their genetic status to themselves. Access to records enables them to acquire the information that they want in order to make choices. Where children are concerned, problems are created by the involvement of parents in health care decisions. If the argument set out in the previous paragraph is accepted, then genetic information that is available may need to be withheld from parents because, if they are given access to it, the child will not be able to decide later to keep it secret. Usually, parents are entitled to see their children's records under the Access to Health Records Act 1990 (applying to manual records created after 1 November 1991) and the Data Protection Act 1984 (for computerized records). However, health professionals are entitled to refuse access where they believe that revealing the information would cause serious harm to the physical or mental health of the child or others. As a result, genetic counsellors are not obliged to reveal information on the genetic status of a child when they believe it would harm the well-being of the child. This might include undermining their chances of taking decisions for themselves later.

This approach is inapplicable to those with a mental handicap, but it would be wrong to assume that it is therefore legitimate to make their genetic status public knowledge. It remains important to preserve the dignity and privacy of those with learning difficulties even though they will never be autonomous. In this case, it is perhaps necessary to link confidentiality with the principle of non-maleficence rather than autonomy. Where exposing genetic deficiencies would adversely affect the client's position it clearly should not be done.

THE INTERESTS OF FUTURE CHILDREN

A different set of problems arises when the interests of future children are considered. How far are those being counselled free to disregard the fact that the choices that they make may affect the position of a person who is yet to be conceived? What responsibilities do genetic counsellors have to potential children? The first argument that must be appraised is whether these future children have a right to be born, so that contributing to a decision to prevent their conception or birth is immoral. The second contention is the opposite of the first, that it is actually in the interests of some people who would have genetic diseases not to be born. This debate involves an imaginative leap, for it is difficult to make sense of the idea of a non-existent being having interests. Yet the very project of genetic counselling is built on the premise that at least some clients believe that it is better to avoid some types of life. This position can only be sustained if unborn and also as-yet-unconceived children have no right to be brought into the world, for if they do it would be wrong to deny them the chance to be conceived. Instead we must show that prospective parents are free to judge whether they wish to risk creating a life that is marred by a genetic defect.

It is certainly plausible to suggest that in most circumstances some life is better than no life at all. At least then there is a chance to make something of existence. On this view, unless the predicted genetic condition is incompatible with any tolerable quality of life, it is arguably in a person's interests to be born. Even if this were accepted, however, it would be very much more difficult to build out of the argument a right to be conceived. It would entail a complete ban on contraception and could even extend to an obligation to have intercourse.

Fortunately, this extreme position can be avoided. It is clear that in English law there is no principle that life must be chosen instead of death at all times and all costs. One illustration of this point is the fact that the Abortion Act 1967 (as amended in 1990) permits the termination of pregnancy where the fetus is expected to be seriously handicapped. Another is that the courts have recognized that a sane adult may refuse life-saving treating, because they are entitled to choose what happens to their bodies. Perhaps the clearest indication of all is that the courts have been prepared to authorize health professionals to refrain from ventilating a severely handicapped baby, holding that it would not be in his interests to continue (*Re J* 1990).

However, the fact that there is no right to be born does not mean that it would be a breach of a child's rights to permit it to be conceived with a genetic defect. Sometimes children claim that their condition is such that they should not have been conceived or that their life should have been terminated before birth. This type of action is called 'wrongful life': 'a claim by, or on behalf of, a person born with predictable physical or mental handicaps that, but for the defendant's negligence, the person would not have been conceived or, having been conceived, would not have been born alive' (Dickens 1989: 82–3). Although some parts of the USA allow such actions, the English courts have rejected the suggestion that it can be a legal wrong to be born (Dickens 1989: 91–6, although see Fortin 1987 for the view that such actions are still open). The fact that wrongful life actions have been rejected is important, because it undermines the claim that prospective parents must avoid having children with genetic disease on the basis that it contravenes the rights of those potential children. It may be in the interests of those children not to be born but it is not their right. In law, therefore, genetic counsellors are free to disregard the personal interests of future children. Their immediate clients are free to decide what risks to take of a child being conceived as there are no legally recognized rights to constrain their choice.

CONCLUSION

The discussion has identified a number of interests that children and
those with a mental handicap have. Many of these are essentially the
same interests that 'normal' adults possess. However, the approaches
that are necessary in order to respect those interests in relation to
those unable to choose for themselves may differ from those adopted
by genetic counsellors. This concluding section focuses on the
roles of parents, carers and professionals in protecting the rights
and interests of the incapacitated. In part this can be seen as the
framework in which the rights that have been discussed are protected
and vindicated.

The first problem concerns the status of the family. Some believe
that it should be up to them to decide whether genetic testing, and
related counselling, should go ahead. This raises difficult questions
about the place of children and those with a mental handicap within
families. English law has rejected the traditional assumption that
parents could exercise their parental rights in whatever ways they
liked. Instead they are entrusted with responsibility for promoting
the welfare of their children and are expected to make choices in
order to further that aim, although the needs of other members of the
family are legitimate considerations if the child's interests will not
be compromised. Consequently, it is no longer enough to assume that
what parents choose is acceptable, consideration must be given to
whether the child's interests indicate that testing is appropriate.

Recent developments in child law, most importantly the decision
in *Gillick* v *W. Norfolk & Wisbech HA* (1985) and the Children Act
1989, have considerably altered the legal status of children. Whereas
it was previously possible to regard children as little more than the
property of their parents, this is no longer the case. Instead, parents
have responsibility for the care of their children rather than rights
over them, and are expected to act in their best interests. Parental
decisions should therefore be made according to whether the child
will benefit, not in order to relieve the anxieties of the parents. This
is in contrast with the position in most US states, where family
autonomy is supported by the law with little recognition that the
interests of the child and the family may diverge (Pelias 1991).

In the context of genetic testing it is sometimes difficult to
separate the interests of children from those of other members of the
family. However, if children are to be given the respect that is due to
them in English law it is necessary to do so. Parents who disregard

their children's interests will be abusing their powers. Although it will be rare that child protection procedures would be appropriate, it may be necessary for genetic counsellors to take on the role of protector for child clients. It would be unethical, for example, to allow the interests of a child to be damaged in order to reduce parental anxiety. Professionals may sometimes need to use their rights to refuse to carry out tests or disclose information in order to protect children from their parents. If necessary, in cases of dispute, a court can be called upon to determine whether a particular child should be tested, or access to their records be given. Decisions would be taken according to the best interests of the child as judged by the court.

To some genetic counsellors, the suggestion that they have an active role in protecting the interests of children against those of their parents may seem improper. It compromises their objectivity and aversion to coercing clients. However, even if such an extreme non-directive model of genetic counselling is attainable (and it may not be: Clarke 1991), it is inappropriate in the context of children and those with a mental handicap. While parents will mostly act in the interests of their children, counsellors must be wary lest they do not. Here they have a watching brief. If they sense cause for concern, they can take the matter to court. When mentally handicapped adults are involved, counsellors are obliged by law to take responsibility for judging what is in their client's best interest.

It is the fact that counsellors cannot restrict themselves to a merely advisory role that marks the most significant difference between clients who can decide for themselves and those who lack the capacity to do so. In this context, genetic counselling cannot be purely concerned with promoting reproductive autonomy. Nor can criticism of the legal framework within which it operates confine itself to examining how far reproductive autonomy is guaranteed (Chadwick and Ngwena 1992). The rights and interests that are at stake are broader than this implies. Further, genetic counsellors are themselves among those entrusted with the task of protecting them.

REFERENCES

Beauchamp, T. L. and Childress, J. F. (1989) *Principles of Biomedical Ethics*, New York: Oxford University Press.
Bolam v *Friern HMC* (1957) 1 *Butterworths Medico-Legal Reports* 1.
Chadwick, R. and Ngwena, C. (1992) 'The development of a normative

standard in counselling for genetic disease: ethics and law', *Journal of Social Welfare and Family Law*, 276–95.

Clarke, A. (1991) 'Is non-directive genetics counselling possible?' *Lancet* 338: 998–1001.

Re D (1976) *Law Reports, Family Division* 185.

Dickens, B. (1989) 'Wrongful birth and life, wrongful death before birth, and wrongful law', in S. Mclean (ed.) *Legal Issues in Human Reproduction*, Aldershot: Gower.

Dworkin, G. (1988) *The Theory and Practice of Autonomy*, Cambridge: Cambridge University Press.

Eekalaar, J. (1986) 'The emergence of children's rights', *Oxford Journal of Legal Studies* 6: 161–82.

F v W. Berkshire HA (1989) *All England Reports* 2: 545.

Fortin, J. (1987) 'Is the "wrongful life" action really dead?' *Journal of Social Welfare Law*, 306.

Furniss v Fitchett (1958) *New Zealand Law Reports* 396.

Gillick v W. Norfolk & Wisbech HA (1985) *All England Reports* 3: 402.

Gillon, R. (1986) *Philosophical Medical Ethics*, Chichester: Wiley.

Re J (1990) *All England Reports* 3: 930.

Re J (1992a) *Medical Law Reports* 3: 317.

Re J (1992b) *Butterworths Medico-Legal Reports*, 9: 10.

Montgomery, J. (1992) 'Parents and children in dispute: who has the final word?', *Journal of Child Law* 4: 85–9.

Pelias, M. Z. (1991) 'Duty to disclose in medical genetics: a legal perspective', *American Journal of Medical Genetics* 39: 347–54.

Pullen, I. (1990) 'Patients, families, and genetic information', in E. Sutherland and A McCall Smith (eds) *Family Rights: Family Law and Medical Advance*, Edinburgh: Edinburgh University Press.

R v Secretary of State for Social Services, W. Midlands RHA & Birmingham AHA, ex parte Hincks (1980) *Butterworths Medico-Legal Reports* 1: 93.

R v St Mary's Hospital, ex parte Harriott (1988) 1 *Family Law Reports* 512.

Re R (1991) *All England Reports* 4: 177.

Raz, J. (1986) *The Morality of Freedom*, Oxford: Oxford University Press.

Re T (1992) *All England Reports* 4: 649.

Chapter 10

Confidentiality in genetic counselling

Paula Boddington

INTRODUCTION

The issue of confidentiality in genetic counselling is highly complex. One aim of this chapter is to examine the issues in a broad framework, discussing different approaches to genetic counselling and their differing implications for confidentiality. Hence, as well as discussing confidentiality directly, I also look at viewpoints that might tend to support it, or that might have no such inbuilt tendency.

There is a large difference between two possible approaches. In one approach, genetic counselling aims to enhance individual choice, autonomy and decision-making in reproduction by providing relevant information to those considering parenthood, as well, of course, as often being directly relevant to individuals wishing to ascertain their own disease status. In a contrasting approach, the goal of counselling is the implementation of some wider public policy towards the elimination of certain genetic disorders, or, more sinisterly, to general 'population improvement' or 'race hygiene'.

Regard for confidentiality fits naturally into the first approach since, broadly speaking, to regard genetic information as confidential is to regard it as the especial concern and property of the individual, and, where important decisions such as those concerning reproduction will be affected by genetic information, protection of confidentiality also protects the individual's right to make such decisions without outside interference: protecting the privacy of the information protects the privacy of the action decided upon in the light of the information. In the second approach, wider public concerns are given emphasis and the individual's interests and wish for privacy and confidentiality may be overturned by appeal to notions of prevention of harm to others, or to the promotion of good.

Whilst someone might wish to adopt such an approach and also maintain a respect for confidentiality, such respect does not arise as naturally as it does in the first, reproductive autonomy model.

Appeals to public good, with scant regard to individual rights, are of course well known to have been made earlier this century by many proponents of the eugenics movement. For example, speaking to the Second International Congress of Eugenics held in the United States in 1921, Leonard Darwin, son of Charles Darwin and president of the Eugenics Education Society of Great Britain, claimed that:

> efforts must be made to ascertain and to make known the rules by which each individual ought to strive to regulate his own conduct in regard to parenthood in accordance with the laws of heredity in so far as they are now surely known. Lastly, the action which the state should take in order to stimulate and to enforce conduct productive of racial progress must be considered a line of advance to be advocated, however, with great circumspection when compulsion is concerned.
>
> (Darwin 1985a: 7)

His 'great circumspection' with regard to compulsion did not prevent him from claiming that 'nevertheless we should not be quite blind to the example set us by Nature in her readiness to sacrifice the individual for the sake of the race' (ibid.: 15) and to suggest, for example, that the right method to adopt, as a rule, for 'mental defectives' is segregation of the sexes, with minimal scope for choice (Darwin 1985b). Moreover, it is vital to recognize that his claim that voluntary methods were in general best, was not made out of concern that individual choice be paramount in reproductive decision-making:

> what we want to know is the rules which ought to guide each individual in deciding his own voluntary actions in all matters relating to racial progress . . . in regard to any proposed line of conduct, we have to weigh in the balance as well as we can its moral effects, the immediate material advantages or disadvantages to the family and to the state which are likely thus to arise, and the benefits or injuries which it will confer or inflict on the race in the future.
>
> (Darwin 1985a: 11)

The 'responsible' individual then is encouraged to think in terms of whether reproduction would benefit the human race as a whole.

Protection of individual privacy and confidentiality has no ensured place in such a view.

Let us turn to examine the suggestions of another discussion document. Whilst claiming not to make any guidelines for practice, this report is important for our purposes because it 'suggests reasons for reconsidering whether, in certain limited cases, the usually accepted rights of patients and others to autonomy and confidentiality should be reconsidered' (Royal College of Physicians 1991: 3). It goes on to suggest that if people have the right to make decisions for themselves on whether to conceive children, then they may perhaps have the right, or even the duty, to make these decisions against the background of as much information as possible. Hence the following conclusions (amongst others) may possibly be drawn:

- Individuals should not necessarily have the right to refuse genetic testing on themselves or their relatives under all circumstances.
- Family members might be entitled to know about their genetic background even against the will of their relatives, and even where the information carried implications about dark family secrets.

If people should have the right to make decisions about having children against a background of full information, this would additionally imply:

- Conveying information about an individual's genetic background to potential spouses or sexual partners should be the normal practice.

If, more strongly, people should have a *duty* (emphasis original) not to make decisions about having children without full information, this would additionally imply:

- Individuals at risk of transmitting some genetic disorder should always be informed of the fact.

(ibid.: 9)

It is enormously interesting that this report switches from a reproductive autonomy model, talking about individuals having the right to make decisions about conceiving children, to the right to do this against a background of full information, which may enhance their autonomy but which does nothing for the autonomy of those who are thereby going to be badgered into a denial of their own right to confidentiality, to talking as if a natural progression of moral reasoning is to a duty to have children only against a background of

full information. This putative duty in fact directly undercuts reproductive autonomy.

In this respect the report has much in common with the claims of
Leonard Darwin. In particular, talk of a possible duty not to make
decisions about having children without full genetic information,
even without any suggestion of enforced state interference, is
directly at odds with the notion that reproduction is a private action
to which is owed the protection of confidentiality. There is no
suggestion that the duty is to oneself: other possible candidates to
whom the duty is owed are one's descendants, or society in general.
To this extent, then, the model of genetic counselling as enhancing
individual reproductive freedom shifts to the public policy or 'larger
good' model.

Seventy years lie between Leonard Darwin's claims and the
report just cited: it was produced by the Royal College of Physicians
of London in October 1991. Yet the two documents have much in
common. What I hope to do here is to illustrate some of the
importance of the issue of confidentiality in genetic counselling,
and to offer some suggestions as to why it should be safeguarded
very carefully.

WHEN MIGHT ISSUES OF CONFIDENTIALITY ARISE IN
GENETIC COUNSELLING?

Genetic counselling poses problems of confidentiality such as those
that are found elsewhere in medical practice, but additionally, because of the specific nature of genetic knowledge, it also poses
distinctive problems of its own. Moreover, because of the specially
sensitive nature of genetic knowledge, many of the problems of
confidentiality take on particular urgency.

Who might wish to have access to information regarding an
individual's genetic makeup? Possible interested parties include,
in the public sphere, employers, insurers, educators, loan companies,
adoption agencies and, in case we forget the lessons of history,
agents of the government. There are obvious reasons why an
individual may wish to keep medical, and in particular genetic,
information from such parties. In the more personal sphere, other
members of an individual's family may wish to have genetic
information about that individual to be able to determine their own
position in relation to a genetic condition, such as whether they are at
risk from Huntington's disease, or whether they are at risk of

transmitting a particular disorder to their offspring. Partners may also have an interest in genetic information when considering sharing parenthood with that individual.

What is distinctive about genetic information is that it is shared information amongst individuals who are genetic relatives: to find out that one's father has Huntington's disease is to find out that one is oneself at risk; to find out that one's brother has inherited a different marker gene for Huntington's from oneself is to find out that he has a different risk status to oneself. So, very often people will wish to have knowledge concerning their relatives, and often knowledge about one person will automatically reveal information about another. The genetic information involved may concern more than disease or carrier status: for instance non-paternity may be an issue that brings potential difficulties. Protecting the confidentiality of one member of a family may be fraught with difficulties. Moreover, since genetic information has this quality of being shared, questions arise about the right of access to this information. If a family member refuses to be tested, then other relatives may be unable to discover information concerning themselves: to what extent does someone have the right to withhold testing in such circumstances? Furthermore, if someone expressly does not wish to know their own genetic status, this wish may be thwarted if other family members obtain information that automatically reveals information about others. The right to confidentiality may be thought to rest at least partly on the notion that information is one's own, is private to oneself. The nature of genetic information challenges this view.

If, as the Royal College of Physicians' Report suggests is possible, one has a duty to obtain genetic information about oneself before making decisions about reproduction, information may then be forced on one against one's will. This can also be seen as an issue of confidentiality. If confidentiality is to protect the ability of the individual to control private information, then to force that information on them against their will can be seen to be a breach of their rights similar to that of revealing it to others against their will.

THE IMPORTANCE OF MEDICAL CONFIDENTIALITY

There are different sorts of justification given for protecting medical confidentiality. One approach is the consequentialist argument, that only by guaranteeing confidentiality can trust be built up between medical staff and the patient. Without such trust, the patient may be reluctant to reveal information that might be vital to successful diagnosis and treatment. The goal of good health care is so important that it justifies the strong protection of confidentiality, even, very often, when there might be other reasons to break confidentiality.

Other justifications make appeal to notions of the protection of privacy, and it is these that I shall be chiefly considering, since I regard them as providing the most revealing analysis of the particular case of confidentiality of genetic information. To protect our individuality, our sense of ourselves, and in recognition of our human vulnerability, privacy needs to be respected. A model of concentric spheres of privacy is often used and is very helpful, although it may not always be possible to delineate these spheres too sharply or without argument. There is some information about ourselves which is readily accessible public knowledge, information that others can get simply by looking, for example, or the sort of information that is on public record and to which the government may have an acknowledged right. There is information that one would reveal to, for instance, one's employer, information one would reveal to a casual acquaintance, to a close acquaintance, to a best friend, a relative, a spouse, a therapist, and information one would reveal to nobody (perhaps, it might be added, not even to oneself). So the whole world might be able to see that I am overweight; the shop assistant may have to know what size I am but my nosy next-door neighbour isn't finding out; I won't tell my mother how much I weigh but unfortunately the doctor has to weigh me; only my husband knows about my midnight frenzies with the icecream, and only my therapist has any idea why I do this (and even she doesn't know the whole story). In general, and other things being equal, the closer information is to the inner sphere of most private information, the more pressing is the need to maintain confidentiality.

Privacy of knowledge is only one aspect of privacy: to this must be added privacy of action. Another way of characterizing the domain of privacy of action is that it is a domain where the individual should be allowed full autonomy. Just as some information is one's own personal concern alone, so some actions are. For instance, the whole sphere of family life, what one does within the home, one's sexual life, is generally (although not without exception or limit) accorded the respect of privacy (see, for example, Wasserstrom 1986).

There are important links between privacy of action and privacy of information: for our purposes, it is necessary to note that the latter may often be needed to safeguard the former, since outside agencies might be tempted to try to interfere if they knew what was going on.

GENETIC INFORMATION AND PRIVACY

Why should we feel a need to keep genetic information within a sphere of privacy? Especially where it concerns genetic disease or disorder, this may be thought simply to belong to the realm of medical information and to be treated as private simply for all the reasons normally given for medical confidentiality. All such reasons can be taken as read: here I wish to pursue the question of whether there is anything distinctive about genetic information that means its privacy and confidentiality should be especially safeguarded.

Spheres of privacy deserve protection, amongst other reasons, when they touch on our sense of individuality and identity. Indeed, this could be one of the reasons for protecting confidentiality with regard to ill-health. Especially where one has to live with a severe, long-term or life-threatening condition, the illness may come to be a crucial part of one's own identity and may be felt to be highly personalized.[1] Conversely, though not necessarily in conflict with this, one may wish for medical confidentiality precisely to avoid being labelled and related to by others as 'a sick person'. And in regard to genetic information, this may be further highlighted: if we regard our identities as constructed out of our genetic makeup, information about that makeup will concern the very nature of our beings. Especially in a world without a soul, where the frontiers of scientific knowledge simply are the frontiers of knowledge, the Human Genome Project is mapping the deepest recesses of the human essence, genetic knowledge of an individual is, in one important sense, as deep as one can go in the discovery of that individual. For these reasons, such knowledge requires to be handled with the utmost sensitivity and respect.

Furthermore, this argument can be strengthened by considering that, in respect of privacy, it is important not just that what is essential to a person's sense of identity should be protected, but that what they feel to be so should be protected; injury and hurt can still be done to them, based on what they feel is important for maintaining a proper sense of inviolate identity.

There is a double edge to this project in pursuit of genetic knowledge, for while it may seem to get to our very essence, it may also seem to dissolve any such notion of essence (Brock 1991). This is in so far as the pursuit of such knowledge is a reductionist project. In one way of looking at this, the human being may be seen to disappear under a welter of chemical formulae. We find no soul, no ME, and rather than being a journey that leads to the essence of the self, it may be seen as a journey that leads to the destruction of the self, like one of those fairy stories where greed leads to total impoverishment and dispossession of all that one holds dear. This is further highlighted by the possibility of genetic manipulation: if a person's genetic makeup is constitutive of their identity, what happens to that identity when genes are altered? Is one then a different person? The difficulty of these questions highlights a sense of insecurity about our very natures. For as well as being an indicator of our true identity, and hence to be regarded as private, genetic knowledge may simultaneously and contrarily be regarded as a threat to any notion of individuality and identity. As potentially threatening information, this then gives a further reason why genetic information should be treated with respect and regarded as belonging to the especial province of the individual. With the newness of this scientific progress, with declining religious accounts of the self, for many people this is a time of flux and of remaking or reinventing the fragile notion of self and of individuality. From two seemingly opposing features of genetic knowledge, we reach the same result: strong reasons for the protection of confidentiality.

What of privacy of action with regard to genetic knowledge? I shall look at the claim that reproduction is a private act, and hence that information relevant to reproductive decisions, as genetic information may be, should be kept confidential to protect the individual's freedom of action. Matters which are of concern to the family, sex and home life are generally viewed as belonging to the private sphere. Having children can then be regarded as belonging to this sphere. Declarations of human rights typically see the freedom to found a family as an extremely important one. Reproduction is widely recognized as central to individual autonomy (Robertson 1991; Clayton 1991). Moreover, the crimes of enforced sterilization of certain groups, the splitting of families, and all the horrors attendant upon such deeds go a long way to support the reproductive freedom of the individual.

But unfortunately there are complexities in this situation. It is necessary to try to spell out the sense in which reproduction can be seen as a private action: not all private actions can be understood in the same sense. Take consenting sexual behaviour between two adults in private. This may be thought to lie in the sphere of private action because it affects no one else, so is no one else's business, and is important and intimate behaviour for the two people concerned, so is very much their business. But note: even in this sphere, regulation of behaviour may be acknowledged to be legitimate, for instance, if one or both are under a certain age, or if there is a financial transaction involved, or certain sado-masochistic practices take place. To point this out is not to enter the debate about whether these particular interferences are justified, but only to illustrate that the meeting of the private and the public spheres takes place at a confused and disputed boundary.

What of having children? It certainly is important and intimate behaviour for the parents, but it is not true that it could strictly be said not to be anyone else's business: it is at least the business of the children. Moreover, since new members of society are produced, then the larger social world will be involved. It is not open to say, as it is with much other private behaviour, that no one else will be affected by it. And if others are affected, this immediately becomes a reason to consider their points of view as well as those of the potential parents.

It could perhaps then be said that having children is in two domains, the private AND the public.

LIMITS TO PRIVACY OF GENETIC INFORMATION

It is thus necessary to discuss further how problems arise with any simple view that privacy of information and action should always and without exception be protected with regard to genetic information.

First, I have tried to argue, the privacy of genetic information should be safeguarded because it is highly personal information close to the centre of our identities as individuals. But it is vital to note the complications observed above (p. 227), that genetic information about one person may also be vitally important for another interested relative. So, although the information may be the especial concern of one individual, it may also be of equal concern to others. The interests of others in no way detracts from the sense in which any one individual has a close interest in the information: it's not like sharing a cake where, the more people who share it, the less it is mine and the smaller the slice I can legitimately hope for. My concern is not diluted by yours; your claim has no straightforward effect of diminishing mine. Here, as so often, we bump against the edges of the myth of inviolate individuality. The reality is that our identities are linked in many ways. The reality of the genetic heritage that goes to make up one unique individual is that it is a shared heritage that spills over into the unique genetic heritage of others.

Second, to consider the privacy of reproduction: it is instructive to point out that there do seem to be limits to the extent to which individuals are left free to make their reproductive choices without any outside moral judgement, and that this at least sometimes seems justified. At least where others are requested to assist, as medical personnel may be, the approach to genetic counselling that aims to enhance individual autonomy can be argued to have limits. There is not pure consumer choice in the sense that the medical personnel offering information and possibilities exercise judgement to the extent that only choices thought to be morally neutral or morally good are offered; or if it is thought that morally suspect choices are being offered, or choices are being offered without sufficient thought having been given to the moral issues, unease is often expressed by others (Clarke 1991; Lippman 1991). For instance, there is room for much debate here about what choices should be offered: for example, how serious a condition should be before it is screened for. This can be illustrated by considering the hypothetical and almost unimaginable case of a couple requesting genetic counselling to ensure that they produced a diseased child: what genetic counsellor would go along with this? (Of course there are complications in the scope for dispute about what conditions are harmful, or might bring benefits.) The example can be changed to one that is more imaginable: picture a couple who would dearly love a son, perhaps because males are more highly prized, perhaps because they have many daughters, in a situation where any sons are in danger of suffering from a serious sex-linked disorder and their daughters are not.[2] I would guess that many people would shrink from helping them to achieve this goal. This widespread opinion that places a limit on reproductive autonomy can also be illustrated by the common unease with abortion simply on grounds of fetal sex, and by the many legislatures which permit abortion within a certain framework only (e.g., not on demand, or with time limits). The crucial question, of course, is whether such limits on individual reproductive autonomy are justified. These difficulties must be pointed out, for they temper the framework of individual reproductive autonomy which supports confidentiality in genetic counselling. This is not in itself to argue that any direct threat to confidentiality has been found here, but, as I stated earlier, I am also concerned in this chapter to discuss the broader framework within which justification for confidentiality arises.

REASONS FOR OVERRIDING GENETIC CONFIDENTIALITY

What the above discussion has attempted to do is to show how there are very strong reasons to protect confidentiality and privacy of genetic information, but that complications exist which might be thought, in some circumstances, to limit the claims of the individual to absolute privacy, confidentiality and control of information and action. The Royal College of Physicians' Report expresses the point:

> There are ... reasons for considering whether in the context of genetics these prima facie rights to autonomy and confidentiality should be regarded as secondary not only to the need to prevent exceptional harm, but also to conflicting rights of other people to obtain genetic information.
>
> (Royal College of Physicians 1991: 7)

Are any reasons there might be to override the confidentiality of genetic information ever strong enough to do so? It will be helpful to start by examining two instances where it has been argued that it is justifiable to override medical confidentiality, instances that may sometimes be used as analogous to the situation of genetic information.

The two instances are tests on drivers for blood alcohol, and notifiable diseases (Royal College of Physicians 1991; Edgar 1991). The first may be seen to have analogies with the question of whether someone has a right to refuse to be tested for genetic information. We have, then, a possible parallel with the limits on the right to refuse testing given in law in relation to possible drunken driving. Just as confidentiality may be overridden here to prevent the harm to the public from drunken drivers, so, it may be thought, confidentiality may be overridden to prevent harm such as the harm to a relative of being denied access to genetic knowledge that is important to them.

In the case of notifiable diseases, it could be claimed that, in order to prevent the spread of a disease amongst the population, thus causing great harm, it is justifiable to require that information about numbers of people who have the disease be made known. This case could be of especial interest to those seeking an analogy which will allow genetic counselling to be seen from the perspective of public population policy. One instance of this would be screening for Down syndrome, where one aim is not simply to enhance reproductive autonomy, but to cut down on the numbers of people with Down syndrome in the population. This is not to say that there is any direct link between such an aim and any notion of force, or any straight-forward breach of confidentiality: I do not wish to overstate my case. My point is to spell out as carefully as possible the general frames of reference in which confidentiality may be firmly safeguarded, or those in which it may be, in some circumstances, under potential attack.

Overriding confidentiality is very often justified, then, on the grounds of trying to prevent great harm. But it is vital to see that the formula '"Prima facie reason for confidentiality" versus "aim of preventing harm"' is only a simplified version of the story. It is necessary to examine, in individual cases, the nature of both sides of the formula, and whether there are any other factors that might alter the particular situation.

First, with blood alcohol tests, the glaring disanalogy with genetic testing is the factor that there is a suspected and rather grave offence. Indeed, routine blood alcohol testing can be seen, with good justifi-cation, to be an infringement of civil liberties. It is widely acknowl-edged that one needs a licence and certain level of competence to drive: no such test is required (yet! one might add) for parenthood. I would suggest there is no useful parallel with genetic testing to be found here. Moreover, I would like firmly to counter any such suggestion, precisely because this example involves a suspected offence: having or carrying a genetic disorder is not an offence. Yet there are grave dangers attached to any suggestion that it might be some kind of offence. There are implications for the stigmatization of individuals, and it also raises the highly problematic possibility of wrongful life suits. As I shall try to show in relation to the alleged analogy with notifiable diseases, the idea of seeing genetic disorders as threats to the public comes up again in a different guise. This is an immensely dangerous pattern of thought to slip into.

What of the side of the formula 'prima facie reason for con-fidentiality'? Confidentiality relates to privacy and there is more than one type and sphere of privacy. The three cases, blood alcohol, notifiable diseases, and genetic conditions, relate to different types of information about a person. For this reason alone, any analogy starts to weaken. Blood alcohol levels relate to a temporary state of the individual, notifiable diseases relate to infections which are acquired and may be temporary states of the individual (with exceptions such as infants born with HIV, in places where this is a notifiable condition). Moreover, infectious diseases can be viewed as conditions stemming from outside the individual, from the organism that is the source of the infection, and to this extent, further out in the spheres of privacy than genetic conditions. Although there may be a genetic component in terms of susceptibility or resistance to an organism, the definition of the disease is located externally, in the foreign entity. Although it has to be recognized that genetic conditions may have an element of interaction with the environment, and may be late-onset conditions, nevertheless, they all have the essential element of a genetic factor which is present from an individual's origins and which is at the core of their physical identity. Thus, it can be argued that there are, from the very beginning, even stronger reasons for protection of confidentiality with regard to genetic conditions than with infectious diseases or blood alcohol. This is not, however, to say that in these latter two cases there may not be other factors I have not here considered or that there are not very good grounds for protecting confidentiality: I am not having a competition. I only wish to demonstrate the nature of the strength of the grounds for confidentiality in the case of genetic conditions, which is that it relates to an innermost sphere of private concern.

What of the other side of the equation, the harm to be prevented? Well, as already shown, blood alcohol tests relate to possible offence, and it is generally recognized that stronger steps can be taken to prevent harm caused by wrongdoing than harm caused innocently. The case of infectious notifiable diseases provides extremely interesting lessons: for a discussion of parallels between genetic disease and HIV with regard to confidentiality, see Edgar (1991). The harm to the population that is to be avoided would be the threat of infection by some outside organism that causes serious disease. An attempt to draw a parallel with genetic disease might be especially seductive if a public population policy, of attempting to control the incidence of a disease in the population, is adopted. But what possible analogy with an outside disease entity could there be in the case of a genetic disorder? Are we under danger of attack by something alien to humanity? Any alleged danger, harm or threat comes, on the contrary, from inside, from our very natures. Moreover, at least at present and for the foreseeable future, steps to prevent the incidence of genetic disorder among the population consist, not exclusively but in the main, not in ensuring that individuals do not acquire the disorder, but ensuring that individuals who would have that disorder are not born in the first place. Thus, the population is not being protected from an outside danger: it could be said that it is being protected from the costs of bearing certain individuals amongst its number, and also that for certain types of individuals, with certain genetic conditions, it is itself a bad thing to be born (a difficult question I cannot examine further here). It is also of course quite fallacious to think of genetic disease 'spreading' in the population in the way that an infectious disease might spread.

One danger here of taking the notifiable infectious diseases model as a model for genetic disease is that, as certain disease organisms may be seen as a threat to humanity, so certain individuals or subgroups may be seen as a threat to humanity as carriers of genetic disorders. The danger in this is connected at least partially with the way that genetic conditions go to the heart of our physical identities, and indeed, the parallel can be made with the way that certain groups have become stigmatized in relation to Aids and HIV. It can be argued that, in some people's minds, infection with HIV regrettably has become part of a way of construing the identity of certain already stigmatized groups. The subgroup of gay men then is construed as a threat to the population, their identity wrongly tied to a disease organism, with many unfortunate results. In this case, the disease organism itself would more accurately be seen as a threat to the population. With genetic disease, however, there is no disease organism in this sense, only genes which are part of the makeup of various individuals. These points apply particularly to the population-based public policy model of genetic counselling, and should be seen as warnings of some of the difficulties of such a model, in dangers posed to individuals and to subgroups in the population.

None of what I have said should be taken as denying that various genetic conditions involve suffering and distress to those who have them and to those who love and care for them. However, it casts doubt on any simple idea that we can characterize genetic conditions as 'harm to population' in the relatively straightforward way that we can with many infectious diseases. Thus, this is an argument against one way of appealing to the existence of great harm as a reason to override confidentiality of genetic information.

There is a great difference between seeing genetic threats as carried by certain members of the population who then have a 'duty' not to contaminate the rest of the population, and seeing us all as sharing a varied genetic heritage.

Moreover, in citing the avoidance of genetic disease as the avoidance of harm, the question is raised of what genetic conditions exactly will count as harmful, and to what degree: furthermore, questions are raised, which will doubtless be hard to answer, of the boundary between genetic disease and simple genetic variation. Given the patterns of genetic variation that are being discovered, it seems built into our very biological natures that the boundary between simple variation and disease is going to be hard to draw (see, for example, Clarke 1991; Clayton 1991; Lippman 1991).

I have tried to show some things that make genetic information special and that have the effect of underlining the importance of confidentiality. I have tried to illustrate the sense in which genetic information is very private information, going in some way to the very core of our identity. I have tried also to demonstrate that it is not unproblematic to say in any straightforward way that genetic disease constitutes a harm to the population, and that, again, the reason for this is the way that genetic disease goes so close to our core identity. In both cases, our identities as individuals, our sense of self-respect, of privacy, is at issue.

It is necessary also for a full discussion to return to the points raised above of the possible limits on the privacy of genetic information and of reproduction, since these limits could potentially be used to override claims to confidentiality. I do not have the space here to give full discussion to these complex issues, but offer instead some preliminary remarks.

Privacy of genetic information may be undermined by the way in which it is shared amongst a group of related individuals. A person may claim that, without information about a relative, they will suffer harm of one sort or another, and also that it is information that they jointly own and thus have a right to.

It is worth pointing out regarding the claim that withholding such information constitutes a harm, that this is a harm dependent upon, first, the development of the technology to discover the information, without which the information cannot be said to be withheld, and second, on the circumstance of someone having appropriate kin upon whom to do the testing. The harm is relative to these two factors, although to say that it is relative is not necessarily to deny its reality.

For a more complete account, the whole notion of shared ownership of knowledge, and the particular case of shared genetic knowledge, needs to be investigated more fully. One suggestion that could be made is that if it really is shared knowledge, then it may be most appropriate to consider that agreement between the parties sharing the knowledge is needed in order fairly to investigate and reveal it. Problems arise, of course, when there is no agreement. It may be asked why, in such a case, it should be the person who does not want the information revealed who will have the upper hand. One answer that can be given to this is that to take sides with the person who wishes to have the information will always be to use force, whether it is the force of taking samples against a person's will, coercion into disclosing information, or the force of using one's superior position to reveal information one already has, perhaps gained in a different context, or to test samples one has already obtained for a different reason. It can also be said that, although information about one individual may be needed to gather information about another, since it directly concerns the first individual's genetic makeup, it belongs to them in a stronger sense. How we should even begin to think about this issue is a question to consider. It could be argued that the language of competing rights between people at odds with each other belongs to a discourse of separate, discrete and autonomous individuals, and that one thing the shared nature of genetic information does is to begin to question the way of seeing people as inviolate separate individuals.

Likewise, the question of reproductive responsibility and reproductive privacy is far too large to cover adequately in the available space. The issue here is more than just the privacy of prospective parents: recall the suggestion of the Royal College of Physicians' Report discussed above that people may have a duty not to make decisions about having children without full genetic information, and that if this is so, then their relatives may also be called upon to be tested or to reveal information. I suggested above (pp. 227–8) that having private information forced on one is akin to, or could be seen as, a violation of confidentiality. A few points can briefly be made. First, we should note the difficulty of making any kind of objective judgement about what conditions should be screened for or avoided, and what risks are and are not worth taking. It could be said that those who stand to be most intimately affected will be the parents or potential parents, and for this reason alone it should be their values, experience and judgement that inform the decision. This could be underlined by the fact that often the potential parents come from families with first-hand experience of the genetic conditions in question. Second, there is the danger of abuse in allowing other agencies a say in an individual's reproductive decision-making. This danger exists even without any formal plan by any body to interfere.

The tendency to 'go the way of technology' should be noted (Clarke 1991; Lippman 1991). Moreover, the potential for arrogance and abuse can be illustrated by the following:

> A major problem in clinical genetics is that, although the doctor has a close relationship with the patient and the patient's family, they often find it difficult to accept advice given on the basis of statistical and population studies applied to them personally. In cystic fibrosis, for example, they very often say 'I will take my chances', even if it is very likely that they will have another affected child who will subsequently die.
>
> (Royal College of Physicians 1991: 15)

This appears as a 'case' in the 'Appendix: Examples of clinical genetics cases which raise ethical issues' in the Royal College of Physicians' Report on *Ethical Issues in Clinical Genetics*. Those who consider such cases a problem may not have considered that such recalcitrant couples who have the wit and strength of mind to resist the advice of professionals may not be suffering from an inability to grasp statistical evidence, but may have different religious beliefs, different moral standards, different assessments of the difficulties of having a child with cystic fibrosis, may place a different weight on the value of having another child, may have a different assessment of the worth of the life of a child with cystic fibrosis, and may simply feel that, whatever these doctors say, for them personally, it is a risk worth taking. That such 'cases' are being presented, in the 1990s, as ethical problems by a body such as the Royal College of Physicians, should warn us that the interfering, 'for-their-own-good' atttitude of the eugenicists of earlier this century is still with us. It is a warning we should take seriously: the potential for abuse and for attack on the individual is too great. Ultimately, the slightest threat of such abuse is one of the strongest arguments for the vigilant protection of privacy and confidentiality in genetic counselling.

NOTES

1 Steve Hornibrook made this point clear to me.
2 I owe the example to Suzanne Uniacke.

REFERENCES

Brock, Dan W. (1991) 'The genome project and human identity', in Mark A. Rothstein (ed.) *Legal and Ethical Issues Raised by the Human Genome*

Project, Houston: Health Law and Policy Institute, University of Texas, 222–43.

Clarke, Angus (1991) 'Is non-directive genetic counselling possible?', *Lancet* 338: 998–1001.

Clayton, Ellen Wright (1991) 'Genetic screening and treatment of newborns', in Mark A. Rothstein (ed.) *Legal and Ethical Issues Raised by the Human Genome Project*, Houston: Health Law and Policy Institute, University of Texas, 116–43.

Conneally, Michael P. (1991) 'The genome project and confidentiality in the clinical setting', in Mark A. Rothstein (ed.) *Legal and Ethical Issues Raised by the Human Genome Project*, Houston: Health Law and Policy Institute, University of Texas, 184–96.

Darwin, Leonard (1985a) 'The aims and methods of eugenical societies', in *Eugenics, Genetics and the Family: Second International Congress of Eugenics, 1921*, vol. I: 5–19, New York: Garland Publishing, Inc.

—— (1985b) 'The field of eugenic reform', in *Eugenics in Race and State: Second International Congress of Eugenics, 1921*, vol. II: 189–202, New York: Garland Publishing, Inc.

Edgar, Harold S. H. (1991) 'The genome project and the legal right to medical confidentiality', in Mark A. Rothstein (ed.) *Legal and Ethical Issues Raised by the Human Genome Project*, Houston: Health Law and Policy Institute, University of Texas, 197–221.

Lippman, Abby (1991) 'Prenatal genetic testing and screening: constructing needs and reinforcing inequities', *American Journal of Law and Medicine* 17: 15–50.

Robertson, John A. (1991) 'Issues in procreation liberty raised by the new genetics', in Mark A. Rothstein (ed.) *Legal and Ethical Issues Raised by the Human Genome Project*, Houston: Health Law and Policy Institute, University of Texas, 116–43.

Rothstein, Mark A. (ed.) (1991) *Legal and Ethical Issues Raised by the Human Genome Project: Proceedings of the Conference in Houston, Texas, March 7–9, 1991*, Houston: Health Law and Policy Institute, University of Texas.

Royal College of Physicians of London (1991) *Ethical Issues in Clinical Genetics: A Report of a Working Group of the Royal College of Physicians' Committees on Ethical Issues in Medicine and Clinical Genetics*, prepared by Janet Radcliffe Richards with Martin Bobrow, London: Royal College of Physicians.

Wasserstrom, Richard (1986) 'The legal and philosophical foundations of the right to privacy', in Thomas A. Mappes and Jane S. Zimbaty (eds) *BioMedical Ethics*, 2nd edn, New York: McGraw-Hill Book Co., 140–7.

Chapter 11

Genetic reductionism and medical genetic practice

Maureen Ramsay

Recent developments in molecular biology and its application to biotechnology have opened up new possibilities for the diagnosis, avoidance and treatment of genetic disease. Molecular studies of genetic diseases are expected to have immediate benefits for the prenatal, preclinical and carrier diagnosis of single-locus, multifactorial and chromosomal diseases (Rossiter and Caskey 1991; McKusick 1991). Advances in genetic knowledge ultimately promise cures and therapies for the major health problems of western society. By uncovering the biochemical basis of the genetic component for common diseases and by discovering genetic markers of susceptibility, recombinant DNA research offers hope for dealing with conditions as diverse as heart disease, stroke, hypertension, diabetes, schizophrenia and manic depression (Baird 1990).

Most clinical geneticists agree that the application of molecular research to genetic disease for the moment must be in developing screening programmes for prevention and avoidance. Prenatal testing for selected birth defects, screening for carriers of a gene that can produce inherited genetic disease, and neonatal and population screening will increasingly be used. These methods, together with prospective and retrospective counselling, can help to prevent the conception or birth of a child with a genetic disorder or can be used to manage and control the effects of the disease once a diagnosis has been made. If genetic screening indicates susceptibility to disease in later life, this will allow early intervention to delay, mitigate the outcomes of, or avoid altogether overt disease and its clinical manifestations.

REDUCTIONISM IN NATURAL AND SOCIAL SCIENCE

The accumulation of genetic knowledge, the promotion of new technologies and the partial success of their applications are influencing thinking about health and illness and legitimizing genetic accounts of the cause and pathogenesis of disease. In these accounts the priority given to genetic explanations can be seen as the ultimate product of an extreme reductionist view of science both natural and social. Reductionism is a set of related ontological, epistemological and methodological theses. That is, reductionism involves linked claims about reality, and about modes of explanation (methodology) and knowledge (epistemology). Particular reductionist theorists emphasize one or other of these claims. However, the key concern for reductionists is the reduction of laws, explanations and properties into a more fundamental theory and the privileging of the description at the reducing level. Reductionists try to explain and understand the properties of complex wholes (for example, biological organisms or societies) in terms of the units out of which those biological or social systems are composed. Reductionist explanations in biology claim that a fundamental understanding of biology comes from the level of DNA, the quintessential component of biological systems. Reductionist explanations in social science claim that a fundamental understanding of society comes from a study of the individuals that make up society. Explicit reductionists argue that the compositional units of the whole are ontologically prior to the whole, that is, the units and their properties exist before the whole and there is a chain of causation that runs from the units to the whole. This view is underpinned by the assumption (shared by many non-reductive materialists) that nature is stratified into various levels of complexity that can be ordered hierarchically. For the study of living organisms the hierarchy of analytic levels reflects the hierarchy of the sciences and runs from the most basic and fundamental units – the physical (atomic and subatomic) – to the biochemical and anatomical, to increasingly complex levels – the physiological, psychological and eventually to analysis at the sociological level. But, reductionism teaches that different levels are not commensurable but reducible. Reductionist methodology collapses higher order levels of explanation into lower order explanations by supposing that, ultimately, higher order levels will be explained in terms of lower order ones, and that these explanations are more fundamental than any other.

Origins of reductionism and influences on western medicine

The origins of reductionist thinking lie in seventeenth-century mechanical philosophy which arose in conjunction with the birth of modern physics. According to this world-view, physical reality is composed of distinct atoms which are related to each other through mechanical causal interactions in accordance with the invariant laws of physics. Phenomena are to be explained in terms of the motions of their constituent parts and the interactions between them. These mechanistic explanations of physical reality informed individualist modes of explanation of social life. Hobbes held that 'it is necessary that we know the things that are to be compounded before we can know the whole compound' for 'everything is best understood by its constitutive causes'. The causes of the social compound reside in 'men as if but even now sprung out of the earth, and suddenly, like mushrooms, come to full maturity, without all kinds of engagement to each other' (Molesworth 1839: 167; ii. xiv; ii. 109). The mechanical vision of the physicists also spilled over into biological explanations, where, on a Cartesian machine image, human organisms are reduced to the sum of their mechanical functions and the operations of their separate parts. According to Descartes there is a dualism of mind and body: 'body' is distinct from 'soul' or 'mind' since 'mind' (the ghost in the machine) is a non-material or spiritual substance which cannot be explained in mechanical terms. Subsequent theorists refused to accept the Cartesian separation of mind and body and adopted a completely materialist metaphysics, claiming that both mental and physical events could be accounted for in terms of physical concepts and laws. In this way, they reduced the mental world to the physical world by arguing that mental events are nothing but a series of physical occurrences that ultimately can be explained in mechanistic terms.

Western medicine, in so far as it is informed by this philosophical legacy, has encouraged thinking about health and disease in a particular way. Health, according to the so-called biomedical model, is understood as the natural functioning of the human organism. Diseases are deviations from natural functional organization. If natural organisms are seen as functional machines, the task of medicine is to understand how the machine works, see where it deviates and how it can be repaired and returned to normal working order. Medicine prescribes its interventions in relation to standard functioning, organic structure and physiological processes and so emphasizes curative medicine with surgical, chemical or technical solutions to maintain or restore natural functional organization. Dualist explanations in which body is distinct from mind and materialist explanations where body is identical to mind both separate what is natural functioning from an individual's experience of it. Diseases as biological dysfunctions are certain sorts of abnormalities that occur in people's bodies and are distinct from an individual's experience of and feelings about illness. Health and disease have empirical indicators which form objective data identified by medical science, the subjective data of feelings and emotions being largely irrelevant to medical practice.

On a reductionist model, disease is located in the atom of society – the individual – who is then reduced to his or her constituent parts. Medical science is applied to parts of bodies, not people. Bodies, in accordance with mechanistic explanations, are thought of as complex biochemical machines, and the unbroken chain of cause and effect in physical disease is attacked at its most fundamental level – the level of the individual nervous system or metabolism. Hence, the task of the science of biological organisms is to reduce the individual's behaviour and interaction with the world to particular molecular and electrochemical configurations, disturbances or abnormalities.

Health and disease then become phenomena relating to the individual abstracted from social, political and cultural contexts. This has the following consequences. It may be assumed that health can be quantified and objectively described in relation to the norms for populations or groups of individuals within them. The criteria of group or population normality by itself, though, cannot provide an objective definition of health. There are many deviations from the average, such as the possession of great strength or ability, which cannot be classified as examples of ill health. Moreover, the frequency of dysfunction could be endemic or universal, as when whole populations are infected with diseases. If health is defined solely in terms of normality, then it becomes difficult to distinguish unhealthy conditions from social deviancy, abnormal, subnormal, nonconforming or maladaptive behaviour. This can result in improper descriptions, stigmatizations and social control of people who behave in disturbing or inappropriate ways. Particular cultural or social norms which vary over time and between societies may partially define what is thought of or valued as natural or deviant. The claim of objectivity here may serve as the cloak for a relativism which justifies accepting certain physical or psychological states which by other standards would be judged unacceptable.

The separation of individual and society in reductionist explanation also tends to obscure the socio-economic causes of and
remedies for ill health. Starting from the uncontroversial fact that
disease is located within the individual, reductionist methodology
can lead to a situation where inappropriate emphasis is placed on the
individual who becomes sick, rather than the social, economic and
environmental factors which may cause them to be sick, with the
consequence that it is the individual illness which is treated in
isolation from, or instead of, other relevant circumstances.

Reductionism in molecular biology

That health and disease are increasingly being interpreted in the light
of developments in genetics is the culmination of a reductionist
philosophy of science (both natural and social) which derives from a
mechanical materialist view of the world. The science of molecular
biology is the final stage in the process of dissecting people into
discrete and disconnected bits of chemical machinery. Steven Rose
(1982: 16) explains that reductionism in microbiological explanations begins with the fundamental unit of biological systems,
the level of DNA, and from this progresses via a direct causal
chain to explanations of higher level outcomes. 'DNA determines
primary protein structure, determines cellular architecture, determines function, determines organismic behaviour.' Applying this
model to disease, it could be said, for example, that a recessive
mutation causes the production of a haemoglobin module with a
particular amino-acid substitution, which causes alterations in the
kinetics of oxygen binding to the haemoglobin molecule, which
causes sickle-cell anaemia. The phenylketonuria mutations cause
an enzyme deficiency which ultimately causes irreversible mental
retardation; defects in single genes cause dysfunction in the metabolic mechanisms which cause the diseases cystic fibrosis and
Huntington's chorea. Where the sequence of events is not fully
known or understood, it could be assumed that if we were able to fill
in the 'gaps' in levels of reality we could legitimately say as a kind
of shorthand statement that particular DNA polymorphisms cause
heart disease (Leppert *et al.* 1986; Langlois *et al.* 1988), Alzheimer's
disease (St George-Hyslop 1987) and polycystic kidney disease
(Reeders *et al.* 1985). It is this kind of reductionism that allowed
such claims as: manic depression can be caused by a single gene on
chromosome 11 (Engeland *et al.* 1987); changed dopamine levels

cause schizophrenia; and a configuration of XYY chromosomes causes violence in men (Rose 1982: 16).

In this way explanation of a whole range of single-gene and multifactorial diseases and abnormal and deviant behaviours can be reduced to particular molecular events. The result of talking about health and disease along these lines exacerbates the tendencies latent in the reductionist biomedical model. That is, genetic determination can be seen as the privileged way to explain health and disease. Differences between people are reduced to their genetic individuality, thus promoting technical solutions to individualized problems.

What's wrong with reductionist explanations?

Reducing the social to the individual

The relationship between genes, individuals and society is more complex than reductionist explanations suggest. The view that the atom or molecule is ontologically prior to the organism and the individual is ontologically prior to society overlooks the fact that phenomena are both individual and part of a greater unity, and that it is the interrelations between them that co-determine the course of events.

From the truism that society consists of human individuals it does not follow either that these individuals are in principle separable from social wholes or that facts about society or social phenonema are to be explained solely in terms of facts about individuals. The assumption that individuals are in principle separable from social wholes implies that logically, if not empirically, individuals can be abstracted from their social context. Their essential characteristics are given and can be understood independent of the socio-historical circumstances within which they are expressed or experienced. They are not determined or affected by them. But this abstract idea of human beings is conceptually as well as empirically incoherent. It is impossible to conceive of individuals as having material properties, being subject to physiological and psychological states, experiencing beliefs, desires and emotions or acting to achieve purposes without presupposing a social context (Lukes 1977). This model of human nature denies the importance of the historical, social, economic and political forces which determine the content, expression and inter-pretation of any individual's experience and behaviour. It has been a commonplace, at least since the time of Marx, that the concept of the abstract individual used as an object of explanation is epistemologically inadequate, that human beings cannot be understood in abstraction from their social circumstances. Real living individuals always exist in some specific social context and it is this to which we must refer in order to understand both people already formed in society and their capacity to transform it. Human activities presuppose a social context as a precondition for any individual action, but the nature of that social context is a consequence of human activity. The position I am defending here is elaborated by Roy Bhaskar (1979). He argues that societies are not reducible to people, 'that social forms are a necessary condition for any intentional act, that their *pre-existence* establishes their *autonomy* as possible objects of scientific investigation and that their *causal power* establishes their reality' (p. 31). This entails what Bhaskar calls 'the transformational model of social activity'. 'Society is both the ever present *condition* (material cause) and the continually reproduced *outcome* of human agency' (p. 43).

> [P]eople do not create society. For it always pre-exists them and is a necessary condition for their activity. Rather, society must be regarded as an ensemble of structures, practices and conventions which individuals reproduce or transform but which would not exist unless they did so.
>
> (p. 45)

Social structures and human agency are existentially interdependent, but distinct. The transformational model of social activity allows us to avoid the ontological errors of reification and voluntarism, and the epistemological errors of social determinism and methodological individualism. 'Society does not exist independently of human activity (the error of reification). But it is not the product of it (the error of voluntarism)' (pp. 45–6). Individuals are not completely determined by social forms (social determinism) nor does the sum of their behaviours adequately explain them (methodological individualism). Individuals cannot be explained apart from social structures, and social phenonema cannot be explained in terms of facts about individuals. Social structures are the necessary condition for human activity, and human activity is always expressed within, and itself expresses, some social form. But human activity can both reproduce and transform those social structures so that society is both a means to and a consequence of human agency.

Reducing the individual to the sum of its parts

Just as society cannot be reduced to individuals, neither can individuals be reduced to, identified with or explained in terms of their genes. If facts about an individual's genetic makeup are used exclusively in reductionist explanations to explain and predict facts about individuals (for example their attitudes, behaviour, susceptibility to disease or disease outcome), then, as Steven Lukes (1977: 185) points out, one of two equally unacceptable and implausible alternatives must follow. Either it is necessary to back up this claim with a theory which will explain the historical, economic and social context in which various behaviours and diseases are experienced in terms of biochemical configurations, or it is necessary to demonstrate that this context is a backdrop against which quasi-mechanical genetic forces are the sole causal influences at work.

Facts about individual behaviour, health status or susceptibility to disease, and differences between individuals, may be related to facts about and differences in their biochemistry, but the biological facts are not necessarily decisive and these acting alone are not always sufficient to cause definite higher level outcomes. To suppose that an outcome at the level of an individual organism can be explained in terms of its biochemical components is to assume that we can dispense both with higher level explanations and with the plurality of causes which co-determine higher level outcomes. There is no reason why properties of wholes should not explain those of their component parts, for it is the organization of an environment that determines what happens within it, the state of society that determines when and how biological determinations apply. Human beings as causal agents, though subject to biological processes, can influence the conditions under which biological laws take hold, by creating, destroying, modifying and transforming the conditions under which they operate and produce effects. Furthermore, because there can be a multiplicity of causes (natural, social, psychological, physical, physiological, biochemical) which combine to produce effects, several kind of causal mechanisms may be involved in the explanation of any event, behaviour or disease. Some of these may not be identifiable or quantifiable. For this reason, it is not possible to explain or predict outcomes in a straightforward deductive way. Because it is not possible to reduce this multiplicity of causal mechanisms to a single level, reductionist explanations cannot be a means of guaranteeing knowledge of higher specific order outcomes.

In the case of genetics, the sheer complexity of a system may make reductionist explanations impossible. Tauber and Sarkar (1992: 223) argue that there is no practical way to predict or characterize biological behaviour or function at the molecular level from DNA sequence information alone, first, because of the 'protein folding problem'. It is assumed that the primary structure or amino-acid sequence of a protein determines its three-dimensional conformation. Therefore it should be possible to calculate the conformation of the sequence. However, Hubbard (1982: 70) argues that:

> even if DNA could be shown truly to 'determine' (not bio-chemically, but in the 'information' sense) the amino-acid sequence of a protein (its so-called primary structure), that does not determine either how the protein folds up into three-dimensional structure, or its function . . . they depend on many factors and interactions that themselves fluctuate over time and are in no sense 'determined' by DNA.

This information is not explicitly contained solely in the properties of the individual molecular components. Second, Tauber and Sarkar argue that what matters most in typical biological processes such as development is the timing of the action of genes (Davidson 1986) and this information is partly environmental. Third, the complexities of interaction between genes and the amount of variability in the human genome of groups and populations is so extensive that a possibility of reductionist explanation from sequence information alone is both unlikely and impractical.

They further complain that the problem of reductionism in its extreme form is that it precludes investigation at levels higher than DNA and this is essential for actual explanation and effective intervention in disease processes. Even in diseases caused by single Mendelian gene disorders, where DNA diagnostic tests are available, as with sickle-cell anaemia, effective intervention is still not guaranteed (Bunn and Forget 1986). Current evidence suggests that in the etiology of genetic disease several loci are almost always involved simultaneously (Williamson and Kessling 1990). Moreover, there is a wide variability within the clinical expressions of genetic disorders (Vogel and Motusky 1986). A child with sickle-cell anaemia may live a full life with minor symptoms, another may suffer excruciating painful crises, damage to organs and early death (Bowman 1977). Down syndrome children may be severely or moderately retarded, but can still lead full and satisfying lives. Hence, it is not possible to trace a causal pathway from the presence of an extra chromosome in order to predict, account for, or explain fully, the severity of the disease in the phenotype. In such cases extragenetic factors, perhaps other biological processes, must be involved in the explanation of the etiology of the disease.

Integrating the biological and the social

For complex disease processes involving poorly understood and multifactorial disease-producing mechanisms, sequence information alone has limited explanatory power. What has to be explained is the interaction between biological processes, and between these and environmental and social factors. Heart disease, stroke, hypertension, diabetes, various cancers and psychiatric illnesses may have a strong genetic component. Genes, or several genes at different loci, may underlie the predisposition to these diseases. However, genetic predisposition is a necessary, but not sufficient, condition for actually contracting many of these diseases. The gaps in our understanding of the multiplicity of causal mechanisms at work in the production of disease, the variations in their clinical outcomes and the sometimes recognized, but unquantifiable, effects of environmental causes make reductionist explanations incapable of producing adequate accounts of the presence of disease at the level of the organism.

A more adequate understanding demands an integration of the biological and the social in which neither is given ontological priority in causation. The biological and social are understood as being related to each other on a transformational model which sees that organisms are not simply products of their social environment but that they are also causes of it. This approach distinguishes epistemologically between levels of explanation relevant to the biological and levels relevant to the social domain without reducing one to the other or denying the existential independence of each, but recognizes their interconnections and their powers of transformation.

It is a mistaken dichotomy to suppose that human beings and human disease are either totally biologically determined or totally socially determined. An adequate understanding of biological and social determinants in the production of human beings and society can only be possible following the recognition that both genes and environment are necessary to explanations of human behaviour and disease. This does not mean that it is possible to quantify on a linear scale the proportion determined by environmental factors and the proportion determined by genetic influences. Genes and environment are not two separate and static quantifiable forces, but interact with each other.

Human beings are biologically determined, and they may have genes or chromosomal abnormalities which predispose them to susceptibility to specific diseases, but what is central to the concrete effects of those determinations is how the environment interacts with the genes and how it can be modified or transformed, how diseases are perceived and how value is conferred on them, and the way in which differences are lived and experienced. This does not mean that biological facts are reducible to social relations and cultural explanations or that biological dysfunction should not be treated by physical intervention. It does mean that we can examine aspects of a social context in order to assess the extent to which biological determinations are socially mediated and therefore socially transformable, and the extent to which they will persist and prevail despite any attempt to transform them. And it is this, this power to transform ourselves and our possibilities, that is significant. There may be genetic factors involved in the onset and severity of chronic obstructive pulmonary disease, there may be suspect genes for common cancers, cardiovascular disease and mental illness, but instances of emphysema, asthma, bronchitis, cancer and mental illness are socially determined by exposure to dust, fumes, carcinogens, and stressful living and working conditions. Because they are socially determined they are within our power to alter. We may have a genetic malfunction which is a necessary and sufficient condition for suffering from a disease outcome, but it would be inaccurate to explain the experience of this disease solely in terms of genetic malfunction. How society regards genetic disease and the kinds of resources available to cope with it make it more or less of a problem. Though there are genetic diseases which can be avoided and treated at a biochemical level, the outcome of genetic malfunction may be transformed by modifying the environment, including attitudes to genetic defects and other forms of handicap. We may be the partial constructs of our genes, but we are able to investigate and intervene in the genetic process. We can find means of overcoming the effects of genetically transmitted disease; we have the ability to intervene in our genetic nature at levels higher than its action site. We are capable of transforming nature and making ourselves.

THE IMPLICATIONS FOR THE SUPPORT AND CARE BY PROFESSIONALS AND SOCIETY OF THOSE WITH INHERITED DISEASE

Advances in genetic knowledge and associated technologies offer new opportunities for the prevention, avoidance and management of genetic disease. Genetic knowledge, screening programmes and counselling procedures can help families plan their reproductive options, identify individuals with defective genes so that appropriate management can avoid complications, alert those at risk giving the opportunity to develop preventive strategies and therapeutic programmes. However, if this technical capacity to monitor individual genetic makeup is seen in the context of a reductionism which locates the social in the individual, and the individual according to their genes, there are a number of major implications for the support and care by professionals and society of those with inherited disease. Concentration on technical knowledge in the context of genetic individuality and individual risk has implications for autonomy and control, the kinds of treatment and support provided, societal attitudes and discriminatory practices.

Whatever the good intentions of geneticists or counsellors, screening procedures take place against a background of social, political, professional and commercial interests. Those responsible for developing and promoting testing and the uses to which it is put control the agenda, and may have interests that are not identical to those affected by genetic disease. Governments can decide what tests can be carried out and on whom. Clinicians, specialists and geneticists determine what can be tested for and can influence who is tested. Governments and clinicians have in turn been influenced by other professional and commercial interests that have developed the diagnostic and screening tests in question. Workplaces and insurance companies may demand tests and use the results in discriminatory ways. Furthermore, because access to diagnostic and counselling services may be limited, only 'at risk' groups are likely to be offered screening services and it will be the most articulate and informed, that is the professional and educated classes, that will make most use of any services available. In the case of carrier-screening and prenatal testing, there will be an increase in the proportion of disabled children born to those with the fewest material and non-material resources to care for them and with less ability to press for change. If the future of genetic screening lies in the ability to detect susceptibility to disease in later life, those with the most resources are going to be the people who take advantage of it. This will benefit those affected but will ultimately increase the already significant gap in class differences in health, reinforcing patterns of inequality in access to health care and in health status itself.

Screening presupposes that it is undesirable to have a genetic disease or to bring people into the world with genetic defects that can be avoided. Of course, there are good reasons for this belief, but if it is informed by a reductive individualist approach avoidance becomes an individual responsibility. So if a woman decides against prenatal screening or abortion when she is found to be carrying a fetus with a genetic defect, it becomes her shame, her guilt, her responsibility for the way the baby turns out (Hubbard 1984: 224). The end result becomes not her fate, but her fault (Hubbard 1986: 227). Similarly, if people do not take advantage of susceptibility screening, or ignore its recommendations for their own future health, and they later contract a genetic disease, they have only themselves to blame. This puts pressure on people to reject a less than perfect baby and to feel personally culpable for their problems of ill health. Given the variation between and within disorders, the multifactorial nature of disease, and the variations in class, culture, education levels and socio-economic circumstances, it is impossible to predict with any accuracy the impact of a genetic defect or susceptibility on any one individual. Interactions with other biological processes and environmental agents, differences in resources – money, time, energy, levels of isolation and support – can determine differences in outcomes of and responses to genetic problems. Different responses also depend on the attitudes and beliefs of those concerned. Weil (1991) draws attention to a variety of investigations which show that factual information provided by counsellors aids understanding and acceptance of the cause, nature and probable consequences of disorders, but personal and religious beliefs play an important role in facilitating coping and adjustment. Beliefs that personal attitudes, actions and place in the world were in some way connected to the disorders, and beliefs that the disorder resulted from substances in the environment; or that the subjects were chosen, singled out or blamed; or that the disorder was a test or opportunity for growth; or that God's actions were involved, contribute to the differing responses to genetic problems. These variations mean it is difficult to assess just how undesirable a genetic problem is and whether action at the level of the individual's genes is likely to benefit them.

Molecular biology and genetics have made possible the recognition of over 3,000 distinct conditions and characteristics which are transmitted genetically from parents to child (McKusick 1983). These include serious disorders which result in early death and for which there is no treatment, such as Tay-Sachs disease, where the causal pathway from base changes in DNA to the appearance of the disease in the phenotype is well understood. This is the paradigm case of successful reductionism, where clinical features of a disease can be accounted for at the level of a metabolic gene defect, and where avoiding the outcome is clearly desirable. However, this paradigm case cannot be applied to other areas of genetic impairment where the issues of cause, consequence, undesirability and intervention are more complex. Moreover, as genetic knowledge increases and more suspect genes are discovered, the boundaries between what is genetically desirable and what is undesirable will change in accordance with the values of those who select the criteria for what counts as a genetic defect or handicap (Thomas 1982: 3–20). The classification of defects may be based on subjective and ideological beliefs about the costs and benefits to society, the value or availability of certain qualities or characteristics. What is not perfect has limitless boundaries if it ever became possible for designer genes to reflect the latest fashion and to determine what kind of future people there could be.

Within a reductionist framework the concern for genetic control of disease could have elitist and discriminatory consequences. Because conditions that are screened for could have been avoided, attitudes towards and facilities for the disabled may worsen. Genetic knowledge has already led to unjustified discrimination against black people, who have been affected by employment restrictions placed on carriers of the sickle-cell trait although they did not actually have the disease (Reilly 1976: 159–84). Some males with an XYY chromosomal complement have suffered continued imprisonment as a result, despite evidence that the genetic defect was not the cause of the problem (Beckwith and King 1974: 475–6). Workplace screening, in which job applicants and employees are tested for inherited traits that may predispose them to industrial disease, has led to exclusionary practices at work (Draper 1991).

In so far as genetic diagnosis reduces complex disease patterns and processes to a biomedical problem, it marginalizes the extent to which genetic disease can be environmentally caused and controlled. In industrial societies the major killers and disabling conditions are heart and cerebrovascular disease, cancer, emphysema, arthritis and diabetes. Whatever the genetic susceptibility to these diseases, incidence of each of them is closely related to lifestyle and environmental factors, for example industrial pollution, working conditions, diet, smoking, stress and lack of exercise. This suggests that reductions of instances of these diseases could come about through environmental, socio-economic and educational measures rather than medical intervention. Moreover, patterns of health and disease within an industrial population are not evenly distributed between social and occupational classes. Townsend and Davidson (1982) showed that class differences in mortality and morbidity rates are constant features throughout all age groups under 65. There is a mass of data to support the general argument that social and economic factors influence health, and that it is the level and nature of production, what is available for consumption, as well as how goods and services are distributed, that are significant determinants of health.

In the case of mental health, it has been argued that there is a potential biochemical basis to mental disorder of all kinds. It is thought that there may be a genetic predisposition to certain functional psychoses such as schizophrenia and manic depression, and it has been suggested that there is a genetic contribution to alcoholism, anxiety reaction, obsessionality and paranoid reaction (Slater and Roth 1969; Martin 1977), but the extent to which the genetic basis of these diseases is a necessary or sufficient condition for their development is unclear. In cultural behavioural explanations a causal role is given to the characteristics of the individual, their intelligence, skills and dispositions, the way they live their lives, their ideas and behaviour at the onset of illness. Despite the lack of concrete knowledge of the causes of mental illness, it is possible to identify conditions associated with the presence or absence of illness in various sections of the population and partially explain illness in terms of those factors which are related to high prevalence rather than focusing on those idiosyncratic factors which determine individual differences in health. Whatever the genetic or biochemical basis of susceptibility to mental illness, the differences in the patterns of mental health and illness that are found between different social classes, the unemployed and employed, men and women, testify to the significance of socio-economic determinants in the explanation of the distribution and occurrence of mental illness within a given group (Plog and Edgerton 1969; Coulter 1973).

Because both the experience and the outcome of genetic disease are affected by a multiplicity of factors at different levels of explanation, the reductionist model does not adequately explain genetic disease. This does not mean, however, that genetic disease is reducible to social experience, circumstances or influences or that there is no such thing as genetic disease in the biomedical sense or that genetic knowledge is not important. There are some diseases that cannot be explained in terms of their social determinants, or as departures from socially acceptable behaviour incompatible with the norms and expectations of a particular social or cultural system. Lung cancer and muscular dystrophy are diseases not because society believes them to be or devalues them, but because they are caused by biological dysfunction. Acknowledgement that there is a biological basis to disease need not lead us to concentrate exclusively on intervention either at the level of genetic dysfunction or at the level of the individual, or to obscure the socio-economic causes of ill health. We need not neglect alternative forms of treatment and support, holistic approaches or the social etiology of disease. We can distinguish between individuals who become sick and what makes them sick, what is ill health and what will produce it. There is no contradiction between saying that disease is located within the individual as the subject of illness and saying that diseases have socio-economic causes. From the claim that disease is found in the individual, it does not follow that diseases are caused by individual genes, the individual is responsible for their own (ill) health or that diseases are caused by treating individuals in particular ways or in isolation from other factors. The emphasis on social determinants merely serves to remind us that, in so far as diseases are influenced by socio-economic factors, then preventive and remedial socio-economic measures and public health policies are necessary to prevent disease and restore health. This is important, because if these diseases are thought of as primarily genetic in origin on a re-ductionist model, then the implications for the support and care of those with or at risk from genetic disease are quite different from those which take account of the multiplicity of causes that determine who gets a disease and how they experience it. Emphasis on the primacy of genetic explanation could lead to a proliferation of screening and counselling services to prevent those with genetic handicaps being born. This could divert resources that could be used to develop treatment programmes, provide support, respite care and domestic alternatives for parents with afflicted children. Less attention may be paid to policies to avoid discrimination against and provide facilities for handicapped people.

If a reductive genetic framework is used to assess workers at risk from industrial hazards, there is the danger that the genetic makeup of workers comes to be understood as the core problem of industrial disease. This has impact on how professionals and policy-makers view the workplace and responsibility for disease. Industrial practices and social policies on health and safety shift their concern from chemical hazards to the personal characteristics of the workers, the result being that it is the workers who are denied employment, rather than the hazard treated at source by reducing toxic chemicals for all and tightening health and safety legislation generally.

If genetic screening and counselling ultimately can provide susceptibility profiles for those at risk from genetic diseases, then the outcome could be that individuals are given their own personal action plans for changing their lifestyles. Although this may prevent any particular individual from becoming ill, it does nothing to change the socio-economic and environmental conditions that are partially responsible for the major diseases of western society. A reductive individualist approach is especially alarming when it is in tandem with government policies on taxation, monetarism and the minimal welfare state, which advocate the entrepreneurial spirit, individual initiative, self-reliance and personal rather than public responsibility. In this context a genetic approach to health individualizes and privatizes health problems without challenging the system that creates ill health.

If genetic knowledge is seen in a reductionist light, the possibilities for its use can lead to undesirable consequences: first, as an instrument of social policy, where this embodies interests which may be detrimental to the autonomy of individuals, this is clearly undesirable; second, as a means of expanding choice for individuals, the coercive context of that choice may determine the decisions people make and so shape and constrain them. The effects of individual choices may serve to limit the freedom of others and lead to the undesirable consequence of creating a more unequal society. Third, the uses to which genetic knowledge is put may divert attention from other causes and cures for diseases and lead to a worsening of attitudes towards those who suffer from them. But there is no a priori reason why these consequences need to follow from the understanding of disease at a molecular level. Understanding the genetic determinants of disease is not just in the interests of power-holders and policy-makers, but is in the interests of those whose lives could be enhanced by such knowledge. This does not entail pursuing a narrow kind of preventive treatment to the exclusion of other approaches, or justify policies which focus on individual susceptibility, personal culpability or shifting lifestyles. Such understanding could be seen as part of a society's shared search for health, which acknowledges that disease also has social causes and mediations, and which sees public and collective health measures aimed at the prevention of disease as the means to ensure that all individuals have the ability, opportunity and resources to meet their health needs and to prevent and manage disease.

We can accept that genetic explanation and biomedical technology has a part to play in the avoidance and treatment of genetic disease, without accepting a reductionist explanation of its causes, or an individual solution to the problems of genetic disease. If we reduce societies to individuals and individuals to their genes, we cannot put the pieces back together again and expect to understand them, for we deny the interaction between genes and the environment, the individual and society. Though biological and social determinations may be the context in which we select our goals, our biological and social nature is such that we can transform those conditions and strive to shape our lives and destinies.

ACKNOWLEDGEMENTS

The author thanks Andrew Belsey, Angus Clarke and Harry Lesser for comments on this chapter.

FURTHER READING

Rose, S., Kamin, L. J. and Lewontin, R. C. (1984) *Not in Our Genes: Biology, Ideology and Human Nature*, Harmondsworth: Penguin.

REFERENCES

Baird, P. A. (1990) 'Genetics and health care: a paradigm shift', *Perspectives in Biology and Medicine* 33 (2) 203–13.
Beckwith, J. and King, J. (1974) 'The XYY syndrome: a dangerous myth', *New Scientist* 14 November.
Bhaskar, R. (1979) *The Possibility of Naturalism*, Brighton: Harvester.
Bowman, J. E. (1977) 'Genetic screening programs and public policy', *Phylon* 38: 117–42.

Bunn, H. F. and Forget, B. F. (1986) *Hemoglobin: Molecular, Genetic and Clinical Aspects*, Philadelphia: Saunders.

Coulter, J. (1973) *Approaches to Insanity: A Philosophical and Sociological Study*, London: Martin Robertson.

Davidson, E. H. (1986) *Gene Activity in Early Development*, 3rd edn, New York: Academic Press.

Draper, E. (1991) *Risky Business*, Cambridge: Cambridge University Press.

Engeland, J. A., Gerhard, D. S., Pauls, D. L., *et al.* (1987) 'Bipolar affective disorders linked to DNA markers on chromosome 11', *Nature* 325: 783–7.

Hubbard, R. (1982) 'The theory and practice of genetic reductionism – from Mendel's laws to genetic engineering', in S. Rose (ed.) *Towards a Liberatory Biology*, London: Allison & Busby, 62–79.

—— (1984) 'Personal courage is not enough: some hazards of childbearing in the 1980s', in A. Arditti, R. D. Klein and S. Minden (eds) *Test-Tube Women: What Future for Motherhood?*, London: Pandora Press.

—— (1986) 'Eugenics and prenatal testing', *International Journal of Health Services* 16 (2) 227–42.

Langlois, S., Kastelein, J. J. P. and Hayden, M. R. (1988) 'Characterisation of six partial deletions in the low-density-lipoprotein (LDL) receptor gene causing familial hypercholesterolemia (FH)', *American Journal of Human Genetics* 43: 60–8.

Leppert, M. F., Hasstedt, S. J., Holm, T., *et al.* (1986) 'A DNA probe for the LDL receptor gene is tightly linked to hypercholesterolemia in a pedigree with early coronary disease', *American Journal of Human Genetics* 39: 300–6.

Lukes, S. (1977) *Essays in Social Theory*, London: Macmillan.

McKusick, V. A. (1983) *Mendelian Inheritance in Man*, 6th edn, Baltimore: Johns Hopkins University Press.

—— (1991) 'Current trends in mapping human genes', *FASEB Journal* 5: 12–20.

Martin, B. (1977) *Abnormal Psychology: Clinical and Scientific Perspectives*, New York: Holt, Reinhart & Winston.

Molesworth, W. (ed.) (1839) *The English Works of Thomas Hobbes*, London: Bonn.

Plog, S. G. and Edgerton, R. B. (eds) (1969) *Changing Perspectives in Mental Illness*, London: Holt, Reinhart & Winston.

Reeders, S. T., Breuning, M. H., Davies, K. E., *et al.* (1985) 'A highly polymorphic DNA marker linked to adult polycystic disease on chromosome 16', *Nature* 317: 542–4.

Reilly, P. (1976) 'State-supported mass genetic screening programs', in A. Milunsky and G. J. Annas (eds) *Genetics and the Law*, New York: Plenum Press.

Rose, S. (ed.) (1982) *Towards a Liberatory Biology*, London: Allison & Busby.

Rossiter, B. J. F. and Caskey, C. T. (1991) 'Molecular studies of human genetic disease', *FASEB Journal* 5: 21–7.

St George-Hyslop, P., Tanzi, R., Polinsky, R. J., *et al.* (1987) 'The genetic defect causing familial Alzheimer's disease maps on chromosome 21', *Science* 235: 885–90.

Slater, E. and Roth, M. (1969) *Clinical Psychiatry*, London: Ballière, Tindall & Cassell.

Tauber, A. I. and Sarkar, S. (1992) 'The Human Genome Project: Has blind reductionism gone too far?', *Perspectives in Biology and Medicine* 35 (2): 220–35.

Thomas, D. (1982) *The Experience of Handicap*, London: Methuen.

Townsend, P. and Davidson, N. (eds) (1982) *Inequalities in Health (The Black Report)*, Harmondsworth: Penguin.

Vogel, F. and Motusky, A. G. (1986) *Human Genetics: Problems and Approaches*, 2nd edn, Berlin: Springer.

Weil, J. (1991) 'Mothers' postcounselling beliefs about the causes of their children's genetic disorders', *American Journal of Human Genetics* 48: 145–53.

Williamson, R. and Kessling, A. M. (1990) 'The problem of polygenic disease', in D. C. Chadwick (ed.) *Human Genetic Information: Science, Law and Ethics*, Chichester: Wiley.

Index